To: Tailon Chi

The Bank for
International Settlements

The Bank for International Settlements

Evolution and Evaluation

JAMES C. BAKER

QUORUM BOOKS
Westport, Connecticut • London

Library of Congress Cataloging-in-Publication Data

Baker, James Calvin, 1935–
   The Bank for International Settlements : evolution and
evaluation / James C. Baker.
      p.   cm.
   Includes bibliographical references and index.
   ISBN 1–56720–518–6 (alk. paper)
   1. Bank for International Settlements.   2. International
finance.   3. Banks and banking, Central.   I. Title.
HG3881.B253   2002
332.1855—dc21   2001049184

British Library Cataloguing in Publication Data is available.

Library of Congress Catalog Card Number: 2001049184
ISBN: 1–56720–518–6

First published in 2002

Quorum Books, 88 Post Road West, Westport, CT 06881
An imprint of Greenwood Publishing Group, Inc.
www.quorumbooks.com

Printed in the United States of America

∞™

The paper used in this book complies with the
Permanent Paper Standard issued by the National
Information Standards Organization (Z39.48–1984).

10 9 8 7 6 5 4 3 2 1

To **Lee C. Nehrt**
who introduced me to a world of
international financial institutions

Contents

Illustrations

Preface

This monograph is a study of the Bank for International Settlements (BIS) and its evolution, administration, operations, and evaluation. The BIS is the oldest international financial institution, having been established in 1930. It survived the conclusion of its major initial objective, a global economic depression, a world war, and an everchanging international monetary and financial system in which major banks have failed, banks in general have been inadequately capitalized, financial derivative instruments have been misused, currency crises occurred in Asia, Europe, Mexico, and Russia, the U.S. dollar was devalued twice within two years, and charges of laundering gold for the Nazis in World War II have been made against the BIS.

The principal hypothesis of this book is that, enigma that it may be, the BIS is the only financial institution which could have accomplished what it did over its seven decades of existence. It has brought some semblance of stability to the international monetary and financial systems and to international banking, specifically by formulating rules for banking authority responsibility when foreign affiliates of a bank fail and for maintenance of more adequate capital by banks with a means to account for riskiness of their assets. It has studied other global financial issues and promulgated proposals in the areas of financial derivative instruments, payment and settlement of cross-border financial transactions, and computer problems such as the Y2K issue at the end of the 1990s.

In addition to these major studies and pronouncements by the BIS, it has maintained extraordinary relationships with central banks and international financial institutions around the world by carrying out functions with them in a discretionary and confidential manner so that its operations have gained a wide reputation and credibility with the international financial system and its institutions. Government officials and academicians look to its studies and reports for helpful financial statistics and analysis and its annual report is highly anticipated for its analysis of international banking and financial markets.

The BIS is without a peer in what it has accomplished. Despite the fact that it has been involved in some very shady operations before and during World War II, it has since maintained a highly professional demeanor toward international bank supervisory and regulatory problems in a way that no individual central bank or even group of central banks could have done. Its leadership in problem solving and coordination of efforts to alleviate regional economic problems, although not always successful, has helped to ease many of these crises.

The objective of this treatise, therefore, is to discuss and analyze the major attributes of the BIS including how and why it was established. The contributions made by the BIS to a more stable international financial system will be evaluated along with their consequences. The discussion is not meant to compare the BIS with other multilateral financial institutions as no other comparable international financial institution exists.

Some critics of the BIS have labeled it as an obscure and secretive organization as though it were involved in a broad conspiracy to corner the global financial markets. It would be difficult, if not impossible, for one institution to do this in a world of instantaneous electronic publication of financial news. But confidentiality must be maintained in international financial transactions, especially those in which central banks are involved.

The BIS is particularly designed to offer discretion and confidentiality to central banks and other multilateral financial institutions in these endeavors. Thus, the public needs to become aware of its usefulness in dealing with the myriad issues that stem from the international financial system, so that the BIS becomes less obscure and secretive in its operations. It is for this purpose that this book has been written.

Acknowledgments

As in all writing endeavors, others must be acknowledged for their assistance in the writing or research involved and for their contribution to the success of this project. My doctoral research assistants found much of the material in the last three years. They are Chun-Ming Zhao, Amit Sinha, and Sue Edwards, whose assistance was coupled with their own doctoral studies in our PhD Program. During the past several years, the Bank for International Settlements has been a subject for discussion in my undergraduate and graduate international financial management courses. Student dialogue concerning the Bank for International Settlements, derivatives in general, and, specifically, exotic derivatives has contributed greatly to the book. Some of these students should be mentioned for their stimulating contributions. These are Amy Augustyn, David L. Baker, Teresa M. Ballinger, Yan Bao, Mike Biffl, Nicholas J. Boulter, Jay Buser, Thomas Clarke, Allison E. Dreier, Richard C. Grimm, Robin Evans, Mike Heineman, I-Lei Huang, Sudesh Indran, Sigurdur Johannesson, Thomas D. Klisuric, Chris Luchs, David Powers, Hector M. Sanabria, and Elizabeth Seliga. Discussions about insurance industry regulation with Dr. Frederick Schroath, Associate Dean of the Kent State University Graduate School of Management, enhanced the section devoted to the BIS relationship with the International Association of Insurance Supervisors. Editorial assistance from Lynn Zelem and Lottie Schnell of Greenwood Publishing Group certainly enhanced the readability of the book and suggestions from the principal editor for the book were very helpful. The Greenwood staff is appreciated for their patience and advice.

Gremlins sometimes invade a project, and the author remains totally responsible for any of these glitches.

Acronyms

ACC	Asian Consultative Council
ASSAL	Association of Insurance Superintendents of Latin America
BCCI	Bank for Credit and Commerce International
BIS	Bank for International Settlements
CGFS	Committee on the Global Financial System
CHAPS	Clearing House Automated Payments System
CHATS	Clearing House Automated Transfer System
CHIPS	Clearing House Interbank Payments System
CPSS	Committee on Payment and Settlement Systems
DVP	Delivery versus payment
ECB	European Central Bank
ECNs	Electronic communications networks
EMCF	European Monetary Cooperation Fund
EMU	European Monetary Union
EU	European Union
FATF	Financial Action Task Force on Money Laundering
Fed	U.S. Federal Reserve System
FSF	Financial Stability Forum
G10	Group of Ten

IAIS	International Association of Insurance Supervisors
IASC	International Accounting Standards Committee
IBS	International Banking Standards
ICSID	International Centre for Settlement of Investment Disputes
IDA	International Development Association
IFC	International Finance Corporation
IIF	Institute of International Finance
IMF	International Monetary Fund
IOSCO	International Organisation of Securities Commissions
ISDA	International Swaps Dealers Association
LDCs	Less-Developed Countries
LIFFE	London International Financial Futures Exchange
LTCM	Long Term Capital Management
MATIF	Marche a Terme International de France
M&A	Mergers and acquisitions
MIGA	Multinational Investment Guarantee Agency
MNCs	multinational companies
NAIC	National Association of Insurance Commissioners
OECD	Organisation for Economic Cooperation and Development
OGIS	Offshore Group of Insurance Supervisors
RTGS	Real-time gross settlement
SWIFT	Society for Worldwide Interbank Financial Telecommunications
VAR	value-at-risk
WTO	World Trade Organisation
Y2K	Year 2000

CHAPTER 1

Introduction to the Bank for International Settlements

INTRODUCTION

Today's world of business is in an environment of borderless finance. The volume of international financial transactions has increased significantly during the past few decades. World trade and investment is now measured in the trillions. For example, more than $1.5 trillion of foreign currency is traded every day. New financial instruments are being created on an almost daily basis. Banks are becoming larger and more sophisticated as a result of cross-border merger and acquisition activity and innovations in electronic technology.

All of this growth has produced four developments which have significantly affected international commerce. These global changes are (1) an acceleration of cross-border capital flows, (2) overwhelming new challenges in emerging markets, (3) growing dominance of capital markets, and (4) new challenges for risk management. These global changes in the international financial system require regulation and oversight that is global instead of the national central banking supervision within a country's borders. The new international financial system requires an international agency which can coordinate the activities of national banking regulatory and supervisory bodies. The Bank for International Settlements (BIS) is such an agency.

The Bank for International Settlements is many things. The BIS is a global financial institution with a regional background. It is a bank for central banks. It is the oldest international financial institution now operating. It is a private institution with shareholders but it does operations for public agencies. Such operations are kept strictly confidential so that the public is usually unaware of most of the BIS operations. In fact, if a random sample survey were taken of citizens of the nations whose central banks are shareholders of BIS, the vast majority would know little or nothing about the BIS. Although it has not functioned as a facilitator of reparations settlements for nearly 70 years, the role for which it was formed, it has survived by adapting to the needs of a well-regulated and stable system of international financial arrangements. As one analyst suggested, it has been a valuable institution as a "talking-shop and meeting-place."[1]

The advent of the BIS was characterized by bankers to be a number of things. At that time, one Chase Manhattan Bank official believed the BIS to be "a positive agency of collaboration between central banks . . . to further central bank solidarity" and that it would be a cooperative venture "rid . . . of political entanglements," able to help "relieve credit dislocation, to build a bridge between countries overstocked with capital and those understocked with it."[2]

It is also one of the more enigmatic international financial institutions operating today. In fact, "the BIS has deliberately shrouded itself in mystery."[3] Part of this characterization stems from the reason for which the BIS was established. The organization was formed in 1930 by the so-called Young Plan, also referred to as the Dawes Plan under the Hague Agreement to facilitate and coordinate the reparations payments or settlements—thus the name Bank for International Settlements—by the German government after World War I.[4] An explanation of this plan is found in Chapter 2. Its major function at that time was to assist the delivery of reparations payments to the victorious Allies. A second objective which has involved the institution is its service as a coordinator of the operations of central banks around the world.

The method to facilitate German reparations adopted by the victorious Allied nations after the establishment of the BIS included the reduction and commercialization of the German reparations payments under the supervision of the BIS. Loans were floated by Germany and Austria and the BIS supervised these loans and managed them until the beginning of World War II, even though the reparations process itself had ended years earlier.[5]

Since 1930, the BIS has developed other roles in the field of international banking, especially after reparations payments ceased in 1932.[6] These functions have included assisting gold transactions among global central banks, research on major banking issues since World War II, promulgation of international rules dealing with foreign bank supervision and bank capital adequacy, and the issuance of research reports on subjects as diverse as derivatives trading by banking institutions and the Year 2000 (Y2K) problem before the end of 1999.

The original operations for which the BIS was established as well as its many other functions will be discussed in this monograph. The evolution, history, administration, and operations, in general, will be discussed and analyzed. In addition, BIS involvement with central banks around the world will be included in the analysis. Enlargement of its board of directors and the reasons for the opposition by the U.S. Federal Reserve Board from officially joining BIS operations will also be discussed. The modus operandi of the BIS including its confidentiality when dealing with and for central bank members will be included in the discussion as will some of the more enigmatic operations carried out by the BIS in World War II.

A chapter will be devoted to some of the latter operations. During the 1930s and 1940s, BIS operations involved transactions between Swiss banks and Nazi Germany in financial and gold dealings. These remain very controversial banking operations and must be a part of the overall analysis of the BIS. The final chapter will include an evaluation of the operations of the BIS carried out over the past 70 years.

Historical Evolution of the BIS

Its Location. As mentioned earlier, the BIS was established to coordinate the payment of reparations by the German government to the Allies. It was also intended to be an institution designed to promote cooperation among central banks in various countries. Its headquarters was established in Basle, Switzerland.[7] Several reasons can be cited for this location. Geographically, Basle is located near the border of Germany, France, and Switzerland. It is a central railroad terminal which facilitated access to other European capitals. Since neutral Switzerland has been famous for its banking establishments and financial operations, the BIS could facilitate the reparations payments quite well from this location. Since the end of World War I, Swiss banks had been a safe haven for international payments in currency and gold. Swiss banks in Basle, Zurich, and other cities in Switzerland had been given a vote of confidence by private and corporate customers globally. Few, if any, official controls were imposed on the movement of money in Switzerland. Finally, some have described Basle as a very attractive city on the Rhine River in which to do business.[8]

The BIS offices are located in a round, modern high-rise building within steps from the main railway station. Keeping with the discretion of a highly secretive organization, the BIS building has no outward sign of identification. Leading central bankers can meet in this place several times annually and draw little or no notice.[9]

The present modern high-rise building in which the BIS is located is in a part of old Basle center city. It is such a modest structure that what surrounds it is often mistaken by the media. The BIS was said to be located between a tourist agency and a watch shop by *Time* magazine. It was said to be situated between a tea shop and a hairdresser by *The Sunday Times*. One author of a book about European financiers thought it was located between a jeweler and a sweet shop.[10]

Reparations and the Young Plan

The Young Plan, named after Owen D. Young, was essentially a decision made by the representatives of the victorious Allied nations to exact a certain amount of reparations from the German Government as well as its allies for its role in World War I. It is often referred to as the Dawes Plan, named after Charles G. Dawes. Young and Dawes were experts appointed in 1923 by President Calvin Coolidge to a commission to investigate German finances. The Dawes Plan was adopted in 1924 and is discussed in more detail in Chapter 2. A form of annuities was created, permitting payments by means of international loans. An institution was needed to coordinate this method of payments and, thus, the BIS was established for that reason at an international meeting known as the Hague Conference, for its location in The Hague, Netherlands. In addition to the reparations settlement function, the BIS was also appointed to act as Trustee for reparations payments made by Bulgaria, Hungary, and Czechoslovakia.

The Young Plan was made effective when documents were drawn up in three meetings. These were held in The Hague in 1925, Baden-Baden, Germany, in 1929, and at a second meeting in The Hague in 1930. In the Baden-Baden meeting, the relations between other governments and an institution such as the proposed BIS, as well as its location, were subjects for discussion. During the second Hague meeting, the BIS was established and the choice of its first operating officials was discussed. The BIS began operations as an international organization governed by international law with privileges and immunities necessary for the performance of its functions.

However, by 1932, reparations payments had ended and the primary reason for the BIS caused a movement to elevate the importance of the second objective mentioned earlier. Since the beginning of the century, officials of the industrialized national governments believed a need existed to centralize regulation of the international banking system. After World War I, the United States became a major international trading nation. The British Commonwealth and other European nations became aware of the importance of international business. To facilitate international trade and investment, a strong international banking system was necessary. These governments desired to establish a regulatory agency which could supervise international banks. Thus, the BIS became, in a manner, that agency.

Its operations were to be funded initially by the central banks of Belgium, France, Germany, Italy, Japan, and the United Kingdom. The promotion of international financial stability became a primary concern of the BIS. Thus, any plans to abolish the institution since its establishment never went further than the backrooms of its planners.

Original Membership, Directors, and Ownership

The BIS began operations with the legal structure of a limited company with an issued share capital. This legal form of organization was desired by the founders of the BIS because they believed the institution should be insulated from governmental interference as much as possible.[11]

BIS activities were funded with the financial resources available to it. These funds had various sources but the major amount came from assessments of the participating central banks. A second major source of funds included long-term deposits made primarily by central banks and other financial institutions according to the trust agreement which established the BIS. The BIS currently holds and invests 10–15 percent of the world's currency reserves.[12] A third resource was represented by treasury funds deposited with the BIS by central banks. Finally, central banks augmented the BIS reserves with money they deposited for their own accounts.

The founders of the BIS included the central banks of Belgium, France, Germany, Italy, Japan, and the United Kingdom along with three leading commercial banks from the United States, including J.P. Morgan & Company, First National Bank of New York, and First National Bank of Chicago. Each central bank subscribed to 16,000 shares and the three U.S. banks also subscribed to this same number of shares. In all, 23 shareholding institutions from different nations subscribed to 112,000 of the 165,100 shares outstanding in the first year of BIS operations. The BIS was authorized to issue 600,000 shares and 529,165 of these are currently outstanding. At the time the initial capital of the BIS was issued, some of the Belgian and French shares and all of the American shares were sold to the public. At the end of 2000, 86.3 percent of the outstanding shares were owned by central banks while the remainder were privately owned, although this will change drastically, as discussed later. Only central banks have voting power. Although the BIS is an organization with outstanding shares and has the legal structure of a limited company, it behaves more like a cooperative form of organization in terms of its central bank members.

An Extraordinary General Meeting of the BIS on January 8, 2001, approved a proposal to restrict ownership of BIS shares to central banks.[13] The privately-owned shares, 13.7 percent of all shares, were withdrawn and shareholders were paid approximately US$10,000 per share. The BIS Board voted unanimously to take this action, which affected some 1,000 institutional investors. Some private investors in BIS shares were not happy about this decision even though the offer made by the BIS was at least a 95 percent premium over the exchange-traded price of BIS shares. The BIS admitted that the shares' net asset value was at least 18 percent higher than the buyout price. A major shareholder has sued in court to stop the action.[14]

The BIS rationalized this decision on the grounds that its public mission was to promote cooperation among central banks and contribute to international financial stability. The major goal of the private shareholders was to maximize their financial investment, an objective which does not conform to the international role of the BIS or its mission.[15]

The U.S. Federal Reserve System and the BIS

The U.S. Federal Reserve System, represented by its Board of Governors, had the right to join the BIS Board of Directors from the beginning. However, this right was not consummated until 1994, even though the Federal Reserve Board had been represented ex-officio at important meetings promulgated by the BIS. A number of reasons for the absence of the Federal Reserve can be cited.[16] First, at the time of the inception of the BIS in 1929–1930, the principal function for the BIS was to coordinate Germany's war reparations. The Federal Reserve believed it was not appropriate for it to join the BIS Board since the United States was not a party to Germany's reparations settlement.

During World War II, some attempts were made to abolish the BIS, so the Federal Reserve delayed joining its Board. After the war, the International Monetary Fund (IMF) and the World Bank were established at the Bretton Woods, New Hampshire, conference to form agencies to facilitate the finance and development operations of the United Nations. U.S. officials believed the BIS operations might be co-opted by these new agencies. However, the United States' position on this matter was mellowed by the belief that the BIS might be able to perform beneficial operations in conjunction with the IMF especially and, perhaps, with the World Bank.

During the first 20 years after World War II, the United States delayed joining the BIS Board, again for a number of reasons. If the United States joined the BIS Board, it was felt that this might be taken as preferential treatment of the BIS to the disadvantage of the IMF. Second, the BIS had a distinctively European flavor and some believed that it was more a regional institution rather than an agency which could facilitate international financial matters on a global basis. Third, if the Federal Reserve were to become involved in the BIS gold operations, such cooperation might be construed as self-centered in an operation with international economic policy implications. Finally, the BIS had played a more direct part in gold transactions with South Africa. U.S. policy toward South Africa, at that time, would be adversely affected by such Federal Reserve/BIS cooperative efforts in the gold market.

The U.S. Federal Reserve did eventually join and participate directly with the BIS Board of Directors in 1994. This move and the reasons for it will be discussed in Chapter 7.

Original Objectives

As mentioned earlier, the major objective mandated by the founders of the BIS was the coordination and settlement of Germany's World War I reparations payments. As an adjunct function to this objective, the BIS was appointed Trustee for reparations payments by Bulgaria, Hungary, and Czechoslovakia for their actions in World War I. A more general objective for the BIS was the promotion of cooperation among central banks and the provision of additional facilities for international financial operations. Some original officials involved in the establishment of the BIS believed a global institution was needed to regulate and supervise the operations of international banks because of the significant increase in international trade and investment after World War I. However, this function was not adopted by the BIS until the 1970s.

Since World War II, the BIS has broadened its role as an international financial institution. Its operations have expanded to cooperation not only with individual European central banks but to those members of the Group of Ten, or G10 countries. The Group of Ten are the central banks of the 10 leading industrialized countries: Belgium, Canada, France, Germany, Italy, Japan, the Netherlands, Sweden, the United Kingdom, and the United States. The Swiss central bank, despite Switzerland's neutrality, has also become a member. The BIS facilitates meetings with the G10 and other important international financial entities to discuss important global financial issues. The agency has established several committees which have dealt with important international bank supervision, capital adequacy, and international financial problems and has issued a number of highly beneficial reports. Its own annual report is one of the most highly sought documents for its analysis of international financial and monetary market issues. Its committees have promulgated important regulations which have been adopted globally in the areas of foreign bank supervision and international bank capital adequacy. These topics will be discussed in detail in subsequent chapters of this treatise.

BIS Functions Since 1930

In this section, the functions performed by the BIS since its establishment will be summarized. The major operations will be discussed in more detail in subsequent chapters. The summary will cover three distinct periods since the BIS began operations: the early period, 1930–1970; the middle period, 1970–1990; and the recent period, since 1990.

Early Period, 1930–1970. The BIS began operations by coordinating the settlement of reparations payments by the German government and its allies after World War I. However, this function ended in 1932 when reparations payments ended. The BIS continued to be a "central bank for central banks" by facilitating gold and foreign exchange transactions in the global financial markets. These operations were accomplished with the greatest degree of confidentiality. Thus, the BIS became an international financial institution respected by national governments and central banks as well as the private international banking community for its secrecy and integrity.

During the global depression in the 1930s and world war and its aftermath in the 1940s, the BIS remained an obscure institution performing its operations and maintaining its confidentiality with central banks, primarily those located in Europe. Its research and analysis of international financial markets and affairs continued to be performed throughout the 1950s and 1960s.

Middle Period, 1970–1990. During this period, the BIS began to expand its focus. Until the 1970s, its relations had been primarily with central banks. The organization became involved with the world of private international banking during this period.

The primary reason for this change of reference stemmed from the failure of two banks in 1974. These bank failures were Franklin National Bank in New York and Bankhaus Herstatt in Germany. Both failures were the result of overextension in foreign exchange trading.[17] Criminal activity was proved in the Franklin National Bank case—at that time, the largest bank failure in U.S. history—when Michele Sindona, an Italian banker with ties to Franklin National Bank, was later convicted and jailed for bank fraud. Herstatt's failure seemed more of an accident than illegal activity, although some of its officers were convicted of German banking violations. Its officers had speculated in foreign currencies and owed more on these transactions than the bank's resources and, thus, the bank had to be closed rather than default on its debt.

The global issue from these bank failures became one of fault and who should pay the creditors. In the case of Herstatt, many accused the Deutsche Bundesbank, Germany's central bank, with acting too slowly and failing to regard the time difference between European and New York foreign exchange markets, during which foreign exchange transactions could not be settled.

The issue came to a head when the G10 central bankers with the cooperation of the BIS formed a committee to resolve this question. This committee was formerly known as the Basle Committee on Banking Supervision but came to be known as the Cooke Committee for its first chairman, Peter Cooke. The Cooke Committee formulated and negotiated the Basle Concordat of 1975 which attempted to settle the question of responsibility in the cases of foreign bank failures at that time. This promulgation will be discussed in detail in Chapter 4.

The 1975 Basle Concordat was tested in 1982 and found wanting. The president of Italian bank Banco Ambrosiano was found hanged beneath the Blackfriars Bridge in London.[18] The bank was found to have uncovered debts totaling $1.3 billion, mostly incurred by its holding company registered in Luxembourg. The Bank of Italy aided the parent bank but argued that the Luxembourg banking authorities were responsible for the failed subsidiary in that country. However, Luxembourg had no central bank and was part of a monetary union with Belgium. Thus, Luxembourg denied any responsibility for assisting the failure. Again, responsibility for the failure of a foreign banking affiliate was in question.

The Cooke Committee responded by revising the Basle Concordat in 1983. This revision held parent banks responsible for supervision of their holding companies or subsidiaries whether located abroad or in the home country. Central banks in the home country of the parent bank could close any subsidiaries deemed not adequately supervised by the parent bank.

Finally, the BIS became involved in another issue dealing with private international banks during this period. Another concordat was promulgated in 1988 dealing with rules for international banks in the maintenance of capital adequate to support their operations. Studies during the 1970s and 1980s had shown that, first, banks were inadequately capitalized given their riskier activities and, second, that no rules were in place mandating higher capital ratios for international banks which resorted to risky lending operations.[19]

The 1988 Concordat, prompted by pressure from the U.S. Federal Reserve Board, set rules for standard methods in the determination of capital and reserves for international banks sufficient to support their assets, primarily loans. Foreign banks were held to the same capital adequacy standards as were U.S. banks. The 1988 Concordat, often referred to as the Basle Accord on Capital Adequacy, will be discussed in more detail in Chapter 5 along with the subsequent proposed revisions.

Recent Period Since 1990. One of the first issues facing international banking regulators in this period had begun in the 1970s, continued throughout the 1980s, and reached its zenith in the early 1990s. This issue stemmed from the problems created by the Bank for Credit and Commerce International (BCCI).

BCCI had been formed in the late 1970s with the alleged objective of furnishing an international banking institution which would cater directly to the banking needs of the less-developed nations of the world. Its founder was a Pakistani citizen who quickly pushed BCCI to become one of the more significant international banks of its time. BCCI avoided national supervision for years because it operated out of Luxembourg, a country with liberal and, perhaps, lax banking rules, and was registered in the Cayman Islands for tax purposes.

BCCI, however, began to violate national banking regulations as it grew by acquisitions. First, the bank began to acquire one or two influential banks in a number of the industrialized nations. In the United States, BCCI acquired banks in Washington, D.C., and Atlanta, Georgia. BCCI majority control of these banks was acquired somehow without permission of the Federal Reserve Board, the regulator responsible for foreign banking operations in the United States. Its policy seemed to be one of placing individuals in command of these banks who had had some major influence on national governments in the parent countries. Second, BCCI became suspected of laundering drug money and funding some kind of illegal arms operation. At that time, some in the media began to refer to the institution as the "*B*ank for *C*rooks and *C*riminals *I*nternational."

Finally, national banking supervisors in Great Britain and 60 other countries closed BCCI offices on July 5, 1991. Over the next several months, an investigation showed that BCCI was the center of an international web of crime, espionage, and intrigue. Its depositors had unwittingly financed a "rogue empire."[20]

The BCCI case, coupled with other cases in the 1980s including the technical failure of Continental Illinois in 1984 and the rescue of Johnson Matthey banking subsidiaries by the Bank of England, resulted in the BIS taking an even more active role in the private international banking world, primarily through its cooperation with the G10 central bankers.

These cases pointed out to BIS officials that bank capital adequacy was an even more important issue than was thought in 1988 when the Basle Accord was promulgated. The inadequacy of bank capital among international banks could and did undermine consumer confidence in the banking world as was reflected in the investment market's reaction to the prices of international banks' equity. By the end of the 1990s, it had become apparent that the 1988 Basle Accord on bank capital had not been fully successful. Questions arose about whether the BIS rules pertained to all banks or only to international banks. The off-balance sheet items, especially derivatives used for price hedging purposes, needed better definition and rules for disclosure. Thus, the capital accord has been revisited. These discussions and results will be discussed further in Chapter 5.

Other issues, some related to the bank supervision and capital issues, have been the focus of BIS committee research and discussion. These include derivatives and their use. Several financial problems plagued banks and companies globally which were blamed on the use and lack of control of derivatives. Examples of these included U.S. companies Procter & Gamble and Gibson Greetings, Metallgesellschaft of Germany, Bank One in the United States and Barings, the over-300-year-old British merchant bank. In addition, the studies included clearing arrangements such as bilateral and multilateral netting arrangements, and the Y2K problem which plagued the financial world during the last few years of the 1990s. These issues and BIS studies of them will be discussed more fully in subsequent chapters.

The BIS, of course, has carried on several activities with and for central banks around the world. These operations include deposit-taking and loans, gold operations, foreign exchange operations, settlement activities, and dealing with Latin American Brady bonds. The Brady Plan had been implemented in 1989 as a solution to the ongoing Latin American debt crisis. Brady bonds were named for Nicholas Brady who was the U.S. Secretary of the Treasury at that time. He put forth this method which emphasized debt relief through forgiveness of loans instead of new lending. Banks were given a choice under the Brady Plan. They could make new loans or they could write off portions of their existing loans with a Latin American government in exchange for new government securities whose interest payments would be backed by funds from the IMF. These debt instruments were called Brady bonds and commercial banks had to make new loans at the same time that they were writing off existing loans for the plan to work.

Brady bonds are usually collateralized by U.S. zero-coupon bonds of various maturities. Thus, the principal is guaranteed but most of these bonds' interest is not. If the country cannot pay the interest on these bonds, investors can collect 100 percent of the principal at maturity, but they lose the interest and the bonds carry an opportunity cost because the investor must tie up the money until maturity. If the interest is not paid, the bonds' value falls on the secondary market. Currency crises such as the Mexican peso devaluation can cause Brady bonds to be very volatile.[21]

The BIS also makes available services to central banks which are referred to as facilities. These are liquid resources which the BIS advances to central banks and include currency swaps for gold, credits advanced against gold pledges, marketable short-term securities, and, occasionally, unsecured and standby credits.[22] In addition to liquidity advances to central banks, the BIS has provided financial assistance to countries when it is guaranteed by a group of leading central banks. One example of this support was the 1998 credit facility arranged by the BIS for Brazil and funded primarily by the United States.[23] Chapter 7 is devoted to a discussion of these functions performed by the BIS.

A major banking activity in which the BIS is involved concerns the management of central bank funds deposited with it.[24] Any funds not needed for lending to central banks are invested in the international financial markets. The BIS deposits some funds with commercial banks and also invests in short-term negotiable instruments such as U.S. Treasury bills.

In addition to its relationships with national central banks and the private international banking community, the BIS has also developed joint and cooperative activities with other multilateral financial institutions. These include the IMF, World Bank, and other international development banks. These activities will be discussed in Chapter 9.

The BIS has expanded its operations with central banks and international banking supervision to include relationships with the international insurance industry. The agency has formed a working relationship with the International Association of Insurance Supervisors (IAIS). BIS work in this area will be discussed in Chapter 10.

BIS' Center for Monetary and Economic Research has performed a function which has not been well publicized. Its research of international financial markets and related activities has been a significant contribution to the literature in this area and to national policy-makers in the international economics arena. Its publications include a quarterly review, annual report, and miscellaneous documents. The BIS Annual Report is published in a number of languages and is difficult to obtain because of the great demand for its analyses of international financial markets. This area will be discussed in detail in Chapter 11.

As mentioned previously, the BIS performed a function in the 1930s and 1940s which has clouded the evaluation of its activities as a leading international financial agency. Nazi Germany transferred gold and other valuables to Swiss banks. Much, perhaps most, of these assets were alleged to have been stolen from Jewish citizens who were sent to the work and death camps as part of the Holocaust. The BIS facilitated some or all of these transfers in the apparent laundering of these commodity assets into money assets to be used by the German war machine. This issue will be discussed in detail in Chapter 12.

The final chapter will be devoted to a summary of BIS operations. Potential areas of study will be discussed. The chapter concludes with an evaluation of the operations of the world's oldest international financial institution.

ADMINISTRATION AND FINANCIAL DATA

Administration

The BIS administrative framework is comprised of the General Meeting and the Board of Directors. The General Meeting is held annually, usually in June, but an Extraordinary General Meeting may be called at any time by the Board of Directors when necessary. One such meeting was last held on January 8, 2001, for the purpose of suspending private ownership of the BIS.

The Board of Directors is comprised of the governors of the central banks of Belgium, France, Germany, Italy, and the United Kingdom. The Chairman of the Board of Governors of the U.S. Federal Reserve System sits on the Board of Directors as an ex-officio member. A maximum of nine governors of other member central banks may be elected to the Board. Currently, the governors of the central banks of Canada, Japan, the Netherlands, Sweden, and Switzerland have been elected to the Board.

The BIS Board of Directors elects a Chairman from among its members and appoints the President of the BIS. Both offices have been vested in one person since 1948. In addition to these governmental decisions, the Board also appoints a General Manager of the BIS as well as other management officials. Current staff of the BIS numbers more than 500 and comes from 35 countries.

Financial Data

According to BIS, *First Annual Report*, the BIS showed total assets as of March 31, 1931, of 1,901,148,912.91 in Swiss gold francs. These assets were held in time deposits, commercial bills, bankers' acceptances, and treasury bills.

As of March 31, 2000, according to BIS documents, the agency's balance sheet showed total assets of 75 billion gold francs with capital and reserves of 3.2 billion gold francs. In terms of the market price of gold at that time, BIS total assets were US$147 billion and its capital and reserves amounted to US$6.7 billion. The exchange rate used at that date was 1 gold franc = US$1.94 and the price of gold used for these calculations was a fixed rate of US$208 per ounce of fine gold. The gold franc of the BIS has a gold weight of a little more than 0.29 grams of fine gold, identical to the gold parity of the Swiss franc at the foundation of the BIS in 1930 until September 1936 when the Swiss franc's gold parity was suspended. Changes in the organization of the BIS including changes in its administration and financial operations will be discussed in more detail in Chapter 2. The most recent financial statements for the BIS are found in the Appendices.

SUMMARY AND CONCLUSIONS

The BIS is the oldest international financial institution still in existence. It has operated as a "central bank for central banks" and has moved into the area of facilitating the regulation of activities of private international banks. It has been instrumental in defining national bank supervisory responsibility for foreign banking institution failures and promulgation of capital adequacy rules for international banks. Its studies of international financial payment and settlement systems and issues such as derivatives use and the Y2K problem have been highly received by the international financial community. As shall be seen in subsequent chapters, the BIS has an excellent international staff and has the respect of the global central banking community.

The Basle Committee on Bank Supervision has gained an international reputation for the work it has accomplished since the mid-1970s. Its two Basle Concordats, to be discussed in detail in Chapter 4, have defined the responsibilities of bank supervisory authorities in the case of foreign bank unit failures. Its work on bank capital acequacy spelled out in the Basle Accords of 1988 and 2001, to be discussed in more detail in Chapter 5, have placed banks on notice to maintain more capital to cover risky loans and investments. Its work with national bank supervisory authorities after the BCCI case has facilitated the progress in the coordination of bank regulatory policy. This work was designed originally for the central banks of the G10 countries but much of it has been applied generally to banks in emerging and transition economies and to smaller banks in industrialized nations.

Most of the operations carried out by the BIS have been highly positive and have contributed significantly to central banking efficiency and bank supervisory activities. However, it has a clouded past, especially with regard to its relationship with Nazi Germany's banks and the Swiss banking industry in the 1930s and 1940s. More light needs to be shed on this part of the BIS' past.

Finally, the decision made by the BIS Board on January 8, 2001, to restrict shareownership to central banks and to compensate private shareholders for their shares needs a comment. The BIS Board rationalized this decision by stating that the objectives of the BIS and the private shareholders were in conflict and implied that the private owners might somehow hinder the fulfillment of the BIS' goals. This conclusion seems interesting in view of the fact that only central banks are permitted to vote outstanding shares. How private shareholders could affect BIS decisions when they could not vote their shares remains a mystery.

NOTES

1. Paul Ferris, *The Money Men of Europe* (New York: Macmillan, 1968), p. 24.

2. Shepard Morgan, "Constructive Functions of the International Bank," *Foreign Affairs*, Vol. 9 (July 9, 1931), pp. 583, 588.

3. "Lenses of Last Resort," *The Economist*, 6 June 1998. Available from *Economist.com*, 7 July 1999, by Internet.

4. See Richard B. Morris, ed., *Encyclopedia of American History* (New York: Harper and Brothers, 1961), pp. 320–321.

5. Ray August, *International Business Law: Text, Cases, and Readings* (Englewood Cliffs, NJ: Prentice Hall, 1993), p. 397.

6. See Henry H. Schloss, *The Bank for International Settlements*. (New York: New York University, 1970), for an early discussion of this institution.

7. This book will use the American style spelling of the city in which the BIS is located, i.e., Basle. The European style, Basel, will be used only in citations of literature.

8. Melvyn Westlake, "Into Basle's Inner Sanctum," *The Banker*, Vol. 144 (March 1994), p. 14+.

9. Donald A. Ball and Wendell H. McCulloch, Jr., *International Business* (Chicago: Irwin, 1996), p. 133.

10. Paul Ferris, *The Money Men of Europe* (New York: Macmillan, 1968), p. 252.

11. Ray August, *International Business Law: Text, Cases, and Readings* (Englewood Cliffs, NJ: Prentice-Hall, 1993), p. 395.

12. Ibid.

13. "BIS Press Release," January 8, 2001, p. 1.

14. "Greenspan: Shareholder Foe?" *Institutional Investor*, Vol. 35 (March 2001), p. 13.

15. "BIS Press Release," January 8, 2001, p. 2.

16. Charles J. Siegman, "The Bank for International Settlements and the Federal Reserve," *Federal Reserve Bulletin*, Vol. 80 (October 1994), pp. 901–902.

17. Susan Strange, *Mad Money: When Markets Outgrow Governments* (Ann Arbor, MI: University of Michigan Press, 1998), pp. 158–159.

18. See Larry Gurwin, "Death of a Banker," *Institutional Investor*, Vol. 16 (October 1982), pp. 258–275, for a complete analysis of the Banco Ambrosiano case.

19. James C. Baker and Raj Aggarwal, "Variations and Trends in Capital Ratios of Large Banks: Implications for International Bank Safety and Regulation," *Akron Business and Economic Review*, Vol. 15 (Summer, 1984), pp. 25–32.

20. Ethan B. Kapstein, *Supervising International Banks: Origins and Implications of the Basle Accord* (Princeton, NJ: Princeton University International Finance Section, December 1991), p. 1.

21. Joan Warner, "Brady Bonds: Are They Worth the Risk?" *Business Week*, November 25, 1996, p. 152.

22. August, *International Business Law: Text, Cases, and Readings*, p. 396.

23. "Bank for International Settlements Profile," p. 5, found at www.bis.org/about/profil2000.htm.

24. Maurice D. Levi, *International Finance: The Markets and Financial Management of Multinational Business* (New York: McGraw-Hill, 1996), p. 222.

CHAPTER 2

Changes in BIS Organization, Administration, and Financing

INTRODUCTION

The BIS was formed in 1930 and, as was discussed in Chapter 1, was established primarily to facilitate German reparations payments after World War I. Establishment of an international financial institution with the form of BIS had been discussed since the beginning of the 20th century, as international trade and investment began to increase significantly. The BIS was created when the Young Plan was adopted by the Hague Conference in 1930.

The Young Plan, most often referred to as the Dawes Plan, was initiated December 15, 1923, when U.S. President Calvin Coolidge appointed Charles G. Dawes, Henry M. Robinson, and Owen D. Young to serve as experts on a commission to investigate German finances. On December 26, 1922, and January 9, 1923, Germany had been declared in default on its reparations payments after World War I. French and Belgian troops then occupied the Ruhr Region on September 26, 1923, and the German mark was declared worthless.[1]

The Dawes Plan was formally adopted April 9, 1924, and it proposed to (1) stabilize the German currency by reorganizing the Reichsbank under Allied supervision and (2) make a new schedule of German reparation payments for five years. A foreign loan of 800 million gold marks was made to Germany under the plan with the United States giving US $110 million of this.[2]

The BIS was formed with funding by the central banks of six nations, Belgium, France, Germany, Italy, Japan, and the United Kingdom. In addition, three private international banks from the United States also assisted in financing the establishment of the BIS. The governors of these six central banks became the founding members of the original BIS Board of Directors. The Chairman of the U.S. Federal Reserve Board was also invited to become a member of the BIS Board but declined for several reasons until 1994 to become a member of the Board. This issue will be discussed in a subsequent section of this chapter.

BIS Objectives

As will be made evident in this book, the BIS' original objective, facilitation of reparation payments by Germany and its allies, had ended and the organization, since then, has taken a much broader focus as an international organization fostering international monetary and financial cooperation in its services, primarily rendered for member central banks. In taking on this mandate, the BIS operates as:

1. a forum to promote discussion and facilitate decision-making processes among central banks and within the international financial community;
2. a principal counterparty for central banks in their financial transactions;
3. a center for economic and monetary research on important global issues; and
4. agent or trustee in connection with selected international financial operations.

ADDITION OF CENTRAL BANK MEMBERS

The primary decision-making body of the BIS is its Board of Directors. The present Board of Directors has 17 members of which 11 are central bank governors. The Board chairman is Urban Bäckström, the Governor of Sveriges Riksbank, the central bank of Sweden. The General Manager of BIS, elected by the Board, is Andrew Crockett and the Assistant General Manager is André Icard.

The BIS administration is comprised of three major departments. These are the General Secretariat whose head is Gunter D. Baer, the

Monetary and Economic Department whose head is William R. White, and the Banking Department whose head is Robert D. Sleeper. The BIS' General Counsel is Mario Giovanoli.

Addition of New Central Bank Members

From 1945 until 1994, the BIS Board included only Western European central banks as members. In July 1994, the BIS elected the governors of the central banks of Canada and Japan. Also in 1994, the United States took its seat on the Board, as will be discussed in the next section.

In recent years, BIS leadership believed that additional central bank members from countries other than European would benefit the work of the institution. As of March 31, 2000, 49 central banks had been invited to become members of the BIS with voting rights and authorized representation at the General Meetings. See Figure 2.1 for a listing of these member central banks.

U.S. FEDERAL RESERVE MEMBERSHIP

The U.S. Federal Reserve System (Fed) had been invited to join the BIS Board of Directors in the early years of its existence. The Fed finally accepted membership in 1994. Several reasons had caused U.S. officials to delay this action. At first, the BIS' primary function was to facilitate the reparations payments by the German Government. The United States was not a party to these payments and, thus, U.S. officials believed it inappropriate to join the direct activities and administration of the BIS.

After reparations payments ended in 1932, the depression and World War II kept the U.S. monetary authorities from focussing on international financial affairs. In fact, the liquidation of the BIS was debated during the latter stages of the war, and was supported by the U.S. Government. The newly formed World Bank and IMF were viewed as principal organizations whose objectives were to deal with postwar international monetary affairs. Thus, the United States government held that the BIS was a superfluous organization.

After the war, the U.S. position was reconsidered and Fed officials acknowledged that the BIS might be able to perform some functions beneficial to the international monetary system that the institutions developed at Bretton Woods could not handle, such as certain ac-

Figure 2.1
Member Central Banks of the BIS

Group of 10 Central Banks and European Central Banks

Belgium	Canada
France	Germany
Italy	Japan
Netherlands	Sweden
Switzerland	United Kingdom
United States	European Central Bank

Newly Added Central Banks

Argentina	Australia
Austria	Brazil
Bulgaria	China
Czech Republic	Denmark
Estonia	Finland
Greece	Hong Kong SAR
Hungary	Iceland
Ireland	Korea
Latvia	Lithuania
Malaysia	Mexico
Norway	Poland
Portugal	Romania
Russia	Saudi Arabia
Singapore	Slovakia
South Africa	Spain
Thailand	Turkey

Central Bank Members Pending Yugoslav Legal Issue Settlement

Central Bank of Bosnia & Herzegovina   Croatian National Bank
National Bank of Republic of Macedonia Bank of Slovenia

Source: www.bis.org/about/profil2000.htm, January 8, 2001, p. 7.

tivities with regard to Marshall Plan aid to Western Europe.[3] The Fed reluctance for this reason persisted during the 1950s and 1960s.

Another important reason for the reluctance of the Fed to join the BIS stemmed from the latter's gold transactions. At that time, the U.S. policy concerning South Africa made such an arrangement with the BIS a sensitive issue in U.S. diplomatic relations with other countries. South Africa was the world's leading gold producer and the gold market had important international economic policy implications during that period.

During the 1970s, the Federal Reserve Board reached a consensus that the BIS had become a sufficiently important international monetary institution that the Fed must be a party to its deliberations and, thus, should have representation on the BIS Board of Directors. However, that consensus was never acted upon and the Fed retained its attitude toward the BIS.

During the 1980s, the U.S. Congress requested that the U.S. Secretaries of State and Treasury and the Chairman of the Federal Reserve Board of Governors prepare a report for Congress on the question of Fed membership on the BIS Board. The conclusion of this study was that no urgency mandated a change in the Fed-BIS relationship and that certain technical and policy reservations militated against the Fed's becoming a member of the BIS Board, but that the matter should be reviewed periodically. Whatever these "technical and policy reservations" were, they apparently substantially diminished in the years after that report.

Finally, in 1994, the Chairman of the Board of Governors of the Federal Reserve System assumed the U.S. seat on the Board of Directors of the BIS.[4] The reason given by the Fed for this belated action was U.S. recognition of the role of the BIS as a major forum for consultation, cooperation, and information exchange among central bankers and the anticipation that such a role would have to be expanded. The international banking expansion needed such agencies to study and support international bank supervisory standards. Thus, the United States needed to be a party to the expansion of this focus in the international economic arena. In addition, with the end of the Cold War, U.S. international monetary and financial policies could be broadened to include the jurisdiction of the BIS and its international cooperative objectives toward the international financial system. The bank and savings association failures of the 1980s, many of which were caused by either mismanagement or inadequate capital, may have prompted the Fed's officials' belief that the BIS could play an important role in the alleviation of such bank supervisory issues and, thus, a stronger Fed presence in the BIS operations would be beneficial.

Alan Greenspan, Chairman of the Fed Board of Governors assumed an ex-officio seat on the BIS Board of Directors in 1994 and the United States was not required to make a financial outlay by purchasing shares in the BIS. However, the Fed was entitled to vote the shares issued as part of the original U.S. issue beginning with the June 1995 Annual Meeting.

BIS CONNECTION TO THE GROUP OF 10

The BIS has maintained a very cooperative relationship with the Group of 10 central banks (G10). The staff of these 11 central banks, Switzerland included, carry on joint studies and make recommendations in collaboration with the BIS. The group of 10 includes the central banks of Belgium, Canada, France, Germany, Italy, Japan, the Netherlands, Sweden, the United Kingdom, and the United States. Switzerland has also become a member despite the country's neutrality and, thus, the Group of 10 actually consists of 11 countries. The governors of these central banks frequently meet at BIS headquarters in Basle.

From its beginning, the BIS has participated in G10 meetings. This is facilitated because the G10 governors meet during the regular BIS meetings. Throughout the 1960s, the G10 coordinated their interventions in the international gold markets through the gold pool and this coordination was assisted by contacts with the BIS. A number of activities designed to achieve more international financial stability have been initiated in the G10 meetings and which the BIS has been instrumental in their formulation and implementation. Among these are the monitoring and analysis of monetary and financial markets, banking supervision, and payment and settlement systems.

The G10 governors were instrumental in the formation of the Cooke Committee, or Basle Committee, on Banking Supervision, to alleviate the problems caused by the failures of Franklin National Bank of New York and Bankhaus Herstatt of Germany in 1974. The secretariat of this committee is provided by the BIS and the committee encompasses three major areas: (1) it serves as a forum for discussion of how specific supervisory problems may be handled, (2) it coordinates the sharing of supervisory responsibilities among national banking supervisory authorities with respect to a parent bank's foreign affiliates in the quest for better global banking supervision, and (3) it aims to increase supervisory standards so that international banking soundness and stability can be improved.

In short, the joint cooperative efforts between the BIS and the G10 governors has increased the efficiency of regulatory and supervisory efforts aimed at improving the international banking system. Without this cooperation in the various studies and standards developed, the individual central banks among the G10 would have continued to employ bank supervisory standards which would have resulted in an unstable system of international banking.

ADMINISTRATIVE STRUCTURE OF THE BIS

Shareownership in the BIS

Of the 600,000 shares authorized by the founders of the BIS, 529,165 are currently issued and outstanding. Each share is valued at 2,500 gold francs. The BIS gold franc has a gold weight of slightly more than 0.29 grams of fine gold, with one gold franc equal to US$1.94. The gold content is valued at the fixed rate of US$208 per ounce of fine gold.[5]

The BIS declares an annual dividend and all shares are entitled to this dividend. However, only central banks have voting rights at the Annual Meeting. During the years in which the U.S. Federal Reserve was not a member of the Board, the BIS Board appointed Citibank N.A. of New York to exercise the voting rights of all of the original U.S. shares issued in 1930. Citibank usually exercised these voting rights by appointing the president or general manager of the BIS to act as its proxy.[6]

BIS Board of Directors

Current BIS statutes permit the governors of the central banks of Belgium, France, Germany, Italy, the United Kingdom, and the United States to be ex-officio members of the Board as long as they remain governors of their respective central banks.

Each ex-officio member may appoint to the BIS Board another person of the same nationality from finance, industry, or commerce. These appointed directors hold office for three years and are eligible for reappointment. In addition to these six ex-officio members and six appointed members, a two-thirds majority of the BIS Board may elect as many as nine members to the Board who are governors of central banks that have subscribed to BIS shares and are from countries other than those represented by the ex-officio members.

Elected members of the Board may serve for three years and may be re-elected.

FINANCIAL OPERATIONS OF THE BIS

The BIS performs several banking, trustee, and agent functions for central banks and other international organizations. Among these transactions is the acceptance of currencies and gold as deposits, primarily from central banks. These transactions are carried out with the highest degree of confidentiality. More than 100 central banks have deposits with the BIS. Current financial statements for the BIS are found in Appendix I.

The BIS also invests its assets in international and national money markets and makes loans to central banks. Its trusteeship relations were originally developed from the World War I reparations payments, its first mandate. It has served as a depositary for secured loans of the European Coal and Steel Community, a forerunner of the European Community. The BIS has served as an agent for the European Monetary Cooperation Fund and has recently served as agent for collateral arrangements as a part of the Brazilian commercial bank debt restructuring and as sub-agent for the Federal Reserve Bank of New York with regard to Brady bonds used to collateralize Venezuelan debt.

The concept of Brady bonds was discussed in Chapter 1. These were bonds issued under the Brady Plan, named for then U.S. Secretary of Treasury Nicholas Brady. These were government bonds whose interest was backed by money from the IMF and which replaced bonds underwritten by banks to Latin American countries. Banks would then write off the latter bonds as in default. Many banks used these bonds as a way to exit from the LDC debt market altogether.

Day-to-Day Operations

The day-to-day operations with other central banks or international financial institutions are limited to those permitted by Article 21 of the original BIS statutes and are as follows:

1. buying and selling of gold coin or bullion for its own account or for the account of central banks;
2. holding gold for its own account under reserve in central banks;
3. accepting the supervision of gold for the account of central banks;

4. making advances to or borrowing from central banks against gold, bills of exchange, and other short-term obligations of prime liquidity or other approved securities;

5. discounting, rediscounting, purchasing, or selling with or without its endorsement bills of exchange, checks, and other short-term obligations of prime liquidity;

6. buying and selling foreign exchange for its own account or for the account of central banks;

7. buying and selling negotiable securities other than shares for its own account or for the account of central banks;

8. discounting for central banks bills taken from their portfolio and rediscounting with central banks bills taken from its own portfolio;

9. opening and maintaining current or deposit accounts with central banks;

10. accepting deposits from central banks on current or deposit account;

11. accepting deposits in connection with trustee agreements that may be made between the BIS and governments in connection with international settlements;

12. accepting such other deposits that, as in the opinion of the Board of the BIS, come within the scope of the BIS' functions.

In addition to these day-to-day operations, the BIS may also:

1. act as agent or correspondent for any central bank;

2. arrange with any central bank for the latter to act as its agent or correspondent;

3. enter into agreements to act as trustee or agent in connection with international settlements, provided that such agreements will not encroach on the obligations of the BIS toward any third parties.

The BIS must maintain stable operations with other central banks in these international cooperative activities. Thus, the BIS must have the consent of the central banks it deals with in these international financial functions. In order to avoid any market disruption, if any central bank disapproves of a BIS-proposed operation, the BIS will not execute the transaction.

INCREASE IN BIS RESEARCH STUDIES

During the past three decades, the BIS has initiated or collaborated in a growing number of studies concerning some aspect of international monetary or financial activities. Some of the most significant of these studies and reports will be discussed in more detail in subsequent chapters, specifically Chapter 11. Several reasons can be cited for this increased research activity by the BIS.

Several large banks have failed since the Franklin National Bank and Herstatt failures of the early 1970s. The international banking community has had several episodes of turmoil with banking and savings and loan failures in the 1970s and 1980s. Since 1970, international trade and investment have increased greatly, as has trading in the foreign exchange, equity, derivatives, and bond markets. Foreign exchange trading amounts to more than US $1.5 trillion per day. Banking capital held by the leading international banks was deemed woefully inadequate in the 1970s.

International banking regulatory agencies and international financial organizations began to take action to alleviate these problems and to increase coordination and cooperative efforts in the international monetary and financial system. The BIS developed a number of committees to cooperate with the G10 central banks in dealing with these problems. Thus, a number of issues were studied and research reports were published on a steady schedule by the BIS. Issues covered included which central banking authority is responsible for failures of foreign affiliates of parent banks, rules to insure that banks maintain adequate bank capital to support their assets, how to protect banks and companies from misuse of derivative financial instruments, and what systems are needed to settle the burgeoning amount of cross-border financial transactions. In addition, specific issues such as the Year 2000 (Y2K) problem at the end of the 1990s were committed to BIS committee studies. The work of these committees will be discussed in general in Chapter 3 and in detail in subsequent chapters.

SUMMARY AND CONCLUSIONS

The organizational framework which governs the BIS and its financial structure were discussed in this chapter. The institution began with only six central bank members. Since its inception it has expanded the membership to include 49 central banks with voting rights and representation at the BIS Annual Meeting.

One major omission from its Board was representation of the U.S. central bank, an original invitee to the Board. Several reasons kept the U.S. Federal Reserve from taking its seat in Basle. These reasons persisted until 1994 when U.S. central banking authorities finally decided that U.S. representation in BIS deliberations would benefit not only the international monetary and financial community but the United States as well.

Several problems in the international financial system have arisen since 1970. These problems have mandated in-depth studies by the Group of 10 central banks in cooperation with the BIS. As a result, the BIS has formed several committees to research these problems and to formulate proposals for dealing with them.

The goals of the BIS, including cooperative efforts to ensure stability of the international monetary and financial system, have led the BIS to become involved in several areas in need of rules and international standards. These have run the gamut from banking supervision and bank capital adequacy to payment and settlement systems, derivatives use, and the Y2K problem. The BIS special committees and groups have produced research studies and standards which have improved the international monetary and financial system.

NOTES

1. Richard B. Morris, ed., *Encyclopedia of American History* (New York: Harper and Brothers, 1961), pp. 320–321.

2. Ibid.

3. Charles J. Siegman, "The Bank for International Settlements and the Federal Reserve," *Federal Reserve Bulletin*, Vol. 80 (October 1994), pp. 900–906.

4. Ibid., p. 900.

5. See discussion in Chapter 1 of the decision made January 8, 2001, by the BIS to withdraw all privately-held shares in return for compensation of approximately US$10,000 per share.

6. Siegman, "The Bank for International Settlements and the Federal Reserve, *Federal Reserve Bulletin*, October 1994, p. 904.

CHAPTER 3

BIS Committees and Research

THE BIS AS A FORUM FOR INTERNATIONAL MONETARY AND FINANCIAL COOPERATION

The BIS fulfills its role as a forum for international monetary and financial cooperation by offering its Basle offices as a meeting place for central bankers and secretariats for committees and other groups. Governors and officials of member central banks hold regular meetings in Basle. In July 1998, the BIS opened a representative office for Asia and the Pacific in the Hong Kong Special Administrative Region of the People's Republic of China. Occasional meetings are held at this location. The Annual Meeting of the BIS is held in Basle in June of each year. In June 1999, 92 central banks were represented at the Annual Meeting, 65 at the governor level. Representatives of 13 international financial institutions also attended this meeting.

The BIS also cooperates with the major international financial institutions. The organization participates as an observer at meetings of the Interim Committee of the Board of Governors of the International Monetary Fund (IMF) and of the Finance Ministers of the Group of Ten (G10) countries. These activities will be discussed in detail in Chapter 9.

Introduction to BIS Committees and Other Forums

After World War II, the BIS began to reach out into other areas of international bank regulatory and payments issues. With BIS cooperation, several intra-European payment and settlement arrangements were created. After 1960, the BIS shifted its interest to deal with a number of currency crises in which central banks were involved. After 1962, the Group of 10 (G10) central banks emerged as an important organization in dealing with international monetary and financial cooperation. The G10 countries are the 10 leading industrialized nations and include the central banks of Belgium, Canada, France, Germany, Italy, Japan, the Netherlands, Sweden, the United Kingdom, and the United States. The Swiss central bank has also become a member. The G10 central bank governors began meeting with the BIS on a regular basis and a cooperative spirit developed which has persisted until the present time.

International financial stability was the goal of this BIS-G10 cooperative effort which emerged in a number of areas including the monitoring and analysis of monetary and financial markets, bank supervision, and payment and settlement systems. A number of committees were established to deal with this myriad of global financial issues. Three of the committees established by the G10 central banks and supported by the BIS have been designated as permanent committees with secretariats at the BIS headquarters in Basle. They are the Basle Committee on Banking Supervision, Committee on the Global Financial System, and the Committee on Payment and Settlement Systems. These committees will be introduced in the following sections but their operations will be discussed more fully in subsequent chapters.

Committee on the Global Financial System. In the early 1970s, a standing committee was established and named the Euro-currency Standing Committee. Its focus was the study of international debt problems and their solution, evolution of more efficient financial market structures, derivative instruments and their macroeconomic and prudential implications, and the collection and analysis of new statistical information relevant to these international financial issues. In early 1999, this committee was renamed the Committee on the Global Financial System (CGFS) and changed its focus to monitoring short-term international financial system conditions, long-term analysis of financial markets and their operations, and the formulation of policy recommendations designed to improve market operations and results.

The specific topics studied by the CGFS in the 1999–2000 period included the design of liquid debt markets, market dynamics under stress, transparency in the information provided to market participants, and improvements in the BIS international banking statistics.[1] The CGFS released a report on market liquidity in May 1999 and followed this in October 1999 with a report on how to develop deep and liquid government bond markets. Later the CGFS established a working group to research the current use of stress testing at large financial institutions for use by supervisory authorities and market participants.

The Committee also collaborates on analysis and solution of financial system problems with other international financial institutions such as the IMF. In 1998, the CGFS worked with the IMF to produce a disclosure template for foreign currency assets as well as a more detailed document of guidelines for the implementation of this template in conjunction with other standards formulated by the IMF. The CGFS has formed a working group to study issues such as transparency and improvement of the disclosure of the risk profile of other financial institutions. This group included various international regulatory agencies.

Committee of Experts on Gold and Foreign Exchange. The Committee of Experts on Gold and Foreign Exchange meets at the time of the regular meetings of the BIS. The Committee's functions are to monitor foreign exchange market activities and to analyze their implications for central bank policies and operating procedures. The focus of this committee is on the long-term implications of the stucture of foreign exchange and gold markets. Foreign exchange markets receive most of its focus because of the decline in importance of the global gold markets and the decline in the market value of gold. However, many central banks are currently adopting a policy of selling some of their gold reserves into the international markets and, thus, a cooperative effort, especially from an institution which prides its confidentiality in such operations, may be beneficial to the successful gold operations of member central banks.

Basle Committee on Banking Supervision. After the 1974 failures of Franklin National Bank in the United States and Bankhaus Herstatt in Germany, the G10 governors established a Basle Committee on Banking Supervision to be based at the BIS with the objective of offering solutions to the issues arising when a foreign banking affiliate fails. This committee, known as the Cooke Committee for its charter chairperson, Peter Cooke, as well as the Basle Committee, was responsible for the Basle Concordat written in 1975 and the subsequent revision of that document after the failure of the Luxembourg subsidiary of Banco Ambrosiano, an Italian bank, in 1982.[2]

At the time of the Franklin failure, caused primarily by top management fraud and overextension in the foreign exchange markets, Franklin represented the largest bank failure in U.S. history. Of course, the U.S. bank failures in the 1980s have moved the Franklin failure out of the Top Ten. However, this failure, coupled with that of Herstatt, fostered concern by the international banking authorities that international standards dealing with banking supervision were needed.

After formulating the Basle Concordat of 1975, a standard for central banks dealing with foreign bank failures, the Luxembourg subsidiary of Banco Ambrosiano, a large Italian bank, failed in 1982. This failure severely tested the 1975 Basle Concordat and found it wanting. The Basle Committee drafted a new Concordat in 1983 to deal with such situations. These pronouncements will be discussed in more detail in Chapter 4.

In addition to these rules on foreign banking failures, this committee is also responsible for the bank capital adequacy standards adopted after the 1988 Basle Capital Accord and the current proposals to revise those global capital standards. The 1988 Basle Accord introduced the concept of incorporating risk in the equation to determine the minimum capital required for large banks. These proposals have been published, to be effective in 2004, and they show that the Basle Committee wants operational risk to be included in the regulatory capital standard.[3] It has issued a comprehensive plan for a more effective international bank supervisory system. The Basle Accords will be discussed in more detail in Chapter 5.

Committee on Payment and Settlement Systems. The Committee on Payment and Settlement Systems (CPSS) was established in the early 1990s to examine the efficiency and stability of domestic and cross-border payment and settlement systems. During the last two decades, the increase in cross-border financial transactions and their settlement has become a burgeoning activity for the banking system. Among the issues studied by this committee are transfer systems for large values, foreign exchange settlement risk, securities settlement arrangements, and retail payment systems. This committee works closely with the IMF, World Bank, and the International Organisation of Securities Commissions (IOSCO).

One of the major publications produced by the CPSS is the so-called Red Book, named for the color of its cover. This is a detailed discussion and analysis of the payment systems in effect in the G10 countries. The work of the CPSS will be discussed in more detail in Chapter 7.

Financial Stability Institute. Prior to the formation of the Financial Stability Forum, to be introduced in the next section, the BIS and the Basle Committee on Banking Supervision established the Financial Stability Institute. This institute promotes better and more independent banking supervision based on what it considers the core principles for the supervision of the financial sector. Plans for the Financial Stability Institute include expansion of its effort to payment systems and insurance industry operations.

The BIS Financial Stability Institute disseminates the best practices formulated by the BIS committees and other international financial organizations. This small function contributes to the creation of a more stable international financial system.[4]

Financial Stability Forum. The Financial Stability Forum was established in 1999 to reform the international financial architecture. The activities facilitated by this group include the exchange and coordination of information among national authorities, international institutions, and international regulatory bodies. The General Manager of the BIS chairs this forum and convenes it regularly to discuss cooperative efforts to improve international financial market surveillance and supervision.

The BIS Monetary and Economic Department worked with the Financial Stability Forum in the Mexican peso and Asian currency crises of the 1990s. This department furnished the Forum with analytical and statistical data on these crises. This Forum works closely with the International Association of Insurance Supervisors (IAIS). The work of the Financial Stability Institute and the Financial Stability Forum will be discussed in more detail in Chapter 11.

Relations with the Insurance Industry

In 1994, the International Association of Insurance Supervisors (IAIS) was formed for the purpose of improving supervision of the insurance industry as well as the development of practical standards for insurance company supervision and the mutual assistance and exchange of information in order to promote the development of domestic insurance markets. The insurance industry in general and the international insurance industry specifically have had a reputation of weak or uncoordinated supervisory standards applied by financial regulatory agencies.

In 1998, the Secretariat of IAIS was based at the BIS. Since then, IAIS has issued several international insurance advisory standards as well as guidance papers. Among these are Insurance Core Principles, an Insurance Concordat, principles for the conduct of the insurance business, and a document concerning guidance on insurance regulation and supervision for emerging market countries. The BIS provides support in technical and administrative aspects of IAIS operations but the latter remains independent in the development of global insurance standards, practices, and principles. The relationship between the BIS and the IAIS will be discussed and analyzed in Chapter 10.

Relations with the Securities Industry

The BIS has initiated a cooperative relationship with the International Organisation of Securities Commissions (IOSCO). IOSCO is a loose confederation of national securities commissions or their counterparts from major industrialized nations. It is also closely allied with the BIS and has issued standards for the securities industry. These have included a Supervisory Framework for Markets and Objectives and Principles of Securities Regulation.

BIS Cooperative Efforts with Central Banks

The BIS has convened joint seminars with several regional political associations and institutions or central banking groups in its effort to improve cooperative efforts with central banks. Among these are: Centro de Estudios Monetarios Latinoamericanos (CEMLA), Executive Meeting of East Asian and Pacific Central Banks (EMEAP), Central Banks of South East Asia, New Zealand, and Australia (SEANZA), South East Asian Central Banks (SEACEN), South Asian Association for Regional Cooperation (SAARC), Gulf Cooperation Council (GCC), and Southern African Development Community (SADC).

In addition to these joint seminars, the BIS coordinates technical assistance and training for the central banks of central and eastern

Europe, the Commonwealth of Independent States, and some transition Asian economies and for 20 central banks of industrialized countries. Meetings are held with the IMF and other international institutions and a database is maintained by the BIS concerning coordination of these institutions. The relationship between the BIS and central banks will be presented in more detail in Chapter 8.

Joint Vienna Institute

The BIS also works with other institutions in a training facility, the Joint Vienna Institute, established in 1992, which offers courses for central banking officials and national economic and financial authorities whose economies were subject at one time to central planning. Among these agencies are the European Bank for Reconstruction and Development (EBRD), World Bank, IMF, Organisation for Economic Cooperation and Development (OECD), and World Trade Organisation (WTO).

Other BIS Meetings

Other meetings are convened by the BIS in which central bank economists and other officials discuss economic and monetary issues facing central banks as well as more specific problems dealing with technology, security, legal, and managerial issues. Before 1993, the BIS hosted central bank committee meetings for the European Community as well as the European Monetary Institute. The latter became the European Central Bank with headquarters in Frankfurt, Germany.

The Joint Forum was established in 1996 as a cooperative platform for the Basle Committee, IAIS, and IOSCO to discuss issues dealing with supervision of banks, securities firms, and insurance companies. The Joint Forum has produced a number of extensive papers on proposals dealing with supervisory problems with the three financial sectors. It will be discussed in more detail in Chapter 11.

The BIS also holds meetings in places other than Basle, Switzerland. For example, the BIS convened a meeting of the central banks of 15 major countries in Hong Kong in early 2001 to discuss bank supervision and the new capital accord proposals. This meeting was discussed earlier.

Centre for Monetary and Economic Research

The Centre for Monetary and Economic Research is a BIS depart-ment responsible for the conduct of research about international monetary and financial issues. The economic research and analyses are published in various economic and working papers, academic journals, and conference proceedings of central banks and interna-tional financial agencies.

The BIS Annual Report. Publication of the BIS Annual Report is a major responsibility of the Centre for Monetary and Economic Re-search. It is published in June in at least four languages as well as on the Internet. Its annual publication is greatly anticipated be-cause of the international monetary and financial market analyses which it includes. The BIS Annual Report is so popular that it is nearly impossible to be placed on its mailing list. In fact, the Annual Report is now almost completely available on the Internet at www.bis.org.

The BIS Annual Report contains sections on specific aspects of the international financial and monetary system. These include macro-economic developments in industrial countries, macro-economic de-velopments in the rest of the world, monetary policy in industrial countries, coverage of domestic asset markets and financial institu-tions in industrial countries, exchange rates and capital flows in the industrial economies, capital flows and financial systems in emerging markets, international financial markets, and BIS activities.

The BIS activities discussed include those of its committees and special groups. For example, the 66th Annual Report for the fiscal year ending in 1996 covered the institution's first comprehensive overview of the size and nature of global derivatives markets. It also contained a discussion of the report on exposure of banks to foreign exchange settlement risk which was formulated by the Committee on Payment and Settlement Systems.

Other BIS Research Publications. The BIS publishes its own re-search in its conference and policy papers as well as a quarterly re-view. Its databases include financial statistics on international debt market activities, derivatives trading, and foreign exchange market transactions. These statistics are often published in its *Quarterly Review*, along with a commentary on market developments. The BIS also contributes to a collaborative effort with the IMF, OECD, and World Bank on statistics concerning external debt and is published on the Internet. These and other research publications by the BIS will be discussed in more detail in Chapter 11.

The BIS on the Internet. The Centre is responsible for the BIS web site on the Internet. This has become a very comprehensive web site which has links to other organizations including the IMF, World Bank, IAIS, and IOSCO. The BIS Annual Report as well as reports of all of the BIS-G10 committees and special groups are found at this site. New web pages are produced on an almost daily basis for this site. BIS press releases can be found as well as BIS Economic Papers and other policy statements or documents. Speeches given by BIS officials and G10 central bankers can be down-loaded from this site. Statistics dealing with financial markets and the international monetary system are included at www.bis.org.

SUMMARY AND CONCLUSIONS

This chapter has included a general introduction to the committees and other research functions of the BIS. The work of these committees will be the subject of subsequent chapters. The BIS, with the coordination and cooperation of the Group of 10 central bank governors, has organized these committees to alleviate problems in specific major areas of the international monetary and financial system. Most of these activities have been established since 1970 when the international financial community began to recognize that serious issues could harm the stability of the international financial system unless standards were formulated and implemented to deal with these issues.

The international ramifications of large bank failures in the 1970s and 1980s with international ramifications led to the establishment of a committee to design better supervisory standards for cases in which foreign banking affiliates were involved. These studies and others by central bankers and academicians demonstrated that international banks did not adequately support their assets with sufficient capital. Such inadequacy caused a loss of confidence by the securities markets and banking consumers and may have contributed to many banking failures of the 1980s. Banking regulators were afraid that systemic risk might do irreparable harm to the international financial system. As a result of these banking problems in the 1970s and 1980s, the BIS, through the efforts of its Committee on Bank Supervision, formulated the Basle Concordats of 1975 and 1983 and the Basle Capital Accord of 1988 with current proposals to amend it.

Other problems in the international financial community fostered the development of committees to study these specific issues. Among these were the misuse of derivative financial instruments by banks and companies, the payment and settlement of cross-border financial transactions, and the Year 2000 (Y2K) computer problem at the end of the 1990s. These issues were studied by BIS/G10 officials. Standards and proposals were published which have made progress in the stabilization of the international financial system.

Finally, the BIS has initiated a comprehensive series of publications with its Annual Report serving as its major publication which has become a collector's item for economists, financial institution supervisors, and financial academicians. This document is a valuable source of data on foreign exchange, activities of international financial markets and institutions, macro-economic analyses of both industrialized and emerging countries' activities, and a discussion of the activities of the BIS. It is now found almost in its entirety on the Internet at the BIS web site. This web site, www.bis.org, includes copies of all BIS publications, working papers, economic papers, speeches of BIS and central bank officials, statistics on financial market and monetary system operations, and all BIS transactions with other central banks.

BIS committees and research activities have begun in recent years to move beyond the bank regulation and supervisory function. The BIS has initiated relationships with non-banking financial activities such as insurance and securities market business. It has assisted the International Association of Insurance Supervisors and the International Organisation of Securities Commissioners with their formulation of rules and standards aimed at making both financial areas more stable and sound in their operations.

With its arsenal of publications, policy papers, committee and special group formulations, and cooperative contacts with central bank governors around the world, the BIS has become an important tool in the efforts to increase stability in the international monetary and financial system. These products will be discussed in more detail in Chapter 11.

NOTES

1. Bank for International Settlements, *70th Annual Report* (Basle, Switzerland, Bank for International Settlements, 2000), section on "Activities of the Bank," pp. 159–160.

2. Larry Gurwin, "Death of a Banker," *Institutional Investor*, Vol. 16 (October 1982), pp. 258–275, represents an excellent case study of the Banco Ambrosiano case.

3. Hans-Kristian Bryn and David Gittleson, "An Emerging Discipline," *Financial News*, August 23, 1999, p. 1.

4. William R. White, "The Asian Crisis and the Bank for International Settlements," a paper presented to the Conference on Asia and the Future of the World Economic Systems, London, England, March 17–18, 1999, p. 3.

CHAPTER 4

The BIS and Bank Supervision

INTRODUCTION

Only one international bank of any size failed during the first four decades of BIS operations. Only one clear-cut international monetary system had governed global foreign exchange markets. That was the fixed rate system established at the Bretton Woods, New Hampshire, conference at the end of World War II which replaced whatever remained of the international gold standard. The IMF and the World Bank were established at that conference and the world's currencies had their values fixed on the dollar, which in turn was fixed on the value of gold, priced at US$35 per ounce at that time.

The gold standard had been in effect until World War I. However, after that war, the British pound weakened and countries began to go off the gold standard. For awhile, a gold exchange standard was made operable in which the U.S. dollar and the British pound could be used as reserve currencies to supplement gold in settling global transactions. The world depression in the 1930s and World War II essentially caused the demise of the gold exchange standard.

After the Bretton Woods fixed rate regime was implemented, several major currencies including the dollar and the pound became overvalued. Others, including the Japanese yen and the German mark, became undervalued. Political reluctance to devalue the pound or the dollar, especially the latter, or to revalue the yen or the mark created much speculation in the foreign exchange markets. The international rules for the maintenance of exchange rates around some par relationship to the dollar or to gold could not be maintained. As a result, foreign exchange markets for the major currencies became unstable and international trade and investment by international business firms and banks became difficult to plan because of currency instability.

The United States made the first step when the Richard Nixon Administration devalued the dollar in 1971. At the same time, the yen and the mark revalued against the dollar. This was intended to reduce the volume of dollars held abroad because of the balance of payments trade deficits incurred over several years. This remedy did not stop the U.S. balance of payments problem in 1972 when the U.S. trade deficit increased even more. The first of a series of oil price increases by oil producing countries and the large dependence on imported oil kept the U.S. currency changes from working.

Finally, the United States devalued the dollar again in 1973. During that year, the major trading nations of the industrialized world dropped the fixed rate international monetary regime in effect since 1946 and opted for a new regime in which currency prices would float according to the foreign exchange market prices. This system is not always a freely floating rate system since governments can and do still intervene in the currency markets either to drive a particular currency price up or down. This system is referred to as a dirty floating rate regime.

The final speculative thrust in the global foreign exchange markets in the early 1970s, before the new system was installed, created instability in the international banking system. Banking supervision was primarily a national responsibility if it existed at all and, in some countries, banking supervision might be no more formal than a "wink or a nod" from the central bank governor of that nation, as it was in Great Britain.

Several international banks suffered losses in the foreign exchange markets at this time. Most large international banks maintained insufficient levels of capital to support their loans and investments, some of which were very risky.[1] Bank capital is a proxy, especially in the securities marketplace, for public confidence in the banking system or in any specific bank. The inadequacy of capital in the banking system coupled with, in some cases, managerial fraud, created a risky situation in the international banking arena, especially if national banking supervision was weak.

Significant Bank Failures

Two bank failures occurred in 1974 involving all of the problems just discussed. These were the failures of Franklin National Bank in New York and Bankhaus Herstatt in Germany. Both failures involved an overextension in the foreign exchange markets and inadequate capital to deal with the losses which were incurred. In the case of Franklin, fraud was involved as well and, in the case of Herstatt, management committed illegal acts.

Both banks were very significant failures for a number of reasons. Franklin was the largest U.S. bank to fail in American history at that time. Herstatt was only a small private bank but did a large correspondent business with leading U.S. and foreign banks in the foreign exchange markets. Bank regulators and foreign exchange traders have called the Herstatt failure a watershed case since operations in the markets before the Herstatt failure were not supervised very carefully, whereas since then, regulators and bank managements have taken a very serious look at this banking function. Both parties have demanded greater controls over foreign exchange trading in the global banking system.

In summary, the failures of these two banks had surprised the international banking community. Central bank governors and bank regulatory officials heeded the call for stronger bank regulations and tighter banking supervision.[2]

THE BASLE COMMITTEE

The Franklin National Bank and Bankhaus Herstatt cases prompted the BIS and the G10 central bankers to form a standing Committee on Banking Regulations and Supervisory Practices. This committee was formed in December 1974 and became known as the Basle Committee. It also was referred to as the Cooke Committee, named for its first chairman, Peter Cooke of the Bank of England.

The objectives of this committee were:[3]

1. general education about how banks were and should be supervised;
2. the sharing of sensitive information to banking supervisors;

3. the establishment of an early warning system to detect problems with international banks;

4. research on banking supervision; and

5. the coordination of policy in the supervision of international banks.

The new committee's first order of business was to formulate guidelines for the division of bank regulatory and supervisory responsibilities between national bank supervisory authorities. In other words, the question of whose banking authority is responsible when a foreign banking affiliate or an international bank fails needed an answer. The Basle Committee issued a short document with its answer to this issue. This became known as the Basle Concordat and was endorsed by the G10 central bank governors in December 1975. A concordat is a typically European concept. In the 1920s, concordat was the name given to informal agreements between the Mussolini Government in Italy and the Pope which decided jurisdiction between the Italian Government and the Vatican in matters dealing with education, taxation, and related issues. Although these were not given the weight of treaties in international law, the parties to them accepted them as binding.[4]

The principles incorporated by the Basle Concordat of 1975 were as follows:[5]

1. the supervision of foreign banking establishments should be the joint responsibility of host and parent authorities;

2. no foreign banking establishment should escape supervision;

3. the supervision of liquidity should be the primary responsibility of the host authorities;

4. the supervision of solvency should be a matter for the parent authority in the case of foreign branches and the responsibility of the host authority in the case of foreign subsidiaries; and

5. practical cooperation should be provided by the exchange of information between host and parent authorities and by the authorization of banking inspectors by, or on behalf of, parent authorities of the territory of the host authority.

The Basle Concordat of 1975, at first, was accepted by the G10 central banks but very soon was accepted by central banks outside of the G10 countries. This simple document essentially stated that when banks operated beyond their home country borders, their home country banking authority was responsible for their overall conduct. However, their foreign operations were the responsibility of the host government's banking authorities. Each government's banking authority should exchange information in cases where a banking unit has a problem. The Basle Concordat of 1975 is restated in Figure 4.1.

Problems with the 1975 Concordat

Some weaknesses in the 1975 Concordat were apparent from the beginning even though the Franklin National Bank and Bankhaus Herstatt failures were handled relatively satisfactorily. But of course, they were banks which were located in countries with strong central banks. Other weaknesses would require the first real test of the rules before banking supervisory authorities would clamor for a

Figure 4.1
Basle Concordat of 1975

The supervision of foreign banking establishments should be the joint responsibility of host and parent authorities.

No foreign banking establishment should escape supervision, each country should ensure that foreign banking establishments are supervised, and supervision should be adequate as judged by both host and parent authorities.

The supervision of liquidity should be the primary responsibility of host authorities since foreign establishments generally have to conform to local practices for their liquidity management and must comply with local regulations.

The supervision of solvency of foreign branches should be essentially a matter for the parent authority. In the case of subsidiaries, while primary responsibility lies with the host authority, parent authorities should take account of the exposure of their domestic banks' foreign subsidiaries and joint ventures because of the parent banks' moral commitment in this regard.

Practical co-operation would be facilitated by transfers of information between host and parent authorities and by the granting of permission for inspections by or on behalf of parent authorities on the territory of the host authority. Every effort should be made to remove any legal restraints (particularly in the field of professional secrecy or national sovereignty) which might hinder these forms of co-operation.

Source: Charles Grant, "Can the Cooke Committee Stand the Heat?" *Euromoney*, October 1982, p. 42.

revision. The 1975 Concordat was considered too vague and contained too many loopholes. In some banking operations, one country's banking authority might think the other country's authority was responsible. Some countries, such as Switzerland, did not permit important information to be exchanged with foreign entities. Tax haven countries with their loopholes could invite banks to locate their foreign operations in such countries and supervision could be evaded.

The 1975 Concordat failed to address the question of different supervisory standards from one country to another. For example, the U.S. Federal Reserve became concerned with the inadequate supervision by some parent authorities in 1979. The Fed had proposed that tougher supervisory standards be adopted by the U.S. offices of foreign banks only to draw strong protests from the banks' parent authorities. The dispute between the Fed and other supervisory authorities also revealed different interpretations of the division of responsibilities that had been spelled out by the 1975 Concordat. For example, the Swiss National Bank argued that the Fed had overextended its authority when it and other central banks held to the principle of parental responsibility.[6] Few central banking authorities believed that the Basle Concordat of 1975 could withstand a major banking failure.

Banco Ambrosiano

A foreign affiliate of a large Italian bank, Banco Ambrosiano, failed in 1982. This case tested severely the 1975 Basle Concordat and found it wanting. Roberto Calvi, the chairman of Banco Ambrosiano, a large Italian bank, was found hanging under London's Blackfriars Bridge on June 18, 1982. He had disappeared from his Rome apartment nine days earlier. His life and death had, at the time, dire implications for both the Italian and the international banking systems.[7]

Roberto Calvi had a rich background of international banking before becoming head of Banco Ambrosiano. He had worked for Banca Commerciale Italiana in Milan after World War II before joining Ambrosiano in 1947. This bank was one of the leading "Catholic" banks, founded in 1896, and named after Saint Ambrose, the patron saint of Milan.

In 1969, Calvi became associated with Michele Sindona, who had gained a fortune in banking and securities trading and who owned two large Italian banks, one of which was Banca Privata Finanziaria. Sindona had working relationships with a number of foreign international banks and was highly connected with Pope Paul VI for whom he had been a financial adviser.

With the Sindona connection, Calvi became chairman of Banco Ambrosiano in 1971 and immediately restructured the bank. He established a Luxembourg holding company and operated through subsidiaries of this holding company. Thus, he was able to avoid the supervision of the Bank of Italy, Italy's central bank. When the latter bank wanted information, Calvi would cite Swiss, Bahamian, or other laws designed to keep banking information secret. Calvi was able to put together a financial empire which also included control of a holding company in Italy that controlled marketing and industrial enterprises—activity prohibited by Italian banking law. However, the Bank of Italy seemed to overlook these violations.

Meanwhile, Sindona was convicted of fraud in the Franklin National Bank failure and his Banca Privata was declared insolvent. Sindona worried that Italian authorities would extradite him from the United States. Sindona turned against Calvi in 1977. Years after Calvi's death, Sindona was extradited to Italy, was convicted, and sent to prison. He died in prison after being mysteriously poisoned during his breakfast one day.

In 1978, Italian authorities began to find problems at Banco Ambrosiano. Calvi had sold shares in Ambrosiano to ghost companies in Panama and Liechtenstein and had illegally exported billions of lire from Italy by illegal securities operations. Calvi also initiated banking operations in Latin America. After the lire plunged in value, Calvi's foreign subsidiaries came under financial strain and Calvi himself was finally convicted for illegal currency operations and sentenced to prison for four years. He managed to remain free from prison while appealing his case with the assistance of high government officials.

In the spring of 1982, the Bank of Italy told Calvi that Ambrosiano had a questionable foreign exposure of US$1.4 billion at the end of 1981. Calvi's board asked for an explanation and then voted against his refusal to explain the overexposure. Calvi turned to Bishop Marsinkus, an American cardinal in the Vatican who controlled the Papal finances. Marsinkus turned him down. Calvi then fled the country with the objective of cleaning up the financial problems in his Latin American and Luxembourg subsidiaries. It was during this trip that he was found hanging beneath the Blackfriar's Bridge in London.

When the Luxembourg holding company of Banco Ambrosiano failed, no central bank bailed it out. Some 250 banks lost a total of US$450 million because of the failure.[8] Bankers have generally held to the philosophy that a central bank responsible for supervising a bank should be the lender of last resort when that bank fails.[9] This did not happen in the Banco Ambrosiano case and the Basle Committee had to return to the drawing board to revamp the Basle Concordat of 1975.

Basle Concordat of 1983

The Basle Concordat of 1975, formulated after the failures of Franklin National Bank and Bankhaus Herstatt, had been criticized for its vagueness and imprecision. Basle Committee members, however, held that the desire to enforce the Concordat's underlying motive was more important than its precise meaning.[10] Both the Luxembourg and Italian banking authorities had declined to act as lender-of-last resort in this case. Some raised the question whether public authorities or private lenders should be responsible for such failures.[11] One official of the Luxembourg-based Norddeutsche Landesbank of Germany said, after 22 years of international banking experience, that the actions of the Bank of Italy in this case were totally unacceptable.[12]

After the failure of the the Luxembourg holding company of Banco Ambrosiano and the death of the latter's chairman, Roberto Calvi, the Basle Committee reviewed the 1975 Concordat and issued a revised version. In the Ambrosiano case, both Luxembourg and Italian banking authorities denied any responsibility for the supervision and lender of last resort functions for the Luxembourg company because it was a holding company rather than a bank.

The revised Basle Concordat was less vague in its guidelines for the supervision of foreign holding companies, although very much longer. A version of the Basle Concordat of 1983 is shown in Figure 4.2. It held that the responsibility for the supervision of an intermediate holding company would rest with the parent bank's banking authority. In the case of Banco Ambrosiano's Luxembourg subsidiary, that meant the Italian authorities.[13]

Two issues encountered by the Concordat of 1975 involved the adequacy of supervision and the principle of consolidated supervi-

Figure 4.2
Basle Concordat of 1983

I. Introduction

This report sets out certain principles that the Committee believes should govern the supervision of banks' foreign establishments by parent and host authorities. It replaces the 1975 Concordat and reformulates some of its provisions, most particularly to take account of the subsequent acceptance by the Governors of the principle that banking supervisory authorities cannot be fully satisfied about the soundness of individual banks unless they can examine the totality of each bank's business worldwide through the technique of consolidation.

The report deals exclusively with the responsibilities of banking supervisory authorities for monitoring the prudential conduct and soundness of the business of banks' foreign establishments. It does not address itself to lender-of-last-resort aspects of the role of central banks.

The principles set out in the report are not necessarily embodied in the laws of the countries represented on the Committee. Rather they are recommended guidelines of best practices in this area, which all members have undertaken to work toward implementing, according to the means available to them.

Adequate supervision of banks' foreign establishments calls not only for an appropriate allocation of responsibilities between parent and host supervisory authorities but also for contact and cooperation between them. It has been, and remains, one of the Committee's principal purposes to foster such cooperation both among its member countries and more widely. The Committee has been encouraged by the like-minded approach of other groups of supervisors, and it hopes to continue to strengthen its relationships with these other groups and to develop new ones. It strongly commends the principles set out in this report as being of general validity for all those who are responsible for the supervision of banks which conduct international business and hopes that they will be progressively accepted and implemented by supervisors worldwide.

Where situations arise which do not appear to be covered by the principles set out in this report, parent and host authorities should explore together ways of ensuring that adequate supervision of banks' foreign establishments is effected.

II. Types of Banks' Foreign Establishments

Banks operating internationally may have interests in the following types of foreign banking establishment: **(1) branches:** operating entities that do not have a separate legal status and are thus integral parts of the foreign parent bank; **(2) subsidiaries:** legally independent institutions wholly owned or majority-owned by a bank that is incorporated in a country

(Figure 4.2 continued)

other than that of the subsidiary; **(3) joint ventures or consortia:** legally independent institutions incorporated in the country where their principal operations are conducted and controlled by two or more parent institutions, most of which are usually foreign and not all of which are necessarily banks. While the pattern of shareholdings may give effective control to one parent institution, with others in a minority, joint ventures are, most typically, owned by a collection of minority shareholders.

In addition, the structure of international banking groups may derive from an ultimate holding company which is not itself a bank. Such a holding company can be an industrial or commercial company, or a company the majority of whose assets consists of shares in banks. These groups may also include intermediate nonbank holding companies or other non-banking companies.

Banks may also have minority participations in foreign banking or nonbanking companies, other than those in joint ventures, which may be held to be part of their overall foreign banking operations. This report does not cover the appropriate supervisory treatment of these participations, but they should be taken into account by the relevant supervisory authorities.

III. General Principles Governing the Supervision of Banks' Foreign Establishments

Effective cooperation between host and parent authorities is a central prerequisite for the supervision of banks' international operations. In relation to the supervision of banks' foreign establishments, there are two basic principles that are fundamental to such cooperation and that call for consultation and contacts between respective host and parent authorities: first, that no foreign banking establishment should escape supervision; and second, that the supervision should be adequate. In giving effect to these principles, host authorities should ensure that parent authorities are informed immediately of any serious problems that arise in a parent bank's foreign establishment. Similarly, parent authorities should inform host authorities when problems arise in a parent bank that are likely to affect the parent bank's foreign establishment.

Acceptance of these principles will not, however, of itself preclude there being gaps and inadequacies in the supervision of banks' foreign establishments. These may occur for various reasons. First, while there should be a presumption that host authorities are in a position to fulfill their supervisory obligations adequately with respect to all foreign bank establishments operating in their territories, this may not always be the case. Problems may, for instance, arise when a foreign establishment is classified as a bank by its parent banking supervisory authority but not by its host authority. In such cases, it is the responsibility of the parent authority to ascertain whether the host authority is able to undertake adequate supervision and the host authority should inform the parent authority if it is not in a position to undertake such supervision.

In cases where host authority supervision is inadequate, the parent authority should either extend its supervision, to the degree that it is practicable, or it should be prepared to discourage the parent bank from continuing to operate the establishment in question.

Second, problems may arise where the host authority considers that supervision of the parent institutions of foreign bank establishments operating in its territory is inadequate or nonexistent. In such cases, the host authority should discourage or, if it is in a position to do so, forbid the operation in its territory of such foreign establishments. Alternatively, the host authority could impose specific conditions governing the conduct of the business of such establishments.

Third, gaps in supervision can arise out of structural features of international banking groups. For example, the existence of holding companies either at the head, or in the middle, of such groups may constitute an impediment to adequate supervision. Furthermore, particular supervisory problems may arise where such holding companies, while not themselves banks, have substantial liabilities to the international banking system. Where holding companies are at the head of groups that include separately incorporated banks operating in different countries, the authorities responsible for supervising those banks should endeavor to coordinate their supervision of those banks, taking account of the overall structure of the group in question. Where a bank is the parent company of a group that contains intermediate holding companies, the parent authority should make sure that such holding companies and their subsidiaries are covered by adequate supervision. Alternatively, the parent authority should not allow the parent bank to operate such intermediate holding companies.

Where groups contain both banks and nonbank organizations, there should, where possible, be liaison between the banking supervisory authorities and any authorities that have responsibilities for supervising these nonbanking organizations, particularly where the nonbanking activities are of a financial character. Banking supervisors, in their overall supervision of banking groups, should take account of these groups' nonbanking activities; and if these activities cannot be adequately supervised, banking supervisors should aim at minimizing the risks to the banking business from the nonbanking activities of such groups.

The implementation of the second basic principle, namely, that the supervision of all foreign banking establishments should be adequate, requires the positive participation of both host and parent authorities. Host authorities are responsible for the foreign bank establishments operating in their territories as individual institutions, while parent authorities are responsible for them as parts of larger banking groups where a general supervisory responsibility exists in respect of their worldwide consolidated activities. These responsibilities of host and parent authorities are both complementary and overlapping.

(Figure 4.2 continued)

The principle of consolidated supervision is that parent banks and parent supervisory authorities monitor the risk exposure—including a perspective of concentrations of risk and of the quality of assets—of the banks or banking groups for which they are responsible, as well as the adequacy of their capital, on the basis of the totality of their business wherever conducted. This principle does not imply any lessening of host authorities' responsibilities for supervising foreign bank establishments that operate in their territories, although it is recognized that the full implementation of the consolidation principle may well lead to some extension of parental responsibility. Consolidation is only one of a range of techniques, albeit an important one, at the disposal of the supervisory authorities and it should not be applied to the exclusion of supervision of individual banking establishments on an unconsolidated basis by parent and host authorities. Moreover, the implementation of the principle of consolidated supervision presupposes that parent banks and parent authorities have access to all the relevant information about the operations of their banks' foreign establishments, although existing banking secrecy provisions in some countries may present a constraint on comprehensive consolidated parental supervision.

IV. Aspects of the Supervision of Banks' Foreign Establishments

The supervision of banks' foreign establishments is considered in this report from three different aspects: solvency, liquidity, and foreign exchange operations and positions. These aspects overlap to some extent. For instance, liquidity and solvency questions can shade into one another. Moveover, both liquidity and solvency considerations arise in the supervision of banks' foreign exchange operations and positions.

(1) Solvency. The allocation of responsibilities for the supervision of the solvency of banks' foreign establishments between parent and host authorities will depend on the type of establishment concerned.

For branches, their solvency is indistinguishable from that of the parent banks as a whole. So, while there is a general responsibility on the host authority to monitor the financial soundness of foreign branches, supervision of solvency is primarily a matter for the parent authority. The "dotation de capital" requirements imposed by certain host authorities on foreign branches operating in their countries do not negate this principle. They exist first to oblige foreign branches that set up in business in those countries to make and to sustain a certain minimum investment in them, and second, to help equalize competitive conditions between foreign branches and domestic banks.

For subsidiaries, the supervision of solvency is a joint responsibility of both host and parent authorities. Host authorities have responsibility for supervising the solvency of all foreign subsidiaries operating in their territories. Their approach to the task of supervising subsidiaries is from the standpoint that these establishments are separate entities, legally incorporated in the country of the host authority. At the same time, parent authorities, in the context of consolidated supervision of the parent banks, need to assess whether the parent institutions' solvency is being affected by the operations of their foreign subsidiaries. Parental supervision on a consolidated basis is needed for two reasons: because the solvency of parent banks cannot be adequately judged without taking account of all their foreign establishments; and because parent banks cannot be indifferent to the situation of their foreign subsidiaries.

For joint ventures, the supervision of solvency should normally, for practical reasons, be primarily the responsibility of the authorities in the country of incorporation. Banks that are shareholders in consortium banks cannot, however, be indifferent to the situation of their joint ventures and may have commitments to these establishments beyond the legal commitments that arise from their shareholdings, for example, through comfort letters. All these commitments must be taken into account by the parent authorities of the shareholder banks when supervising their solvency. Depending on the pattern of shareholdings in joint ventures, and particularly when one bank is a dominant shareholder, there can also be circumstances in which the supervision of their solvency should be the joint responsibility of the authorities in the country of incorporation and the parent authorities of the shareholder banks.

(2) Liquidity. References to supervision of liquidity in this section do not relate to central banks' functions as lenders of last resort, but to the responsibility of supervisory authorities for monitoring the control systems and procedures established by their banks that enable them to meet their obligations as they fall due including, as necessary, those of their foreign establishments.

The allocation of responsibilities for the supervision of the liquidity of banks' foreign establishments between parent and host authorities will depend, as with solvency, on the type of establishment concerned. The host authority has responsibility for monitoring the liquidity of the foreign bank's establishments in its country; the parent authority has responsibility for monitoring the liquidity of the banking group as a whole.

For branches, the initial presumption should be that primary responsibility for supervising liquidity rests with the host authority. Host authorities will often be best equipped to supervise liquidity as it relates to local practices and regulations and the functioning of their domestic money markets. At the same time, the liquidity of all foreign branches will always be a matter of concern to the parent authorities, since a branch's liquidity is frequently controlled directly by the parent bank and cannot be viewed in isolation from that of the whole bank of which it is a part. Parent authorities need to be aware of parent banks' control systems and need to take account of calls that may be made on the resources of parent banks by their foreign branches. Host and parent authorities should always consult each other if there are any doubts in particular cases about where responsibilities for supervising the liquidity of foreign branches should lie.

(Figure 4.2 continued)

For subsidiaries, primary responsibility for supervising liquidity should rest with the host authority. Parent authorities should take account of any stand-by or other facilities granted as well as any other commitments, for example, through comfort letters, by parent banks to these establishments. Host authorities should inform the parent authorities of the importance they attach to such facilities and commitments, so as to ensure that full account is taken of them in the supervision of the parent bank. Where the host authority has difficulties in supervising the liquidity, specially in foreign currency, of foreign banks' subsidiaries, it will be expected to inform the parent authorities, and appropriate arrangements will have to be agreed so as to ensure adequate supervision.

For joint ventures, primary responsibility for supervising liquidity should rest with the authorities in the country of incorporation. The parent authorities of shareholders in joint ventures should take account of any stand-by or other facilities granted as well as any other commitments, for example, through comfort letters, by shareholder banks to those establishments. The authorities in the country of incorporation of joint ventures should inform the parent authorities of shareholder banks of the importance they attach to such facilities and commitments so as to ensure that full account is taken of them in the supervision of the shareholder bank.

Within the framework of consolidated supervision, parent authorities have a general responsibility for overseeing the liquidity control systems employed by the banking groups they supervise and for ensuring that these systems and the overall liquidity position of such groups are adequate. It is recognized, however, that full consolidation may not always be practicable as a technique for supervising liquidity because of differences of local regulations and market situations and the complications of banks operating in different time zones and different currencies. Parent authorities should consult with host authorities to ensure that the latter are aware of the overall systems within which the foreign establishments are operating. Host authorities have a duty to ensure that the parent authority is immediately informed of any serious liquidity inadequacy in a parent bank's foreign establishment.

(3) Foreign exchange operations and positions. As regards the supervision of banks' foreign exchange operations and positions, there should be a joint responsibility of parent and host authorities. It is particularly important for parent banks to have in place systems for monitoring their group's overall foreign exchange exposure and for parent authorities to monitor those systems. Host authorities should be in a position to monitor the foreign exchange exposure of foreign establishments in their territories and should inform themselves of the nature and extent of the supervision of these establishments being undertaken by the parent authorities.

Source: "Revised Basle Concordat on Bank Oversight Clarifies the Division of Supervisory Roles," *IMF Survey*, Vol. 12 (July 11, 1983), pp. 201–204.

sion. The 1983 Concordat dealt with these issues. Guidelines were adopted with regard to the problem of uneven supervisory standards from one nation to another. These guidelines gave the host authority the ability to discourage or prohibit the operation in its territory of foreign banking institutions if it found the supervision of the parent institution in the home country to be inadequate. Or the host authority could impose tighter regulations against the subsidiary of such an inadequately supervised parent banking institution. The guidelines also held that, if the host country's supervision is inadequate, the parent authority should extend its supervision to the foreign subsidiary or discourage the parent bank from operating that subsidiary.[14]

With regard to the second issue of consolidated supervision, the 1975 Concordat gave responsibility for supervision of the solvency of foreign subsidiaries to the host banking authority. The new Concordat amended this and gave joint responsibility of solvency supervision to both host and parent banking authorities. However, the supervision of liquidity in both branches and subsidiaries was given to the host banking authorities. Parent authorities under the principle of consolidated supervision have general responsibility for supervision of the liquidity control systems employed by the parent banking groups over which they have oversight jurisdiction.

The Basle Concordat also treated the supervision of the solvency of foreign subsidiaries in its revision of 1983. The 1983 rules stated that, for an evaluation of a foreign subsidiary's solvency to be accurate, it must be based on the bank's consolidated commitments. Thus, the commitments of the parent bank and all of its foreign branches and subsidiaries should be considered together when deriving the capital ratios. The goal of this change was to place additional responsibility on the parent bank to insure that offshore banking centers are adequately supervised.[15]

Implications of the Basle Concordat. The 1983 Concordat removed much of the ambiguity contained in the original Concordat. However, the new version does raise a number of implications for international banking supervisory agencies. First, these rules have no force of law and, therefore, are unenforceable. The only means of "enforcement" is the adoption of these standards by the major central banks and bank supervisory agencies for the purpose of improving the safety and soundness of the international banking system. But some weak central banks will not have the political maturity to adopt these rules. Some of these nations are home to the very banks and financial institutions which create problems for the international financial system. BCCI, discussed in Chapter 1, was chartered first in Pakistan. This is a good example of the lack of political clout to accept the rules in the Basle Concordat.

Second, a supervisory agency may be unable to fulfill its responsibilities under the Concordat. One supervisory agency may be required by the new rules to inform another supervisory agency that its supervision is inadequate. This may place an inequitable burden on the second agency. In the case where a host authority deems that the parent's supervision is inadequate and, therefore, the foreign affiliate should not operate in the host country, the major principle of international banking poses a real issue. That is the principle of reciprocity. International diplomacy in the banking world is a two-way street. In addition, what criteria will a host authority use to declare the parent's supervision to be inadequate? Will objective criteria be used or might the decision be more political than one based on some set measurements?

Third, effective implementation of the Concordat may be impeded by technical barriers. Difficulty in obtaining information and the differences in accounting rules and national laws, especially bank secrecy laws, may pose a barrier to observance of the Concordat. Financial information may not be comparable because of the use of non-consolidated balance sheets in some countries.[16] Transparency is not considered proper usage in many countries.

A fourth implication for banking authorities involves the restrictions on cooperation necessary to foster amicable relations among supervisory authorities in order to implement the Concordat. Supervisory practices differ from one nation to another. Some nations such as the United States have three banking supervisory authorities. Others have only one which may supervise in a very casual manner. Host authorities may not be willing to share responsibility with parent authorities and vice versa.

Finally, the revised Concordat did not address the lender-of-last-resort function. When the supervision of either the host or the parent authority is found wanting when an institution fails, it seems that central banks should share some of the responsibility of the lender-of-last-resort function. From time to time, international financial shocks may occur to the international banking system. Systemic risk may cause failures of institutions on a cross-border basis. The loss of confidence in the banking system needs to be addressed by provision of the lender-of-last-resort function and, on occasion, that function may need to be shared.

Criticisms of the Concordat. Some questions about supervision have been unanswered by the revised Concordat.[17] It still does not precisely address the relationship between the parent bank and its foreign affiliates. The principle of consolidated supervision advanced in the 1983 Concordat assumes that the solvency of a foreign branch is indistinguishable from that of the parent. This may not always be true. The moral and legal commitment of the parent bank to its foreign affiliate often may be vague. Until this weakness is addressed, host banking authorities should more closely supervise any foreign banks established in its country.

The 1983 Concordat divides supervisory responsibilities between parent and host banking authorities by liquidity and solvency considerations. These may overlap at times. However, the Concordat does not indicate where a liquidity problem might end and a solvency problem begins. Without a clear distinction of these functions, the supervision of some banking functions would not overlap and the problem might be overlooked by both the parent bank management and the host banking authority.

The lender-of-last-resort problem was not addressed in the Concordat of 1975 as well. So far, only national lenders-of-last-resort exist to bail out a failed bank, as was done in the 1984 case of the Continental Illinois Bank. In the international case, a national lender-of-last-resort must either have supervisory jurisdiction over an international bank—to date, none do—or be willing to trust another agency exercising such control and with which it shares control of the situation.

Recent Developments

Banking Supervision in LDCs. The Basle Committee initiated two new organizations to cover less-developed countries (LDCs). These are the Offshore Supervisors Group and the Commission of Latin American and Caribbean Banking Supervisors and Regulatory Bodies.[18] These groups have endorsed the Concordat but their activities have been limited. Given that a large part of the world's debt is carried by the countries represented by these committees, their limited work and success is disturbing.

The BIS has begun to take a more intense interest in the banking community in LDCs. The Basle Committee on Banking Supervision announced formal recommendations for the Central Bank of Brazil at the September 1997 IMF/World Bank Annual Meeting. A principal objective of these recommendations was the political independence of supervisory officials in Brazil. Some of the actions stressed by the Basle Committee were as follows:[19]

1. expansion of the power of the Central Bank of Brazil in order to implement preventative measures in financial institutions supervision;

2. empowerment of the Central Bank of Brazil to expropriate the controlling shares of a financial group deemed a problem and the subsequent sale of the shares at a public auction;

3. abolition of the rule that the minimum capital of a foreign bank in Brazil be double that of a domestic bank;

4. increase of the minimum capital required when establishing a new bank;

5. adoption in Brazil of the Basle Accord with regard to the minimum capital necessary;

6. increase in the capital requirements associated with risk-weighted assets from 8 percent to 10 percent for Brazilian banks;

7. supervisory officials must maintain frequent contact with their constituent banks;

8. supervision is to be done on a consolidated basis that includes a bank's holdings in other companies;

9. amendment of the legislation dealing with opening bank branches in foreign countries; and

10. permission for the Central Bank of Brazil to supervise operations of bank offices in foreign countries or business enterprises in which banks hold shares.

Minimum Standards

In addition to the establishment of these committees, the Basle Committee also published a paper entitled "Minimum Standards for the Supervision of International Banking Groups and Their Cross-Border Establishments" in 1992.[20] This was not a quasi-legal document but set forth some minimum standards hoping that banks would adopt them.

Four minimum standards were developed in this paper. They are as follows:

1. all international banking groups and international banks should be supervised by a home country authority that capably performs consolidated supervision;

2. the creation of cross-border banking establishments should receive the prior consent of both the host country supervisory authority and the bank's and, if different, the banking group's home country supervisory authority;

3. supervisory authorities should possess the right to gather information from the cross-border banking establishments of the banks or banking groups for which they are the home country supervisor; and

4. if a host country authority determines that any one of the foregoing minimum standards is not met to its satisfaction, that authority could impose restrictive measures to satisfy its prudential concerns consistent with minimum standards, including the prohibition of the creation of banking establishments.

Core Principles. Following publication of the paper on minimum standards, the Basle Committee released another paper entitled "Core Principles for Effective Banking Supervision." In 1998, the BIS, IMF, and World Bank designated the paper and its 25 core principles as a compliance document for national bank supervisory agencies. However, these institutions have no enforcement powers. Among the 25 principles outlined by the Basle Committee, three are representative of its objectives. First, to prevent abuses arising from connected lending, bank supervisors must require that banks lend to related companies and individuals on an arm's length basis, that such extensions of credit are effectively monitored, and that other appropriate steps are taken to control or mitigate the risks involved in the transaction. A second principle holds that banking supervisors must determine that banks have adequate policies, practices, and procedures in place that promote high ethical and professional standards in the financial sector and prevent the bank from being used, intentionally or unintentionally, by criminal elements. This is a direct reference to the BCCI case. Finally, the third principle states that banking supervisors must require local operations of foreign banks to be conducted with the same high standards as are required of domestic institutions and that these authorities have powers to share information needed by the home country supervisors of those banks for the purpose of carrying out consolidated supervision. Some countries still refuse to share such information.

Long Term Capital Management. During the late 1990s, Long Term Capital Management (LTCM) nearly went bankrupt. This was an investment company which invested large amounts of funds in a highly leveraged manner. The fund had been established with leading financial engineering academicians among its founders, including Myron Scholes and Robert C. Merton. Scholes and Merton were Nobel Prize winners and Scholes had discovered the option pricing mathematical model with Fisher Black. John Meriwether of Salomon Brothers was also one of the founders of LTCM.

The fund was established with US$10 million investments which could not be withdrawn for three years. More than US$4.8 billion in funds was raised in the first three months. The fund managers applied their mathematical equations and dynamic hedging to offset risks with a portfolio containing US$120 billion of borrowed funds. This implied a leverage ratio of 25:1. The fund used derivatives for hedging purposes and had a total gross notional value of US$1.3 trillion. They invested in markets all around the world using these models, coupled with the assumption that the markets would move in the same probability as they had moved in the past. The models worked for the first three years as the fund made annual returns of 20, 43, and 41 percent. In 1997, the market dynamics changed and the fund earned only 17 percent. Competition from other funds using similar techniques began to threaten LTCM. The models stopped working and traders went back to their instincts, becoming quite conservative in their investing.

In 1997, LTCM returned half its capital to investors but kept the fund's level of assets high with large amounts of debt. LTCM began to suffer losses in 1998 but maintained its high level of debt at US$100 billion. Interest rate spreads began to widen in 1998 as a result of the Asian financial crisis and then because of the Russian default in 1998. Losses from the divergence in these spreads caused the LTCM to lose 90 percent of its net asset value. The balance sheet leverage ratio rose to more than 150:1. The models used by the fund were based on normal market behavior but the markets did not behave normally during this period. LTCM was on the brink of bankruptcy in August 1998.

As a hedge fund, its objective had been to provide risk management for a variety of large investors, including international banks. The bankruptcy of this large investment company had dire implications for the systemic risk it posed and could have created a global international financial crisis. If LTCM ceased operations, it was estimated that US$1.25 trillion would be lost. In September 1998, the U.S. Federal Reserve Board and the U.S. Treasury Department intervened to bailout LTCM. A total of US$3.6 billion was injected into the failing fund by 14 Wall Street firms in order to avoid the contagion risk to other financial institutions around the world.

One of the lessons learned from the LTCM case was that credit and market risk are related and may interact and reinforce each other when placed under economic pressure. A more rigorous control system used by the banks making loans to an institution such as LTCM could have warned them of the exposure to risk they faced.

Many banks which loaned money to LTCM underestimated the risks vis-à-vis the hedge fund's strategy in terms of its leverage and the size and scope of its open positions. Firms transacting with LTCM discovered they had larger potential exposure to loss than they had expected. And if LTCM had failed as its positions were liquidated, the exposure to loss would have been indirectly in their own trading books as well as on some of their other outstanding credits. Wide swings in many financial prices and diminished liquidity resulted from concerns about the possible liquidation of LTCM's assets.[21]

Other lessons learned from the LTCM debacle were that such speculative ventures need to be regulated. Hedge funds are, for the most part, not regulated by any national regulatory authority. LTCM was not even required to provide information to investors nor did it do so voluntarily. This was a case of extreme asymmetric information.

Moral Hazard. Bank regulation analysts have suggested that the LTCM case represented a good example of the problem of moral hazard. Moral hazard occurs when insurance, in the form of deposit insurance or lender-of-last-resort action, encourages a financial institution to take risks rather than discourage it from doing so. When moral hazard is present, insurers are faced with increased scope of the risk exposure.[22] Moral hazard was an underlying factor in the failure of many banks and savings and loan associations in the United States during the 1980s when the Federal Deposit Insurance Corporation and Federal Savings and Loan Insurance Corporation furnished deposit insurance to the extent of US$100,000 or more per depositor and the Federal Reserve System acted as lender-of-last-resort in bailing out many of the failed institutions.

The lender-of-last-resort responsibility of a central bank can add to moral hazard. In late 1998, this occurred when the Federal Reserve Board tried to stem a world financial crisis. The Thai baht collapse in July 1997 was followed by currency crises throughout Asia. The Russians defaulted on an international loan in August 1998. The Fed implemented easier monetary policy in late 1998 by providing liquidity to keep U.S. financial institutions from failing as lender-of-last-resort. The increase in moral hazard which resulted had begun with the bailout of the Mexican Government in 1994 and was followed with the economic assistance to Indonesia, Korea, Malaysia, and Thailand and the bailout of Russia as a country "too big to fail" in genre of the 1984 Continental Illinois Bank bailout. Finally, the Fed-sponsored rescue of LTCM added still further to moral hazard even though other culprits could be blamed. These included the IMF and the U.S. Treasury in their mismanagement of the international economy.[23]

After LTCM was rescued, the Basle Committee formed a working group to study the relationship between banks and highly leveraged institutions.[24] The group sought to identify the larger issues the LTCM case raised. Bank supervisory response to such problems was discussed as well as what risk management techniques were needed.

A report on the LTCM issues was published in January 1999. The group had been chaired by Jan Brockmeijer of the Netherlands Bank. A number of problems in banks' risk management practices were identified. Most important of these was the imbalance among key parts of the credit risk management process and, especially, the overemphasis on the role of collateral in protecting against credit loss, i.e., the bank capital required to support some risky assets. The group concluded that banks need to obtain more information about the borrower in order to make better credit decisions. Banks were found wanting in this requirement and were unable to properly assess leverage or risk concentrations in some markets or to develop a liquidity risk profile of individual institutions.[25]

This report prompted the Basle Committee to issue a set of sound practices to guide banks and their supervisors. These were[26]:

1. establish clear policies to govern their involvement with highly leveraged institutions;
2. adopt credit standards to address the specific risks associated with these institutions;
3. establish meaningful measures of potential future exposure as well as credit limits which incorporate the results of stress testing; and
4. monitor exposure on a frequent basis.

Country Risk. The BIS has also begun to place a more serious emphasis on the examination of country, or political, risk in LDCs. Country risk is the risk incurred when operating in a country where political action or economic problems may eminate from the country's environment itself and, thus, adversely affect international commerce with that country. Political risk is generally defined as the risk taken by the host government or one of its agencies that will cause an adverse effect in a trade or investment transaction with a foreign trader or investor. Political risk is comprised of four types: (1) risk from expropriation of property owned by a foreign investor, (2) inconvertibility of the host country's currency so that dividends from a foreign investment may not be remitted or capital from the investment may not be repatriated to the parent firm, (3) interference or repudiation of a contract between a foreign investor and a local business firm or the host government or one of its agencies, and (4) violence from civil strife, insurrection, coup, or war.[27]

The Basle Committee on Banking Supervision formulated a ruling on the exposure to country risk. With regard to banks, the committee defined country risk faced by banks as the situation when one or more borrowers may be unable to service their debts because of events in their own country.[28] The Basle Committee's ruling in such cases placed additional responsibility on the parent bank, particularly with regard to the derivation of their capital ratios and requiring that offshore financial centers be adequately supervised.

The BIS then published a book which contained statistics on countries' indebtedness—a perceived major ingredient of country risk. The Basle Committee then concluded that banks should use a consolidated basis when assessing exposure to country risk.

Credit Risk. To follow up on the political risk work, the Basle Committee issued a press release in April 1999 which analyzed current practices and issues in credit risk modelling, a subject related to country risk. Banks use credit risk modelling to quantify and aggregate credit risk across geographical and business lines. Sophisticated financial institutions find value in credit risk models because such models can give estimates of credit risk caused by: (1) the economic environment, (2) market variables, (3) credit quality, and (4) shifts in business lines. Some of the conceptual approaches to credit risk modelling include deciding on a time horizon, defining the credit loss, and determining how credits can be aggregated and measured in the connection between default events.

Officials of the Federal Reserve Bank of New York, including its President William McDonough, believe that credit risk modelling should be applied in bank management and that it will not only play a critical role in risk management but may also assist in the determination of regulatory capital requirements, the subject of Chapter 5.

Customer Due Diligence for Banks. One of the most recent endeavors by the Basle Committee on Banking Supervision was the publication of a consultative paper on customer due diligence for banks.[29] The paper represents the effort of the Basle Committee to strengthen risk management procedures in banks around the world. Once national bank supervisors adopt the procedures outlined in the paper, a framework can be developed to formulate basic supervisory practices to handle such problems as money laundering and other financial crimes.

The paper provides guidance for national banking supervisors for the establishment of minimum standards and internal controls to guarantee that banks know with whom they do business. The problems incurred in the BCCI case can then be avoided. The paper sets forth essential elements for customer due diligence such as customer acceptance policies, customer identification, monitoring of high-risk accounts, and risk management. One would think that all banks would practice such due diligence but many banks around the world are not sophisticated sufficiently to put into effect such basic controls. Furthermore, many national banking supervisory authorities are not much more sophisticated in their oversight processes.

Other Basle Committee Policy Papers. The Basle Committee released several policy papers and consultative documents during the 1999–2000 period. Among these were releases on the following topics: corporate governance (September 1999), credit risk (July 1999), highly leveraged institutions (January 1999 and January 2000), loan accounting (July 1999), transparency and disclosure (July 1999 and January 2000), and the Year 2000 (Y2K) (September 1999 and March 2000). The consultative papers deal with issues about which the Basle Committee solicits outside opinions before formulating a final principle or standard.

International Conference of Banking Supervisors. Finally, the Basle Committee initiated a biennial International Conference of Banking Supervisors in 1979. These conferences are usually held in Basle and are co-sponsored by the Swiss National Bank, the Swiss Federal Banking Commission, and the BIS. The major topics for the September 2000 Conference were a review of the Basle Capital Accord and the financial industry in the 21st century. More than 300 delegates from more than 120 countries usually attend these conferences.

SUMMARY AND CONCLUSIONS

During the 1970s and 1980s, many banks and savings institutions failed for a number of reasons. A large share of the blame for these failures and the subsequent loss of confidence in the international financial system was inadequate supervision by bank regulatory agencies as well as the lack of coordination among these agencies. After the failures of Franklin National Bank in the United States and Bankhaus Herstatt in Germany in 1973, the BIS took charge and formed, with the coordination of the G10, the Basle Committee on Banking Supervision, or the Cooke Committee, charged with the objective of formulating a standard rule to place the responsibility for foreign bank failures with the appropriate national banking supervisory agency.

This committee formulated the Basle Concordat of 1975, a short and somewhat vague statement holding that when banks operated in a foreign country, the authorities in their home country were responsible for their overall operations. But their foreign operations were the responsibility of the host nation's banking authority. The vagueness of this standard could not hold up when a foreign holding company of Italy's Banco Ambrosiano failed in 1982.

The Basle Committee went back to the drawing board and issued a revision of the Concordat in 1983. The new standard is several times longer than the 1975 version, as can be seen in Figure 4.2. The Basle Concordat of 1983 made parent banks responsible for supervision of their holding companies at home and abroad. It further stated that, essentially, if the parent bank's central bank or other banking authority believed that these units were not properly supervised, it could close them down.

The 1983 Concordat also has had its critics. It was held inadequate in the BCCI case which developed after Banco Ambrosiano and the 1983 Concordat's formulation. But the BIS and the Basle Committee began the work toward a more coordinated supervision of international banks. It has spurred the major central banks to work toward better regulation of activities of large international banks and has begun to move the focus of better bank supervision toward the banking community in the less developed world. A major area in which a gap still exists in the handling of foreign bank failures is the lender-of-last-resort question when a major unit fails. This problem remains to be clarified.

Some problems still exist. The rules formulated by the Basle Committee are voluntary. No international agency, including the BIS, has enforcement powers to insure that the rules are implemented. In addition, the Concordat of 1983 empowers a host supervisory authority to close a banking office of a foreign bank if it deems that the parent bank's supervision is inadequate. But no means to define what is inadequate supervsion are contained in the Concordat.

In conclusion, it should be stated that supervision of international banks was in much disarray before the creation of the Basle Committee. Banking supervisors from one country to another were unaware of where their responsibility ended and where that of another country's supervisor began. The first two major works of this committee were the Basle Concordat and the Basle Accord, the latter to be discussed in detail in the next chapter. These created unified standards for international bank supervisors which, at least, have been a good start toward a more harmonious and coordinated international financial system. The work of the Basle Committee, especially with regard to bank supervision, demonstrates that the BIS has taken a major role in setting new standards for bank safety on a global basis.[30] The most important part of this work has been the formulation of a minimum capital requirement for banks based on the riskiness of their assets. This will be the topic of the next chapter.

NOTES

1. James C. Baker and Raj Aggarwal, "Variations and Trends in Capital Ratios of Large Banks: Implications for International Bank Safety and Regulation," *Akron Business and Economic Review*, Vol. 15 (Summer, 1984), pp. 25–32.

2. L.G. Goldberg and Anthony Saunders, "The Determinants of Foreign Banking in the United States," *Journal of Banking and Finance*, Vol. 5 (March 1981), pp. 17–32; J.M. Gray, "The Multinational Bank: A Financial MNC?" *Journal of Banking and Finance*, Vol. 5 (March 1981), pp. 33–36; W.A. Kennett, "International Banking's Challenge for Supervisory Authorities," *Canadian Banker and ICB Reviews*, Vol. 88 (June 1981), pp. 48–55.

3. Ethan Kapstein, *Governing the Global Economy* (Boston: Harvard University Press, 1994).

4. Susan Strange, *Mad Money: When Markets Outgrow Governments* (Ann Arbor, MI: University of Michigan Press, 1998), p. 177.

5. Charles Grant, "Can the Cooke Committee Stand the Heat?" *Euromoney*, October 1982, p. 42.

6. Ibid., pp. 55–56.

7. For an excellent case study of the Roberto Calvi death and his connection with Banco Ambrosiano, see Larry Gurwin, "Death of a Banker," *Institutional Investor*, Vol. 16 (October 1982), pp. 258–275.

8. Grant, "Can the Cooke Committee Stand the Heat?" *Euromoney*, October 1982, p. 39.

9. Ibid.

10. Ibid., p. 45.

11. Paul Blustein, "Ambrosiano's Fallout on International Banking," *The Wall Street Journal*, September 1, 1982, p. 12.

12. Ibid.

13. "Revised Basle Concordat on Bank Oversight Clarifies the Division of Supervisory Roles," *IMF Survey*, Vol. 12 (July 11, 1983), p. 203.

14. Ibid., p. 202.

15. Richard S. Dale, "International Banking is Out of Control," *Challenge*, January-February 1983, p. 27.

16. John G. Heimann, "The Challenge of International Supervision," *Institutional Investor*, Vol. 13 (December 1979), p. 136.

17. Richard Dale, "Basle Concordat: Lessons from Ambrosiano," *The Banker*, Vol. 133 (September 1983), p. 55.

18. See G.G. Johnson and R.K. Abrams, "The Lender-of-Last-Resort in an International Context," *Essays in International Finance Series*, No. 151 (May 1983). International Finance Section, Department of Economics, Princeton University.

19. "Multilateral Financial Assistance to the Banco Central do Brasil," Bank for International Settlements Press Release, December 10, 1998 found at http://www.bis.org/press/p981210.htm.

20. The Basle Committee on Banking Supervision, "Minimum Standards for the Supervision of International Banking Groups and Their Cross-Border Establishments," (Basle, Switzerland: Bank for International Settlements, July 1992).

21. Laurence H. Meyer, "Lessons from Recent Global Financial Crises," remarks before the International Finance Conference, Federal Reserve Bank of Chicago, October 1, 1999, pp. 1–2.

22. Anthony Saunders, *Financial Institutions Management: A Modern Perspective* (Burr Ridge, IL: Irwin McGraw-Hill, 2000), p. 409.

23. Robert L. Bartley, "The Moral-Hazard Bubble," *The Wall Street Journal*, April 9, 2001, p. A29.

24. William J. McDonough, "Global Financial Reform: A Regulator's Perspective," an address before the Foreign Policy Association Conference, New York, November 17, 1999, and reprinted in the *Federal Reserve Bank of New York Annual Report 1999* (New York: Federal Reserve Bank of New York, 1999), p. 5.

25. Ibid.

26. Ibid., p. 6.

27. James C. Baker, *International Finance: Management, Markets, and Institutions* (Upper Saddle River, NJ: Prentice Hall, 1998), pp. 122–124.

28. G.G. Johnson and R.K. Abrams, "Aspects of the International Banking Safety Net," *IMF Occasional Paper #17*, March 1983, p. 28.

29. Federal Reserve Bank of New York, "Basel Committee on Banking Supervision: Consultative Paper on Customer Due Diligence for Banks," *Banking Information*, Circular No. 11321, February 8, 2001, p. 1.

30. Maurice D. Levi, *International Finance: The Markets and Financial Management of Multinational Business* (New York: McGraw-Hill, 1996), pp. 560–561.

CHAPTER 5

The Basle Accord on Capital Adequacy

INTRODUCTION

During the 1970s and 1980s, many banks and savings institutions were closed by national authorities and, in many of these cases, the cause was insolvency. Many of these financial institutions had inadequate capital to support their assets, particularly risky loans, and other investments. Several studies held that large international banks headquartered in many countries were not adequately capitalized.[1]

Bank capital has many functions. Capital can be used as a cushion to protect against losses. Capital can be a source of funds with which to acquire physical assets. Capital can protect depositors whose accounts are not fully insured. Capital can protect the bank when a liquidity crisis occurs. The larger a bank's capital-to-assets ratio, the more likely it will be to meet its obligations.[2] Stronger capital adequacy standards tend to increase public confidence in banks. This is generally reflected in the market price of a bank's stock as the market places a higher premium on those banks that maintain a higher level of capital in their balance sheets.

In addition to the problem of inadequate capital held by large international banks, BIS member countries as well as other countries used a variety of methods and standards in calculating capital requirements of their banks. Even the definition of bank capital may have been different from one country to another. No country used a system which quantified the capital needs of a bank in relation to the riskiness of that bank's assets.

Bank capital in general eroded as the global economy declined and as international sovereign debt became a problem beginning in 1982. The Basle Committee, discussed in detail in Chapter 4 in its promulgation of the Basle Concordats of 1975 and 1983, began to publish studies concerning the shrinking capital held by international banks. A serious conflict arose at this time as the BIS and the Basle Committee maintained that bank capital was too low while central bankers, some in the G10 countries, apparently were unconvinced of the need to develop a unified standard to deal with international bank capital. BIS management, through its experts on the Basle Committee, seemed to lead another part of the BIS, its Board of Directors, in demanding a unified standard to deal with this problem.

THE BASLE ACCORD OF 1988

The BIS, through its Committee on Banking Regulations and Supervisory Practices, created standards and agreements on capital adequacy which, at that time, leveled the "playing field" for banks. The need for more regulation of bank capital became quite clear as the global financial market and cross-border financial transactions grew larger and larger. The disparity in the ways in which banks could operate widened as central banks and international banking expanded beyond national borders and international competition in trade and investment increased.

Two reasons for new standards dealing with international bank capital were put forth. First, some banks considered capital as equity alone while others included long-term debt or off-balance sheet items. Thus, this inconsistency in the definition of bank capital resulted in inaccurate disclosure of bank capital and the danger that banks could fail because of insolvency. The second reason involved the problem of different degrees of banking supervision from one country to another. Banks in some countries could do things that banks in other countries were prohibited by regulations from doing. For example, banks in Belgium could own industrial companies. U.S. banks could not. Banks in some countries were not as efficient as banks in other nations. Central banks could, themselves, overexpand because of these problems, overextend their resources as lender-of-last-resort as banks failed, and find themselves out of business without government subsidies.

U.S. bank regulatory agencies had worked on the problem of bank capital adequacy during the 1980s. A large number of banks and savings and loan associations had failed during this period. Continental Illinois, the large Chicago-based international bank, had to be bailed out by Federal regulators. Bank of America had been in financial trouble. The Federal Reserve Board, Federal Deposit Insurance Corporation, and Comptroller of the Currency then agreed in 1987 on a proposal for a common standard rule of capital adequacy for banking. This rule was strongly influenced by the work of the Committee on Banking Regulations and Supervisory Practices (now called the Committee on Banking Supervision) at the BIS and was adopted by the BIS and the G10 central banks.

Before the Basle Committee formulated the original Basle Accord, the U.S. and British banking authorities, the Federal Reserve Board, and the Bank of England took a bilateral route to the establishment of bank capital adequacy standards. Supervisors from both countries believed from the beginning that a bilateral strategy on this issue might harm relations between Great Britain and the European Community. The Federal Reserve Board members thought that the bilateral action might harm relations with the G10 central bank governors.

However, the U.S. and U.K. officials continued their strategy. They held talks with Japanese and major West European supervisors and reopened discussions in Basle at the BIS. Thus, the joint U.S.-U.K. proposal put pressure on the Basle Committee to adopt a capital adequacy standard. The accord had to be accepted by the G10 countries and the differences had to be ironed out so that the standard could be enforced domestically in each nation.

For example, Japan was concerned with the accounting procedures for hidden reserves including real estate and corporate equities. A compromise was worked out between the Japanese desire to mark-to-market the values of these hidden reserves and the British-American regulatory prohibition against the use of market value instead of historical value.[3]

Guidelines

The guidelines developed to support this rule were designed to achieve certain objectives, including the following:

1. the establishment of a uniform capital framework which might be applicable to all national bank supervisory agencies;

2. the encouragement of international banking institutions to strengthen their capital ratios; and

3. the reduction of a source of competitive inequality arising from differences in bank supervision from one country to another.

In other words, the Basle Accord was intended to promote competitive conditions from one country to another which are equal for internationally active banks. In addition, it was meant to improve the financial resilience of banks. More than 100 countries have adopted the original Basle Accord.[4]

Risk-Based Capital Ratios. The new capital rules established in 1988 called for the implementation of a risk-based capital ratio to replace the simple capital-to-assets ratio for the measurement of bank capital. This risk-based capital ratio method was phased in at the beginning of 1993 and has come to be known as the Basle Accord. The new rules were aimed primarily at banks in industrialized countries.

The Basle Accord placed a bank's capital into two tiers.[5] Tier I, or core capital, included common stockholders' equity, any cumulative or noncumulative preferred stock, and minority interest in equity accounts of consolidated subsidiaries. Tier II, or supplementary capital, included an allowance for loan and lease losses, preferred stock, any hybrid capital instruments including perpetual debt and convertible securities, subordinated debt and intermediate-term preferred stock, and revaluation reserves on, for example, equity and buildings.

Certain revisions were to be made to each of these tiers. Goodwill was to be deducted from Tier I capital. Other deductions were to be made from the sum of Tier I and II capital. These included investments in unconsolidated subsidiaries, reciprocal holdings of banking organizations' capital securities, and other deductions such as other subsidiaries or joint ventures.

After the measurement of a bank's capital has been done according to these guidelines, the amounts are compared with certain percentage weights. Core capital or Tier I must equal or exceed 4 percent of weighted-risk assets. The total of Tier II capital was limited to 100 percent of Tier I capital. Certain maximum limits were imposed on some of the categories in each tier. The final total of Tier I and Tier II capital must equal or exceed 8 percent of weighted-risk assets.

A bank's assets are risk-weighted in the following manner. Assets are classified according to categories of riskiness and must be supported by capital in relation to the risk of each category. For example, Category 1 assets do not need to be supported by any capital and include cash, balances due from other central banks, and gold bullion held. Category 2 assets must be backed with capital by 20 percent of their value and include cash being collected, short-term claims, certain privately issued securities, and some investments. Half (50 percent) of category 3 assets must be backed with capital and include fully secured loans, bonds, and credit equivalent amounts of interest rate- and foreign exchange rate-related contracts. Finally, category 4 assets must be 100 percent backed by capital and include all other claims, obligations, property, plant, and equipment, real estate, fixed assets, and all other assets.[6]

If a bank, after using these calculations, finds that it is below the Basle Accord capital adequacy standard, it must raise new capital to meet the requirements. If this is not possible, the bank must shrink its assets and liabilities or reduce its net risk exposure by, for example, reducing risky loans or investments.

Off-Balance Sheet Items. One of the objectives of the Basle Accord was to create a system which would consider off-balance sheet items on banks' financial statements. These are items usually not reported in the year-end financial statements. Examples are loan commitments, guarantees, swap and hedging transactions using derivatives, and investment banking activities, among others. Off-balance sheet transactions have had rapid growth in recent years.

These items are now classified under four different conversion factors which convert the face value of an item into the appropriate amount of risk needing capital support. These conversion factors are:

1. 100 percent conversion factor: direct credit substitutes, risk participation in bankers' acceptances and direct credit substitutes, and securities loaned for which the bank is at risk;
2. 50 percent conversion factor: transaction-related contingencies, unused portions of commitments with original maturity, and revolving underwriting facilities and note issuance facilities;
3. 20 percent conversion factor: short-term, self-liquidating trade-related contingencies, including commercial letters of credit; and

4. zero percent conversion factor: unused portions of commitments with original maturity of one year or less or which can be cancelled at any time.

These guidelines now place banks on the same footing, as long as countries agree on the same minimum capital base as measured by the BIS standards.

Tests of the Basle Accord. The Basle Accord was tested in a number of countries during the 1990s. In India, a large number of new private banks were established. The BIS watched the situation in India closely because of financial scandals there. Many of the Indian banks have relied on the Reserve Bank of India to assist them. Most of the capital in these banks is Tier I capital and, thus, it is easier to meet the Basle standards.[7]

Venezuela is another country in which banking problems have occurred. Several banks have defaulted on their clearinghouse obligations. The BIS asked the Venezuelan central bank to intervene by alleviating the default problems and encouraging sounder banking practices. Capital adequacy standards are being strengthened there. Some banking analysts believe Venezuela is overbanked and many bank mergers should be encouraged.[8]

Australia is another country watched by the BIS. However, Australia has not had any financial crises but has incurred an economic boom. Companies in Australia have been financing their own investments and bypassing the banks in order to save interest costs. This practice has left the banking system with extra capital well above the Basle Accord standards. Banks have been easing lending terms to increase the demand for loans. The BIS is worried that the terms might become too easy and that bank failure might occur because of bad loans. The Basle Accord may be applied in such cases.[9]

Some countries' banks have had trouble meeting the Basle Accord rules. Japan's banks, among the lowest capitalized in the world, did meet the new standards but had to scramble to raise the additional capital. Capital is not easy to raise in Japan for many reasons. Japanese banks have been plagued for many years with bad loans. Bank mergers, popular in other countries, are not used in Japan. Japanese banks have not been very profitable and, thus, internal capital has not grown very much.[10] Japanese banks were able to meet the standards by reducing risk in their assets.[11]

Current Developments and Evaluation of the Basle Accord

The Basle Accord applied a standard for measuring capital adequacy in which the riskiness of a bank's assets was considered for the first time. Much change has occurred in international banking since the Basle Accord was formulated and it became apparent that changes in the original standard were necessary.[12] Some in the field believe the method of assigning risk to assets based on the four categories was arbitrary. Loans to, for example, all countries in the OECD does not reflect the inherent risk of all of those loans. Loans to Mexico, an OECD member, are riskier than, say, loans to Germany or the Netherlands or, for that matter, the United States.

In addition, banks have made much progress in the use of internal risk-weighting systems and their sophistication and accuracy. Alan Greenspan, Chairman of the U.S. Federal Reserve Board, gave support to the internal risk-weighting systems used by banks when he urged that regulators examine the banking industry and the merits of such internal systems.[13] One of his motivations in this belief is the method used by the Basle Accord in lumping loans to a blue-chip corporation in the same risk category as a loan to a financially distressed firm.

In fact, other organizations have given support to privately-based risk measurement techniques. The Washington-based Institute of International Finance (IIF) suggested that advances in risk measurement techniques in the private sector were better than the rules imposed by the Basle Accord.[14] This group held that the Basle rules may actually lead to adverse decisions by bank managers. For example, if a bank is required to hold 8 percent in capital reserves for corporate loans, it might be in the bank's best interest to find a loan that has sufficient risk to justify the 8 percent requirement. The bank would have an incentive to ignore safe, low-risk corporate loans because it will need to hold 8 percent in capital reserves despite the fact that its internal risk-weighting system might suggest a lower amount. If the bank is to maximize profits, it must accept loans with sufficient risk to justify the standard 8 percent capital reserve requirement.

Chairman Greenspan further criticized the Basle Accord.[15] He held that: (1) the Basle Accord sets the minimum capital ratio and not the maximum insolvency probability; (2) the Accord accounts for credit and market risk but does not explicitly consider other forms of risk, e.g. operations risk, systemic risk, etc.; and (3) the Basle Accord considers trading-account activities but does not cover hedging, diversification, portfolio management, and other risk management techniques which banks may do.

Finally, some have argued that the Basle Accord only covers international banks, and large ones at that. Thousands of smaller banks have correspondent relations with these banks and systemic risk is always possible. These analysts argue that the Basle Accord needs to have wider application to the international banking system. The 1988 Accord also became the standard in LDCs. Regulators in these countries increased levels of bank capital and, thus, banks in emerging markets became more safe and sound.

PROPOSED CHANGES TO THE BASLE ACCORD

Basle Accord Problems

During the late 1990s, the Basle Committee began to respond to the criticisms and weaknesses of the original Basle Accord. In 1997, the IIF established a task force to study the regulatory implications of changes in risk management.[16] The IIF, with 280 financial institution members around the world, concluded that the Basle Accord rules did not adequately consider changes in risk measurement techniques adopted since its implementation.

The IIF made a number of recommendations. Among them were the following: (1) amend existing risk weights so that internal or external credit ratings are considered; (2) recognize credit risk models which banks were using internally to calculate their regulatory requirements; (3) permit supervisors to adopt qualitative criteria for estimating how losses in a portfolio are to be distributed; and (4) modify the treatment of loan loss provisions by treating them as Tier One capital.

A major disagreement arose at this time among central bankers who were represented on the Basle Committee. German banking regulators wanted to require a minimum amount of capital to back *Pfandbriefe*, bonds issued by German mortgage banks, whose outstanding total value of US $957 billion is more than that of Germany's government-bond market. The present Accord treats these as lower risk assets. U.S. bank regulators believe they are much riskier than the low requirements imply. This treatment of these instruments gives them a competitive advantage and it has been estimated that issuers of these bonds can raise money 15 basis points cheaper than competitive instruments.[17]

Other criticisms of the Basle Accord included the perception on the part of some international banking supervisors that only large international banks were covered by the the capital requirements of the Accord. As has been discussed above, some believe the lender-of-last-resort issue should be resolved. This was not required by the original Accord or by the Basle Concordat.

Another criticism concerned the risk weight formula. Risky assets, such as corporate loans, were weighted at 100 percent. In other words, such loans were to be backed 100 percent by capital. However, debts to OECD country members were considered risk free, i.e., they are weighted at 0 percent. Exposures to banks based in these countries are considered low-risk assets and are weighted at 20 percent.[18]

These loans may, in fact, carry a much higher level of riskiness. But the Basle Accord permits these countries to have a lower cost of debt capital than non-OECD nations. During the 1990s, Mexico, the Czech Republic, Poland, and Korea all became members of OECD and all had economic booms fueled by cheap credit. Within a short period of time, all of these countries suffered an economic downturn.

Editors of *Euromoney*, the journal of international money and capital markets, also criticized the 1988 Accord. They voiced two objections.[19] The first was that regulators around the world were more concerned about their own constituent institutions and would pay only lip-service to the agreement. For example, France and Japan were held to be the worst offenders. In France, state-owned financial institutions have embellished each other's capital through share swaps. In Japan, banks use revaluation reserves and have changed the rules to introduce securitization and new forms of debt capital to skirt the new capital rules. They also have friendly shareholders who supply capital at the lowest cost of capital in the world.

The second *Euromoney* objection to the Basle Accord of 1988 is that it replaces the consultative form of bank supervision with a more legalistic form which relies on the letter of the law more than it does the spirit of the law. The consultative form, *Euromoney* believes, is more subjective than the legalistic form. The journal adds that some overly prudent regulators demand more than the minimum 8 percent capital ratios by using the consultative approach.[20] In short, some banking supervisory authorities have mandated capital rules which were too excessive.

The framers of the Basle Accord did not anticipate the development of new types of secondary and derivatives financial markets whereby banks sell credit risk instead of retaining it as loans on their balance sheet. This is the act of securitization of debt instruments by the banks.

Some banking industry analysts believe that no accord would be better than a bad accord in practice. The Basle Accord, although as suggested above, was aimed at first toward banks in the largest economies, it has since become the *de facto* standard adopted by all banks globally.

The 1988 Accord has become very difficult to revise. U.S. regulators, for example, have pushed the plan to use banks' internal models for allocating capital to credit risks.[21] This was not part of the original accord. Furthermore, in countries with advanced financial markets, many financial institutions have incurred problems because the indicative power of the 1988 Accord capital adequacy ratio in these countries was illusory. Some of these institutions maintained insufficient loan loss reserves while reporting adequate capital ratios just before their financial crisis.

Another major problem was faced by some parent bank authorities such as those in Germany and Switzerland. Secrecy laws in those and other countries legally constrained the types of some information bank supervisors could collect on the foreign activities of their commercial banks.[22] These secrecy laws presented problems not only for national banking authorities but also for international cooperative efforts as well.

In addition to these confidentiality problems, the accounting systems of different countries presented problems when the various unconsolidated financial statements were provided by parent banks and their foreign branches and subsidiaries. Even without secrecy laws, the lack of internationally-accepted general accounting principles and practices compounded the issue of adequate bank supervision.

Finally, evidence from some countries involved in currency crises of the late 1990s has shown that many banks had very overstated capital ratios. They, in effect, had made insufficient provision for their loan-loss reserves.

THE REVISED BASLE ACCORD

In January, 2001, the Basle Committee on Banking Supervision issued a new set of consultative documents and capital adequacy standards for banks. The present committee is chaired by William J. McDonough, President of the New York Federal Reserve Bank. The consultative period ended May 31, 2001, and a new capital adequacy standard was published by the end of 2001, to become effective in 2004.[23]

The current Basle Committee on Banking Supervision is comprised of senior banking supervisory officials from the G10 countries, as well as Luxembourg and Switzerland. It includes representatives from other countries in the consultative process. The Committee has a permanent secretariat at the BIS. These are the officials responsible for formulation of the new Accord.

The new Accord is more extensive and complex than the 1988 Accord. It is more risk-sensitive than the 1988 Accord and contains new options for measuring credit as well as operational risk. But the risk-sensitive part of the new Accord is not very much more complex than the 1988 Accord.[24]

Objectives of the New Accord

The Committee on Banking Supervision stressed five objectives for the new Accord.[25] They are:

1. the new Accord should continue to promote safety and soundness in the financial system and, as such, the new framework should at least maintain the current overall level of capital in the system;
2. the new Accord should continue to enhance competitive equality;
3. the new Accord should constitute a more comprehensive approach to addressing risks;
4. the new Accord should contain approaches to capital adequacy that are appropriately sensitive to the degree of risk involved in a bank's positions and activities;
5. the new Accord should focus on internationally active banks, although its underlying principles should be suitable for application to banks of varying levels of complexity and sophistication.

Some of these objectives were changes from the first Accord. The first two objectives merely confirm the major objectives of the 1988 Accord. The third objective is a change from the first Accord in that it allows options for addressing risks, some of which may be models for measurement of risk which have been developed by banks internally. The fourth objective is intended to catch those activities not well addressed by the 1988 Accord, such as derivatives use and asset securitization, so that they may be appropriately assessed for the weight of their risk. For example, swaps activity by banks, for either interest rate or currency swaps, is undercapitalized. The Basle approach is inadequate because it requires banks to calculate their swap credit exposures on a gross basis. One analyst stated that if banks in general have, for example, a US$210 billion swap portfolio, its net replacement value might be US$1.6 billion, requiring US$64 million in equity if one assumes leverage of 25 percent.[26]

The final objective addresses one of the criticisms of the 1988 Accord. Analysts perceived that it addressed only large international banks. This objective confirms this but holds that the new standards should be adopted by any bank of any level of sophistication. Small banks may add to systemic risk as did Herstatt in 1974. Herstatt was a tiny US$200 million bank but had large correspondent relationships, especially in foreign exchange operations, with large international banks. Its failure caused large losses by several large international banks.

The newly revised Accord is based on a three-cornered foundation, or as the Basle Committee describes it, three pillars. Pillar I links capital requirements more closely to actual risk. Pillar II strengthens the supervisory process for enforcing capital standards. Pillar III enhances the effectiveness of market discipline by imposing uniform bank disclosure. This revision is not solely a capital adequacy standard but a more pervasive change in supervisory behavior.[27]

Pillar I

This section of the revision provides a more detailed system for capital adequacy requirements for various types of risk. This requirement more closely links capital adequacy requirements to risk.[28] Banks will be permitted to use their own risk management system to rate the credit riskiness of their counterparties—but only after banking supervisors approve the bank's model. This is referred to as an "internal ratings based" approach.

The 1988 Accord imposed a maximum credit-risk capital requirement of 8 percent but, under the new proposal, capital requirements might be as high as 12 percent for a counterparty with a poor credit standing. But high-quality corporate credits receive a more favorable risk weight and capital requirements for these exposures might drop from the 8 percent requirement to as low as 1.6 percent under the proposed accord. Banks which are less sophisticated will be given an expanded standard system for classifying banking credits.[29]

Pillar II

This section of the proposed revision of the Basle Accord focuses on the supervisory process.[30] The supervisory process will review the method by which banks assess their own capital adequacy needs. Four key principles of supervisory review were set forth in the proposal. They are:

1. banks must relate their capital needs to their risk profile and have a written strategy for maintenance of the appropriate level of capital;
2. supervisors must review such arrangements and act appropriately if they observe a weakness in the bank's system;
3. banks should operate above the minimum-capital adequacy level and supervisors should be able to require that banks maintain above-minimum levels of capital; and
4. supervisors should intervene before banks fall below the minimum level of capital adequacy.

With regard to the first principle of supervisory review, the Basle Committee believes that a sound capital adequacy assessment process should include policies and procedures designed to identify material risks. Bank management is responsible for the establishment and maintenance of this process including procedures for relating the bank's strategies and level of capital to risk.[31]

Concerning the second principle of supervisory review, the Basle Committee holds that supervisors should review and evaluate banks' internal capital adequacy assessments and strategies in addition to their ability to monitor and ensure their compliance with regulatory capital ratios. If supervisors are not satisfied with any bank's management in the fulfillment of this process, they should take appropriate supervisory action.[32]

In terms of the third principle of supervisory review, the Basle Committee posits that supervisory authorities have a number of ways of ensuring that banks operate with adequate levels of capital. Some authorities may even desire to set higher capital ratios for the entire banking system than the minimum ratios mandated by the new Accord.[33]

Finally, supervisory authorities may consider a range of options if they believe that a bank is not meeting the minimum requirements, according to the fourth principle of supervisory review. Such options may include more intensified monitoring of the bank, dividend payment restrictions, requiring the bank to implement a capital restoration plan, or a requirement that the bank raise more capital immediately.[34]

Pillar III

Pillar III specifies what information banks should disclose. This requirement will be coupled with market discipline and will reinforce it. Banks will be required to furnish much more information than they have in the past. Minimum disclosure includes details of the controlling entities in a banking group. This is aimed at the avoidance of another BCCI case. Such disclosure requirements also include the amount of paid-up capital, disclosed reserves, minority interests, provisions for credit losses, and the composition of capital.[35]

These changes in the Basle Accord have several objectives. They are designed to alleviate or eliminate the problems alluded to earlier in this chapter. They will move away from the risk weights of the original accord and be aimed at other risks such as interest rate and operational risk. The new Accord will look at the riskiness of the entire banking group while, at the same time, examine the safety and soundness of individual banks within the group.[36] Securitization activity by banks may slow since the more risk-adjusted approach makes the securitization of corporate and consumer loans interesting for only lower-rated borrowers and might, in fact, increase the attractiveness of other long-term assets such as mortgages. Synthetic securitization is addressed in the proposal but restrictions which concern structure, risk management, and disclosure may create too many problems.[37]

Criticisms of the New Accord

The new Basle Accord has already faced a number of criticisms. Some of these are aimed at the philosophy behind the new proposals. Some are aimed at the new methodology. Others are speculative in nature and based on assumptions of the new proposal.

The Basle Committee suggested that banks could use private sector credit ratings to weight their assets. Some European borrowers, for example, are not rated at all by any rating agency.

The new proposal also holds that banks should be charged for operational risk. This is the risk of losses which result from processes, systems, external events, and human failure. Construction of a system for monitoring and measuring this type of risk which will be subject to external review will be difficult.[38]

The new proposal has also been criticized for its assumption that banks act independently. In fact, banks operate in a market which may be illiquid at times and in which banks are exposed to a great deal of systemic risk.

The new Accord permits banks to use their own internal credit models to measure their capital adequacy. Some argue that this practice may encourage banks to lend large amounts in boom times and reduce credit in economic downturns, thus worsening economic cycles. Actually, banks in BIS member countries have been allowed since January 1998 to calculate their market risk exposures using either the standardized approach using the Basle Accord formula or they can use their own internal models, provided they obtain supervisory authority approval.[39] Thus, some banks already had experience using internally-developed models.

Furthermore, the internal model-based methodology may mean different things to different bank regulators. National supervisors may treat their constituent banks more leniently than they should. The Basle Committee counters this criticism with the idea that market forces will act as a constraint. If regulators are lenient, banks being supervised by that regulator will be penalized by the financial markets. This phenomenon has been shown to exist by data that banks which maintain high capital ratios are rewarded with higher equity prices.

It remains to be seen how accepted the new Accord proposals become. Some regions have already reported a favorable response to the new regulatory framework. Asian countries are among the nations which have been favorably disposed toward the proposal.[40] At a BIS meeting in Hong Kong early in 2001, Asian central bankers were favorably responsive to the new regulatory framework of the proposed Basle Accord rules, especially the change allowing banks more independence in assessing their capital riskiness.

European Union Capital Adequacy Rules

The European Union (EU) announced in January 2001 that a second round of consultations are to be held in preparation of final drafts of a new capital adequacy standard for the European Union to be made effective by 2004. The proposals will be aimed at amending current EU legislation concerning bank capital. The new rules will require European banks and investment companies to respond rapidly to market change, operate flexibly, and safeguard consistency and proper supervision for customers and consumers. The financing needs of small businesses must be regarded by the new rules.

The EU Commission has worked closely with the Basle Committee on the design of this proposal. In fact, the EU Commission used the Basle Accord as a model in developing its standard. The EU proposal will require banking supervisors to mandate minimum capital held in relation to the risk exposure of the banks in the EU. The objectives of the proposals are:[41]

1. market change will be reflected by considering the different needs of global institutions as well as local institutions;
2. capital charges and underlying economic risk will be more closely aligned;
3. incentives will be provided for enhanced risk mitigation standards; and
4. a framework will be provided to support a comprehensive assessment of the risks to which banks and investment firms are exposed.

SUMMARY AND CONCLUSIONS

The Basle Committee on Banking Supervision has formulated two major documents which have strengthened the supervision of international banks and added stability to the international financial system. These were: (1) the Basle Concordat of 1973 and its revision of 1983, prompted by the failures of Franklin National Bank of New York and Bankhaus Herstatt in Germany in 1973 and by the Luxembourg holding company of Italian Banco Ambrosiano in 1982 and discussed in Chapter 4, and (2) the Basle Accord of 1988, which addressed the capital adequacy, or lack thereof, among international banks and which has recently been revised.

The Basle Accord of 1988 contained a method for capital maintenance in a bank with relation to the riskiness of the bank's assets. Several studies in the 1970s and 1980s concluded that banks in general and large international banks specifically maintained inadequate capital. Bank capital or net worth, essentially the difference between a bank's assets and its liabilities, is considered to be a measurement of confidence in the bank. The lower this item in the balance sheet, or the lower a ratio such as capital-to-assets, the lower the confidence in the bank by its customers and the financial markets.

Capital is a nebulous item and one cannot get one's hands on it. But if it is inadequate to support the bank's assets, particularly its assets such as some risky loans and investments, this inadequacy places the bank in a dangerous position if a run on its deposits occurs, as happened in 1984 with Continental Illinois Bank, or market declines cause its loans or investments to decline in value, as has happened with the Japanese banks during the past decade.

The Basle Accord of 1988 was a work of political diplomacy. The U.S. and British bank supervisory agencies had bilaterally initiated their own capital adequacy standards and joined together to place pressure on the BIS and the Basle Committee to adopt a new standard which would be risk-based in determination of minimum capital adequacy for banks. Compromises had to be made with G10 members because of differences in accounting standards and practices in some countries. These compromises resulted in a new standard in which the G10 countries could seek enforcement in their domestic operations.

The Basle Accord raised the standards for most banks for capital adequacy. It essentially required banks to maintain approximately an 8 percent minimum level of capital, depending on the riskiness of their assets. The U.S. Federal Reserve Board had pressed for years to have international banks support their assets using a risk-based methodology. The Basle Committee finally adopted such a system. Some have held that the 1988 Capital Accord, formulated by the Committee on Banking Supervision and agreed to by the G10 countries, provided the BIS "with its most visible coup in recent years."[42]

In light of the improvement in capital-asset ratios of most banks, the Basle Accord had shortcomings. Some believed it was aimed at only large international banks in the industrialized nations. Many smaller banks maintain correspondent relationships with these larger banks and their risk level may be passed on to the larger banks. The Herstatt case involved a relatively small German bank which had large trading relationships in foreign exchange with leading international banks such as Chase Manhattan Bank. The closing of that bank caused large losses at many of these banks.

In the time since the Basle Accord was formulated, many banks have developed internal models which they use to maintain their capital adequacy minimums. Some of these models are better than the BIS model. Many banks show good capital-to-asset ratios but do not, under the current standard, maintain adequate loan loss reserves. Temporary problems, such as the Asian currency crisis, caused these banks to become insolvent because their capital ratios hid their balance sheet problem.

Some national banking systems want to use the Basle Accord rules to maintain minimum capital against what may be high risk assets needing more capital than the minimum standard requires. The German *pfandbriefe* market is one such difference of opinion. This financial instrument has a very large market in Germany but U.S. central banking authorities believe these bonds, issued by German mortgage banks, are riskier than the standard implies and would like to see higher amounts of capital behind them in banks' balance sheets.

Thus, the dynamic process inherent in the BIS approach to international banking system supervision resulted in the Basle Committee's return to the problem of bank capital adequacy. The new committee, led by the President of the New York Federal Reserve Bank William J. McDonough, returned to the drawing board and drafted a revised Basle Accord. The new accord will go into effect in 2004 and will increase the capital requirements for some assets while lowering it for others. It strengthens international bank supervision and permits banks to use their own internal capital adequacy models, provided they are approved by their national bank supervisors.

The new Accord proposals have been criticized on several levels. It remains to be seen whether the internal models approach, with which banks will be permitted to measure their capital adequacy, will work. It seems that any bank which desires international respectability will use this method as its standard approach.

The argument that the new Accord is aimed solely at large banks in G10 countries and that it is not appropriate for, say, emerging markets may be overcome. The 1988 Accord was ultimately adopted by smaller banks and some in non-G10 countries.

One of the key criticisms of the new Accord which may be difficult to overcome is that its methodology will require more and better national banking supervisory staffs. The internal ratings-based approach will require more expertise among the staffs of national banking supervisory authorities who will need to examine the quality of these approaches. Bank supervisory officials will need to become more knowledgeable of modern risk management techniques. National governments may not place a priority on investment for the acquisition of such staffs. And these governments will need to invest heavily in staff, training, and technology in order to implement the new Accord.

Despite the criticisms directed at the Basle Accord, the Basle Committee itself has an inherent weakness in its role as a forum for collective action. It has no enforcement powers and, in fact, has been held in reserve in the solution of some issues. This was apparent in the debt crisis of the early 1980s. In the initial response to the emerging markets debt crisis, the Basle Committee actually played no role at all.[43]

The new Accord, perhaps, will improve the international banking system. The world of cross-border financial transactions is changing so rapidly that regulators and supervisors have had trouble adapting to the change. Supervisors must keep up with sophistication of banks and capital market participants. They must adapt to and rely on quantitative and sophisticated risk assessment models.[44] Whether the new Accord will increase the stability of the international financial system remains to be seen, especially in the 21st century and the financial environment of electronic communications networks (ECNs) and global custody payment and settlement systems. As was mentioned earlier, no capital standard at all may be better than a poor one.

NOTES

1. James C. Baker and Raj Aggarwal, "Variations and Trends in Capital Ratios of Large Banks: Implications for International Bank Safety and Regulation," *Akron Business and Economic Review*, Vol. 15 (Summer, 1984), pp. 25–32.

2. Lee C. Buchheit, "How to Negotiate the Capital Adequacy Indemnity Clause," *International Financial Law Review*, March 1993, pp. 30–35.

3. Ethan B. Kapstein, *Supervising International Banks: Origins and Implications of the Basle Accord* (Princeton, NJ: Princeton University International Finance Section, December 1991), pp. 21–22.

4. Jan van der Vossen, "The New Basel Capital Proposal for Banks," *Finance & Development*, Vol. 38 (March 2001), p. II of the Bulletin.

5. See Anthony Saunders and Marcia Millon Cornett, *Financial Markets and Institutions: A Modern Perspective* (New York: McGraw-Hill, 2001), pp. 420–421, for an excellent discussion of the Basle Accord for-

mat. Also see Edward P.M. Gardener, *Capital Adequacy and Banking Supervision* (North Wales: University of Wales Press, 1991).

6. James C. Baker, *International Finance: Management, Markets, and Institutions* (Englewood Cliffs, NJ: Prentice-Hall, 1998), p. 218.

7. Alison Warner, "Private Passions," *The Banker*, Vol. 143 (September 1993), pp. 52–55.

8. Michael Camdessus, "Cleaning Up After Latino," *The Banker*, Vol. 146 (June 1996), pp. 18–20.

9. Emilia Tagaza, "Who Needs Money?" *Far Eastern Economic Review*, September 28, 1995, pp. 70–73.

10. Jonathan Friedland, "Yen For Capital," *Far Eastern Economic Review*, April 8, 1993, p. 72.

11. Neil Berhmann, "A Big Boost in Issues Imminent," *Asia Finance*, October 15, 1991, pp. 78–80.

12. Edgar Meister, "Supervisory Capital Standards: Modernise or Redesign?" *Economic Policy Review—Federal Reserve Bank of New York*, Vol. 4 (October 1998), pp. 101–104.

13. Alan Greenspan, "The Role of Capital in Optimal Banking Supervision and Regulation," *Economic Policy Review—Federal Reserve Bank of New York*, Vol. 4 (October 1998), pp. 163–168.

14. "IIF Calls for Review of Basle Ratios," *The Banker*, Vol. 148 (April 1998), pp. 13–14.

15. Alan Greenspan, "Wanted: Bank Regulators Who Act More Like the Market," *Secondary Mortgage Markets*, Vol. 15 (July 1998), p. n.a.

16. "IIF Calls for Review of Basle Ratios," *The Banker*, Vol. 148 (April 1998), p. 13.

17. "Basle Brush," *The Economist*, May 1, 1999, p. 69.

18. Michael Peterson, "Basel Gives Banks the Whip Hand," *Euromoney*, March 2001, p. 48.

19. "More Meddling," *Euromoney*, February 1992, p. 5.

20. Ibid.

21. "Basle Brush," *The Economist*, May 1, 1999, p. 69.

22. Kapstein, *Supervising International Banks: Origins and Implications of the Basle Accord*, p. 6.

23. Jan van der Vossen, "Basel Committee Presents Proposals for New Capital Adequacy Standards for Banks," *IMF Survey*, Vol. 30 (February 5, 2001), p. 37.

24. Basel Committee on Banking Supervision, "Overview of The New Basel Capital Accord," issued by the Bank for International Settlements, January 2001, p. 1.

25. Ibid., pp. 6–7.

26. Simon Brady, "The Ref Gets Rough," *Euromoney*, April 1992, p. 30.

27. Jan van der Vossen, "Basel Committee Presents Proposals for New Capital Adequacy Standards for Banks," *IMF Survey*, p. 38.

28. van der Vossen, "The New Basel Capital Proposal for Banks," *Finance & Development*, p. III of the Bulletin.

29. Ibid.

30. Ibid., p. 39.

31. Basel Committee on Banking Supervision, *Overview of The New Basel Capital Accord* (Basle, Switzerland: Bank for International Settlements, January 2001), p. 31.

32. Ibid.

33. Ibid.

34. Ibid.

35. van der Vossen, "The New Basel Capital Proposal for Banks," *Finance & Development*, p. 40.

36. Michael Blanden, "Basle Faulty," *The Banker*, Vol. 149 (July 1999), p. 25.

37. Birgit Specht, "Synthetic Securitization Enters Next Generation," *The 2001 Guide to Opportunities in Global Fixed Income* (a *Euromoney* supplement), February 2001, p. 29.

38. Ibid., p. 50.

39. Anthony Saunders, *Financial Institutions Management* (Burr Ridge, IL: Irwin McGraw-Hill, 2000), p. 194.

40. "Major Central Banks Expect an Upturn in 2nd Half of 2001," *The Wall Street Journal*, February 13, 2001, p. A18.

41. Found on the Internet at http://europa.eu.int, April 25, 2001, pp. 1–2.

42. Melvyn Westlake, "Into Basle's Inner Sanctum," *The Banker*, Vol. 144 (March 1994), p. 17.

43. Kapstein, *Supervising International Banks: Origins and Implications of the Basle Accord*, p. 8.

44. van der Vossen, "Basel Committee Presents Proposals for New Capital Adequacy Standards for Banks," *IMF Survey*, p. 40.

CHAPTER 6

The Bank for International Settlements and Derivatives

INTRODUCTION

During the 1980s, the volume of cross-border financial transactions increased significantly. New types of financial instruments were invented on an almost daily basis. Risk management became the buzzword among international banks and multinational companies (MNCs). Even state and local governments became active in hedging market and interest rate risk while international firms and banks were concerned about these risks as well as exposure to foreign exchange risk.

The latter type of risk began to emerge after global commerce adopted the floating rate regime as a new international monetary system in 1973. MNCs employed computer software which permitted them to do their own sensitivity analyses with regard to various interest rate and exchange rate scenarios. International banks such as Chemical Bank of New York and Chase Manhattan made available foreign exchange exposure management systems to MNCs.

Derivative financial instruments were devised by banks and financial institutions to be used by firms in hedging these financial risks. A derivative is a financial instrument traded on an exchange or over-the-counter and which is a financial arrangement between two parties. Its payments are based on the performance of an under-

lying financial or commodity asset, i.e., the benchmark. Every derivative, no matter how simple or complex, is derived from some
underlying quantity of an asset or, in some cases, a market index.
These financial instruments can be based on currencies, commodities, government or corporate debt, home mortgages, stocks, interest rates, or a combination of any of these.

Exchange-Traded Derivatives

Derivatives include so-called plain vanilla instruments such as
futures and options contracts which are traded on some organized
exchange markets such as the Chicago Board of Trade, the Chicago
Mercantile Exchange, the Philadelphia Exchange, the European
Options Exchange, or the Chicago Board Options Exchange. Forward foreign exchange contracts traded in international banks are
derivatives since their quantities and quality are based on the cash
market for foreign currencies.

From an international standpoint, few derivatives exchanges operated until the past few decades. The European exchanges have
thrived during the past decade and include markets with some of
the highest volume in contracts traded in the world. These include
the Marché a Terme International de France (MATIF), the Deutsche
Terminbörse—now known as Eurex in Germany, and the London
International Financial Futures Exchange (LIFFE).

Some derivatives are marketed over-the-counter. Among these
are some options, interest rate and currency swaps, and the relatively new so-called exotic derivatives. These contracts are written
by individuals, banks, or companies and some, such as the exotic
derivatives, are custom-designed for one specific type of hedge and
may have a shelf-life for as little as a day or less.

Futures and Forwards. A futures or forward contract is one which
offers a price for future delivery and which is determined by some
type of market. These also include swaps and commit the buyer and
seller to trade a contract for a given quantity of an asset at a price on
a future date. With futures contracts, no money changes hands until the delivery date with regard to foreign exchange contracts where
delivery is usually made. A pure futures contract is usually not delivered at delivery date but offset by the purchase or sale of an offset-
ting contract so that no net open position exists after delivery date.[1]

Options. Options, whether for foreign currencies, company
stocks, or debt instruments, give the buyer a right, but not the obli-

gation, to buy or sell an asset at a predetermined price over some specific time period. The option's price, or premium, is usually a small percentage of the asset's underlying value, or notional value. On the other hand, foreign currency forward contracts and futures-type derivatives present the buyer with an obligation, either the obligation to deliver foreign currency in the case of currency forwards, or the obligation to offset an open position at delivery date on a futures contract.[2]

Notional value, defined above, is not a good indicator of credit exposure and its concomitant risk. Such exposure usually amounts to a small fraction of notional value. For example, settlement and payment risks are additional forms which credit risk can take.

The Over-the-Counter Market

In the over-the-counter market, option contracts and interest rate or currency swaps may be written by individuals, banks, securities firms, or other companies. These contracts permit the dealer to link the contract to a desired interest rate, foreign currency rate, or the price of some other asset.[3] Specifically, an option is a contract which gives the purchaser the right, but not the obligation, to buy (if a call) or sell (if a put) an asset at a stated price—the strike or exercise price—on a stated date—if a European option—or at any time before a stated date—if an American option. A swap is the simultaneous exchange of the interest rate obligation of a variable-rate debt instrument for the interest rate obligation of a fixed-rate debt instrument, if an interest rate swap, or the exchange of liabilities in two different currencies, but packaged as a single transaction rather than as two separate loans.[4]

Most of the trading in derivatives is for speculative purposes, i.e., for the trader to make a profit. However, a significant share of the volume in these financial instruments is used to hedge against price fluctuations in currencies, stocks, bonds, or other assets. The liquidity in these markets is generally furnished by those speculating in the prices of these instruments.

Exotic Derivatives.[5] During the 1980s and early 1990s, banks and other financial institutions began to experiment with a very complex type of derivative. These were called exotic derivatives and were written for the purpose of hedging a very specific risk. They are complex options, hybrid swaps, or combinations of such instruments and are often embedded in securities. They were a direct result of financial engineering by experts in both mathematics and high finance.

Exotic derivatives, structured to respond to a very narrow risk, are priced by simulations of many prices which generate the most appropriate profit margin for the writer and cover the most appropriate risk for the buyer. Margins on exotic derivatives may be as much as three times those on ordinary derivatives and the return on equity from them may run as high as 35–50 percent. Or it could be zero.

Exotic derivatives are written on an over-the-counter basis and traded over-the-counter, if traded at all. A secondary market for these instruments is usually impossible because of the extremely customized nature of such financial instruments. Examples of exotic derivatives include the barrier option, the convertible reset bond, the quanto diff swap, and the index-amortizing option, discussed below.

The Barrier Option. Barrier options can be used for both hedging and speculation. The barrier option contains a special provision that causes premature expiration of the option or causes it to fail to come into existence even after the premium has been paid. In other words, the option is triggered if the underlying market reaches a certain "barrier." These derivatives have very complex risk characteristics. Some of the mathematics behind the pricing of barrier options are so complicated that, in one case, Credit Suisse Financial Products Company had to hire a quantitative expert, who had worked on the Strategic Defense Initiative, for his work on pattern recognition dynamics. This field is a close relative of options theory.[6]

Barrier options are classified into either of two groups, path independent or path dependent options. The path independent barrier option provides a payoff if the price of the underlying asset finishes above or below the strike price by expiration date. The direction of price movement for a payoff is determined at the purchase of the option.

Path dependent options are more complex and, thus, more risky. This option is an ordinary option with an added feature of a second predetermined rate that dictates whether the option will be exercised. The payoff is determined by whether the underlying asset's price passes the pre-set barrier or trigger at any point during the life of the option.

These options are classified as knock-in or knock-out options depending on whether they are activated if the spot price of the underlying asset crosses the set barrier. Furthermore, the knock-in option may be a down-and-in option only if the spot price falls below the barrier during the option's life or an up-and-in option if the spot price rises above the trigger set above the strike price of the option. With a knock-out option, the opposite is true: for a down-and-out option, the option expires as soon as the spot price falls below the barrier. For an up-and-out option, the option expires when the spot price rises above the barrier price.

The Convertible Reset Bond. The convertible reset bond permits the investor to choose between the bond's nominal yield and, for example, the return on another underlying asset. The underlying asset might be, for example, the performance of a stock index. Reset periods can be set to permit the investor a periodical change of mind. Some of these exotic derivatives essentially give the investor a money-back guarantee.

The Quanto Diff Swap. Another popular type of exotic derivative is the quanto diff, or differential, swap which contains embedded options on the inter-relationships of currencies and interest rates. Diff swaps are correlation instruments defined by two characteristics of its cash flow: the cash flow must be a function of two or more risk factors and at least two of these factors must be combined in a non-additive way. The correlation between the two factors determines the price of the diff swap. This derivative permits investors to earn on foreign currency interest rates without incurring currency risk.[7] Many who traded in diff swaps were unaware of the risk exposure they were incurring.[8]

Other Exotic Options. Nomura Securities, a Japanese investment firm, has developed the outperformance, or spread, option, used to hedge against underperformance by a pension fund manager. If one of the pension fund's managers, say of its growth portfolio, outperforms the current value-oriented portfolio by, for example, 5 percent, the institution receives the return on the current portfolio plus 5 percent. But if the growth portfolio underperforms the current portfolio, the manager will lose only the cost of the option.[9]

U.S. investors in fixed income debt instruments can use the index-amortizing swap. This swap can replicate the return on asset-backed securities, especially mortgage-backed securities. With mortgage-backed securities, the disadvantages are that prepayment by mortgagees is difficult to forecast since it is also difficult to predict the direction of interest rates or how fast interest rates will move. The index-amortizing swap is structured to permit the outstanding notional principal to amortize faster, by pre-determined amounts, as interest rates fall. These instruments can be used as investments or as hedges against an investor's position in mortgage-backed securities.[10] Growth of index-amortizing swaps was phenomenal in the early 1990s. Volume increased from nothing in 1990 to US$100–150 billion by the end of 1993.[11]

Finally, the digital option has been developed in the exotic derivatives class. This option pays out a large return at expiration date assuming the rate on which the option is based stays within a predetermined band or below a given strike price. These are also known as binary options which either pay a predetermined amount or nothing at all, depending on whether their underlying index is within a specified range at expiration. A standard option, for example, might pay one cent if it is one cent in the money or fifty cents if it is fifty cents in the money. A digital option would pay, say, US$2 whether it is one cent in the money or US$5 in the money.[12] Digital options are used by investors with strong views about the market's future direction.

Exotic Derivatives for Emerging Markets. Exotic derivatives have been developed for use with investment in emerging markets. Swiss Bank Company issued two low-exercise-price options—deep-in-the-money calls—on stocks from Malaysia and Singapore. The strike price for these exotic derivatives was set sufficiently below the value of the underlying stocks—US$1 versus US$1,409 for the Singapore-Malaysia-Thailand basket of stocks—so that no doubt exists about the options being exercised. Their price behaves not as an option price but as an index. This gives investors the full upside and downside risk.[13]

Benefits of Exotic Options

The benefits of exotic derivatives can be demonstrated by analyzing the difference between a forward contract and a conventional option.[14] With a forward, the investor/hedger can lock in a future rate or price but is unable to take advantage of any favorable movements in the price of the underlying asset. With an option, the investor/hedger can benefit from favorable movements in the underlying asset's price while, at the same time, be protected from any adverse price movements. But this benefit is costly—the premium on the option must be paid.

Investors/hedgers have an alternative to the option and its premium. They can replicate the pay-off profile of the option by buying forward contracts and can create an initial position which is equal to half the desired amount of an option which is at-the-money. As the price of the underlying asset increases, investors/hedgers can increase their forward position, or decrease it as the price declines. The cost of this approach is an incremental cost which is equal to the premium on the option.

But this alternative needs to be monitored constantly. Most investors/hedgers lack the technology, time, skills, or patience to manage such positions. They thus, pay the premium to the option writer to assume the risk and manage the position. Exotic derivatives can be customized to provide such benefits and which permit investors/hedgers to manage only those specific risks in which they are interested. Exotic derivatives of the type discussed above can furnish these benefits and aid investors/hedgers with their specific type of risk. The writer of these derivatives takes on most or all of the risk. But that is why margins and profits on these financial instruments can be quite high.[15]

Providers of Exotic Derivatives. Providers of exotic derivatives can be classified into three groups of financial institutions. The first group specializes in exotic derivatives for cross-border and cross-assets transactions. This group includes Bankers Trust, Credit Suisse-First Boston, Merrill Lynch, and JP Morgan. The second group produces a general set of exotic derivatives. This group includes Lehman Brothers, Goldman Sachs, Salomon Brothers, Morgan Stanley, and Swiss Bank. The third group of 15–25 firms includes U.S. banks Chase Manhattan and Citibank, European banks Deutsche Bank and Paribas, as well as insurance companies AIG, General Re, and Prudential, and investment banks Nomura, Kidder Peabody, and Barclays. The banks and firms mentioned above write the vast bulk of exotic derivatives and are the financial institutions which most concern international financial regulators.

Exotic Derivatives and Regulators. Exotic derivatives at the height of their use never totaled more than 5–10 percent of the total derivatives business. Yet they seemed to occupy an inordinate amount of time on the part of bank regulators and company policy-makers. Even this total amounts to trillions of dollars of outstanding notional value. Notional value is the theoretical value of the underlying securities. The International Swaps Dealers Association (ISDA) estimated that the notional value of all outstanding interest rate and currency swaps alone might be US$5 trillion. These are not, technically, exotic derivatives but the ISDA estimates the notional value of exotics to be in the US$300–600 billion range.[16]

Several adverse possibilities faced the exotic derivatives market in the early 1990s. The margins on these instruments began to decline as more and more banks began to write them. The capital investment in the staff and computer equipment necessary to write such instruments continued to increase greatly, squeezing many financial institutions from the market and creating profit and capital problems for those remaining in the market.

Derivatives Market Activity

The BIS gathers and analyzes data on international financial market activity. The organization publishes a *Quarterly Review: International Banking and Financial Market Developments*. In the March 2001 publication of this report, the dollar value of exchange-traded derivatives activity rose 6 percent in the fourth quarter of 2000. Equity derivative contracts was the most active area and dollar volume of these contracts rose 22 percent to US$11.4 trillion, the result of hedging stock positions by investors, especially in technology equities.[17]

During the 1990s, derivatives market activity increased significantly. In 1992, it was estimated that exchange-traded derivatives had grown in importance relative to the underlying cash instruments. The number of exchanges on which futures and options contracts are traded expanded greatly during the decade. The major exchanges on which derivatives are traded include Eurex in Germany, the Chicago Board of Trade, the Chicago Mercantile Exchange, MATIF in France, the Chicago Board Options Exchange, the Philadelphia Exchange, the European Options Exchange, and the London International Financial Futures and Options Exchange. Investors turned to interest and currency swaps more and more to hedge price positions in a number of assets. Over-the-counter derivatives volume grew commensurately and the exotic derivative in many types was used to the point that losses in ordinary derivative instruments were blamed on these financial innovations.

The Crisis in Derivatives

During the early 1990s, a number of institutions, including the BIS, formed the Group of 30—a research and consultative group, or think tank. It is formally known as the Consultative Group on International Economic and Monetary Affairs, is based in New York, and is financed by the major international financial institutions. It is comprised of 30 hand-picked members from public and private finance and is headed by Paul Volcker, former Chairman of the U.S. Federal Reserve Board. Other members include Jean-Claude Trichet, Governor of the Banque de France, Dr. Jacob A. Frenkel, Governor of the Bank of Israel, and Andrew D. Crockett, General Manager of the BIS. The heads of Morgan Stanley, Merrill Lynch, and the Dresdner Bank are members as are leading economists Peter B. Kenen of Princeton University and Paul Krugman of the Massachusetts Institute of Technology.

The Group of 30 has produced a body of global finance dogma which has gotten wide media attention. Its message is that finance must be modernized, innovation should be encouraged, international regulation should be harmonized, free movement of capital and open markets should be ensured, and the markets' ability to regulate themselves, especially in the areas of hedge funds and derivates, should be trusted by the public.[18]

The Group of 30 became concerned about the exposure to market risk faced by the international banking system from the use of derivatives, especially exotic derivatives. The market risk of concern to these diverse entities was the danger of losses from fluctuations in interest rates, foreign exchange rates, or equity prices. Regulators became concerned that a market decline from misuse of these instruments, coupled with inadequate capital in the banking system, could result in a catastrophic increase in global systemic risk in the international banking system.[19]

In the meantime, several crises involving the use, or perceived use, of derivatives occurred. A number of companies, banks, and governmental institutions incurred severe losses. Among these were Piper Jaffray Company, Procter & Gamble, Metallgesellshaft, Air Products, Atlantic Richfield, Kashima Oil in Japan, Barings Bank, Bank One, and Orange County, California. Selected examples of these will be discussed in the following sections.

Procter & Gamble. On April 12, 1994, Procter & Gamble (P&G), the large U.S. household products company, reported a US $102 million aftertax charge to close out two leveraged interest rate swaps. These were diff swaps. The swaps were arranged by Bankers Trust, a leader at that time in derivatives products. P&G sued Bankers Trust for not accurately and fully disclosing the terms and risks of the swaps.[20]

Metallgesellschaft. Metallgesellschaft, a leading German metals and mining company, nearly went bankrupt in 1993 because of a liquidity crisis. The company had employed a hedging strategy through its U.S. subsidiary, MG Corporation, which used futures contracts to hedge long-term fixed price contracts to supply oil products to small independent service stations in the United States. This strategy was designed to protect the subsidiary from oil price increases and the futures were traded on the New York Mercantile Exchange. As oil prices declined, the value of the futures contracts also fell, causing MG to put up additional margin payments. For each decline of US$1 in the price of oil, MG was required to pay US$160 million in margin. A major shareholder in Metallgesellschaft forced the company to hire new management. One of these managers liquidated many of the futures positions instead of rolling them forward, thus creating a liquidity crisis. Paper losses were converted to real losses, which amounted to US$1.3 billion for Metallgesellschaft.[21]

Piper Jaffray Companies. Piper Capital Management Inc., a subsidiary of the Piper Jaffray Company, a regional brokerage firm based in Minneapolis, lost nearly 50 percent of its stock value in 1994. The company used derivatives in its bond fund for hedging purposes and did not disclose this fact to its investors, which included small city governments and a local symphony orchestra. These instruments lost much of their value and investors sued the company for the losses and for lack of disclosure.

Barings Bank. One of the most notorious cases was that of the demise of Barings Bank PLC, a merchant bank headquartered in London and founded in 1762. Barings had financed Great Britain's war against Napoleon's France and had arranged the U.S. purchase of the Louisiana Territory from France in 1803. The bank became insolvent when it lost more than US$1 billion from trading by a general manager of its Singapore subsidiary named Nick Leeson. Leeson was a rogue trader who bought stock futures contracts in Tokyo and Osaka and sold them in Singapore. The contracts were derived from the Nikkei 225 stock index. Leeson tried to make arbitrage profits in the two markets and also used puts on the Nikkei stock index in Japan to raise cash for margin calls on Nikkei futures contracts in which he had invested bank funds. The result was a loss which exceeded the capital of the parent bank. Barings Bank failed and its assets were sold for £1 to ING Bank in the Netherlands and Leeson went to prison for his misuse of derivatives.[22]

Bank One. Bank One, a large regional bank headquartered in Columbus, Ohio, planned to use company stock to acquire another large bank during this period. At the same time, it had hired experts from another bank acquisition who had experience in derivatives. Bank One began to deal in derivatives for its own account for the purpose of research and development of the product. The bank's management merely wished to determine the value of such financial instruments in hedging the bank's asset-liability position. When it became known that Bank One was experimenting in derivatives, the market penalized the bank's stock price and the planned acquisition, to be made with bank equity, had to be postponed until the stock price recovered. In the meantime, Bank One drastically reduced its experiment with derivatives, thus having its policies changed by the stock market, even though the bank had actually made profits from derivatives transactions.

Orange County, California. The Treasurer of Orange County, California, suffered losses in public accounts from the alleged use of derivatives to hedge the price of debt instruments in which he had invested county funds. This local government official actually incurred the county's losses from the purchase of long-term securities with short-term loans.[23] These were leveraged interest rate instruments provided by a leading brokerage firm. But the perception by the public was that derivatives had been used in this case. The county filed the largest municipal bankruptcy in history. This official was subsequently convicted of misuse of public funds. The media misrepresented derivatives, and especially exotic derivatives, as the cause of Orange County's problem.

Results. Exotic derivatives were not used in any of these cases. These all involved so-called plain vanilla derivatives, ordinary futures or options contracts. However, banks such as Bankers Trust, a leader in derivatives and, particularly exotics, retreated drastically in their writing of exotic options. As mentioned above, several studies were carried out with derivatives in general as their major topic. Bankers Trust was sued by Procter & Gamble. The Bank of England was blamed for overlooking the Barings-Leeson problem. The governor of the Bank of England was quoted as saying that the central banks have many rules but many criminals are also involved.[24]

One of the conclusions reached by some in these cases involving losses from derivatives is that those using derivatives had found that profits from hedging were more than from the investments the hedges were designed to protect. Some of the players became deeply involved in derivatives of all kinds. At the time of the Barings fiasco, a Minneapolis Federal Reserve Bank study found that derivatives represented 46 percent of the assets of Bankers Trust and 37 percent of Morgan Guaranty's assets. Thus, global banking supervisors became very concerned.

THE BIS AND THE DERIVATIVES CONCERN

Several issues regarding derivatives were raised in addition to the losses by leading companies and banks. Creditworthiness became an issue. Creditworthiness of the counterparties to swap transactions gained importance. Strong credit ratings were needed for counterparties as well as swaps dealers. Accounting and tax consequences were identified as results of financial engineering. Derivatives of all types have different tax and accounting implications for corporations. Regulators became concerned about three issues: (1) the fact that market sophistication increased too rapidly for regulators to maintain vigilance; (2) volume growth and market sophistication greatly increased risks faced by banks; and (3) derivatives use increased the systemic risk of the global financial markets.

BIS Reports on Derivatives

The BIS and its major committees have formulated and published a number of reports dealing with derivatives, their use, and implications. The major reports and activities are discussed in this section. See Figure 6.1 for a chronological listing of the major BIS activities on derivatives and their markets.

The Promisel Report. The BIS became concerned that problems stemming from the use of derivatives, especially by banks, and inadequate control of such trading activities might lead to a systemic collapse of the international banking system. Thus, the BIS issued a study known as the Promisel Report, published in 1992. The Basle Committee on Banking Supervision followed up with recommendations for higher capital levels for banks to cover market risk from derivatives trading. These revised capital standards became effective in 1996.[25]

The general manager of the BIS, Andrew Crockett, the first English-speaking chief executive officer of the BIS, became quite con-

Figure 6.1
BIS Development of Derivatives, Regulations, and Disclosures

July 1994	The Basle Committee on Banking Supervision and the Technical Committee of the International Organisation of Securities Commissions (IOSCO) jointly released documents providing guidance on the sound risk management of derivatives activities.
May 1995	The Basle Committee on Banking Supervision and the Technical Committee of IOSCO jointly issued a report, *Framework for Supervisory Information about the Derivatives Activities of Banks and Securities Firms.*
July 1996	The G10 central banks formulated a report, *Proposals for Improving Global Derivatives Market Statistics.* This report outlines a framework for the regular collection of derivatives market data from a small number of leading global dealers.
November 1996	Basle Committee on Banking Supervision and IOSCO released their survey of the disclosures of trading and derivatives activities by banks and securities firms in their 1995 annual reports.
January 1997	The G10 central banks approved regular collection of derivatives market statistics. The approved framework differed from the July 1996 proposals in ways which lessened the burden on reporting institutions. These data will include notional values and gross market values of foreign exchange, interest rate and equity-based derivatives instruments in a wide variety of underlying currencies, interest rates, and equity markets and the statistics will include derivatives-related credit exposures before and after netting arrangements.
November 1997	Basle Committee on Banking Supervision and the Technical Committee of IOSCO released their *Survey of Disclosures about Trading and Derivatives Activities.*
November 1998	Basle Committee on Banking Supervision and the Technical Committee of IOSCO released their *Survey of Disclosures about Trading and Derivatives Activities.* At about the same time, the two committees issued *1998 Supervisory Information Framework for Derivatives and Trading Activities.*

Source: I-Lei Huang, "The Derivatives Regulations of the Bank for International Settlements," unpublished working paper, Kent State University, May 2000, pp. 4–5.

cerned about derivatives. The Glasgow-born, former Executive Director of the Bank of England, stated as early as 1994 that the BIS should play a major role in monitoring the growth of financial derivatives.[26] He believed the topic was one for central bankers to manage but that few central banks have the resources to analyze the problem. Thus, he thought that the BIS could make a major contribution in this area.

The report entitled "Recent Developments in International Interbank Relations" was informally known as the Promisel Report, for its chairman. The report was the work of a G10 committee and called for improvements in the quality and coverage of market data about over-the-counter derivatives, including the exotics.[27] It also was concerned with netting of forward foreign exchange obligations and connected this function with the Basle Accord on minimum bank capital requirements by stating that the only form of netting of such obligation is bilateral netting on the basis of novation.[28]

BIS Guidelines. Between 1993 and 1999, a series of studies and research reports were initiated and published by the BIS about the derivatives problem. The BIS reported a growing concern over derivatives trading and its problems in its 1993 Annual Report.[29] One concern stressed by the BIS was over the proliferation of custom-made products—structured or engineered financial instruments—whose risk/return profile is changed by embedding in the instruments derivative features. The BIS also recognized a growing anxiety over risks involved in the increase of market counterparty exposures, especially in the case of swaps.[30]

In July 1994, the Basle Committee in collaboration with the Technical Committee of the International Organization of Securities Commissions (IOSCO) published a set of guidelines for the sound risk management of derivatives use. In May 1995, this grouping issued a report entitled *Framework for Supervisory Information about the Derivatives Activities of Banks and Securities Firms.*

Proposed Triennial Central Bank Survey. In 1994, the BIS announced an international survey of activity in the derivatives markets to be carried out in conjunction with the BIS' triennial central bank survey of foreign exchange market activity. Before this time, data on derivatives markets were collected by exchanges, various industry groups including the Futures Industry Association and the International Swaps and Derivatives Association, and national regulators.[31] The first survey on derivatives was carried out in 1995 but not published until 1996. The problem with this type study is that much time elapses between the announcement of the study and its publication. In the world of global financial markets and financial engineering, as *The Banker* put it, "things may have moved on by then."[32]

Brockmeijer Report. In February 1995, a report, "Issues of Measurement Related to Market Size and Macroprudential Risks in Derivatives Markets," was published and became known as the Brockmeijer Report, for the committee chairman, Jan Brockmeijer of the Netherlands Bank. This report identified the information requirements of central banks with regard to the derivatives markets. The report proposed two objectives: a comprehensive survey of derivatives markets to be conducted relatively infrequently and a system for the more regular collection of statistics on derivatives activity from a small number of leading global derivatives dealers.[33] In April 1995, the Central Bank Survey of Derivatives Market Activity was conducted. The survey, proposed by the Brockmeijer Report, was conducted by central banks and monetary authorities in 26 countries. The results were published by the BIS in May 1996 in the "Central Bank Survey of Foreign Exchange and Derivatives Market Activity."

In July 1996, the G10 central banks added to the Basle Committee/IOSCO work by publishing a report entitled *Proposals for Improving Global Derivatives Market Statistics*. This report included a framework for systematic collection of derivatives market data from a small number of leading global derivatives dealers, proposed in the Brockmeijer Report.

Euro-currency Standing Committee. The G10 central banks in conjunction with the BIS formed a working group of the Euro-currency Standing Committee, a BIS committee housed in Basle.[34] This working group was charged with the formulation of a more frequent collection of derivatives statistics than the triennial survey discussed earlier. This group was chaired by Shinichi Yoshikuni of the Bank of Japan and its report was presented to the G10 central bank governors in July 1996. The report called for a more regular collection of derivatives activity statistics by the end of 1997. The report also recommended that central banks determine whether another derivatives market global survey be carried out in conjunction with the next foreign exchange market survey, then planned for 1998.

The Yoshikuni Report also discussed alternatives to derivatives in monitoring price risks and exposures in international financial markets. Central banks had not analyzed these alternatives from either a theoretical or quantitative viewpoint.

Triennial Survey Results. In November 1996, the Basle Committee and IOSCO released the results of the first triennial survey conducted in 1995 about trading and derivatives activities by banks and securities investment firms. In 1998, the BIS released its latest survey of such activities entitled *Central Bank Survey of Foreign Exchange and Derivatives Market Activity.* Activity in derivatives increased by 26 percent during the 1995–1998 period but was down from the 45 percent increase during the 1992–1995 period.[35]

According to this report, the global daily turnover of foreign exchange and interest rate derivatives contracts, including traditional foreign exchange derivatives instruments traded over-the-counter, amounted to US$1.3 trillion. Worldwide positions in over-the-counter market derivatives of all types amounted to US$72 trillion. Gross market values of all derivatives, defined as the costs that would have been incurred if the contracts had been replaced at market prices as of June 30, 1998, amounted to US$2.6 trillion, about 3.6 percent of total notional value. The survey also found that the total notional value of the over-the-counter derivatives market was US$70 trillion compared with US$14 trillion for exchange-traded derivatives instruments.

G10 Approval of Regular Collection of Data. In January 1997, the G10 central banks approved the regular collection of derivatives market statistics. This plan places a lighter burden on reporting institutions and requires the compilation of market statistics on the notional values and gross market values outstanding of a wide range of derivatives products. Derivatives-based credit exposures before and after netting arrangements will be required and the results will be published by the BIS.[36]

In November 1997 and November 1998, the Basle Committee/IOSCO group released a survey entitled *Survey of Disclosures about Trading and Derivatives Activities,* and on the latter date, they issued a report entitled *1998 Supervisory Information Framework for Derivatives and Trading Activities.*

This period of intense study of the derivatives markets by the BIS and its related groups has been relatively short. More public disclosure is needed. Many institutions still do not provide sufficient information about key aspects of their trading and derivatives activities including risk profiles and risk management practices.

Accounting Implications

The BIS/IOSCO studies of derivatives market activities also identified the fact that several other national and international bodies had recently issued proposals or standards with regard to the accounting implications of derivatives trading, as a result of the perceived inadequate accounting concepts and principles in this area.[37] The International Accounting Standards Committee (IASC) has issued a standard as well as a discussion on this subject. The IASC is an international body of representatives of the major country accounting societies and is dedicated to the promulgation and adoption of accounting standards which have international application.

The IASC issued International Accounting Standard (IAS) 32, "Financial Instruments: Disclosure and Presentation," in June 1995. IAS 32 includes requirements for disclosure of terms, conditions, and accounting policies for financial instruments, interest rate risk and credit risk data, and the fair value of on- and off-balance sheet financial instruments, including derivatives. Its discussion paper, "Accounting for Financial Assets and Financial Liabilities," was published in March 1997 and advocates the use of fair values of historical costs to account for financial assets and financial information. In addition, it recommends more disclosure about financial risks as well as the objectives and strategies for managing these risks.

The Japanese Ministry of Finance issued new regulations about market value accounting for trading activities to be effective April 1, 1997. Japanese banks were given permission to adopt mark-to-market accounting for their trading activities including derivatives if these banks meet approval standards on international control, valuation, and accounting procedures set by the Ministry of Finance.

The Accounting Standards Board in the United Kingdom issued "Financial Reporting Exposure Draft 13, with Supplement" in April 1997 requiring banks to disclose information about derivatives use. Just prior to this standard, the U.S. Securities and Exchange Commission issued a market risk disclosure rule covering derivatives.

In France, the Fédération des Experts Comptables Européens issued a report entitled "Accounting Treatment of Financial Instruments—A European Perspective" in December 1996 recommending the disclosure of qualitative information about the use of financial instruments including derivatives and the management of related risks.

In-house Models by the Business World

Companies also began to implement better controls internally in their derivatives usage. Some installed in-house software enabling them to do sensitivity analyses of their exposures under a variety of future interest rate and foreign exchange rate scenarios.[38] For example, SBC Capital Markets, an investment banker, developed such software and began making it available for its customers. Senior management of large firms, recognizing the problems of Procter & Gamble, Gibson Greetings, Barings Bank, and Metallgesellschaft, began to educate themselves about derivatives and their benefits as well as their risks. Many of these firms turned away from the complex derivatives, especially exotics, and returned to hedging with plain vanilla derivatives such as futures and options with their highly liquid markets.[39]

In summary, many international reports published about the problems with derivatives and their use placed emphasis on self-regulation by companies, banks, and other entities. It would seem that self-regulation is synonymous with self-interest since high internal standards can result in a triple-A rating for the companies' securities. These studies advocated that companies and banks manage their various risks to a competitive advantage.

One such model prompted by international agencies including the Basle Committee is the use of value-at-risk (VAR) methodology.[40] VAR is a measurement of how much of a firm's money is at risk daily in its various derivatives contracts and other financial strategies. VAR coupled with simple probability analysis can produce one number to quantify with high probability the most which the company could lose in a single day. U.S. banks such as JP Morgan, Chase Manhattan, Bankers Trust, Chemical Bank, and Citicorp were already using VAR analysis to measure market risk. Corporate adoption of the technique, however, has been slow.

The G30 Response

In July 1993, the G30, a banking think tank, issued its report about the global derivatives problem. This was considered by most to be a friendly attack on the industry. The head of the International

Swaps and Derivatives Association (ISDA), the trade association representing the derivatives industry, said of the study that it was a "milestone in broadening understanding of global derivatives."[41]

This report explained the uses of derivatives, primarily to the uninitiated, and outlined the problems concerning valuation, accounting and reporting, market and credit risk measurement, systems and controls, and legal risk, all of which face dealers and end-users of derivatives. The study contained little new material and was criticized for its lack of a timetable or procedure for implementing its recommendations and an identification of just what firms need to implement which of its recommendations.[42]

The editors of *Euromoney*, a leading journal of the world's capital and money markets published in London, criticized the G30 report, referred to it as the Weatherstone Report for Dennis Weatherstone, chairman of JP Morgan and the head of the G30 committee in charge of the report.[43] They said it was unclear what the study was supposed to be. The report contained two dozen recommendations but Weatherstone said the study was not intended to be a manual or code of conduct. *Euromoney* believed the report lacked objectivity because the committee was dominated by top officials of the leading derivatives trading institutions. Third, *Euromoney* believed the report should not be taken seriously because of G30's attempt to present it as entirely separate from the myriad other studies being conducted at that time, especially by central banks and other banking regulators. Finally, the G30 study concludes that concerns about derivatives and systemic risk are misguided and that, according to its data, derivatives volume, when compared with that of other financial assets, is relatively small. They argued that the complexity of derivatives should be of concern only when such trading outweighed the participants' abilities to evaluate and manage the risks associated with derivatives use.

With regard to this last point, *Euromoney* editors were not very reassured by the G30 information. The report states that some firms do not have senior management responsible for derivatives use by their firms. The study found that 93 percent of derivatives dealers have some understanding of the issues at the board level. But when one company derivatives dealer was asked how many members of his company's board really understood derivatives, he responded: "one and a half."[44]

The Industry Response

Several industry studies of the derivatives markets were published during this period. Among the industry associations which studied this problem was the ISDA. Almost all of the leading exchanges where derivatives were traded issued reports on derivatives as well as their own standards. Among these was the Chicago Mercantile Exchange. The Chicago "Merc" issued a report on how to deal with so-called myths about derivatives.[45] The report discussed six myths about derivatives in this report. They are as follows:

1. Derivatives are always dangerous and cause only losses for customers; in fact, derivatives transfer risk from one market participant to another or to the market and someone inevitably loses. However, derivatives may be the lowest cost or most efficient method for hedging financial risks.
2. Most institutional investors take huge gambles with derivatives; in fact, industry data show that institutional investors limit their portfolios to an allocation of derivatives to less than 5 percent;
3. All instances where the media has cited derivatives losses do in fact involve derivatives; in fact, some of these did not involve derivatives instruments at all.
4. Derivatives have no economic value; in fact, according to the BIS itself, derivatives improve the efficiency of financial markets and, by permitting more financial risks to be hedged, may permit some borrowers more access to sources of funds.
5. More government regulation and micromanagement would protect investors from any mistakes; in fact, government regulation did not protect savings and loan investors or taxpayers from the large losses incurred when many of these institutions failed in the 1980s.
6. No guidelines can be found for the prudent use of derivatives; in fact, central banks such as the U.S. Federal Reserve System, as well as the Group of 30, have given guidance to banks that use these instruments or have published guidelines on how to use derivatives and other such instruments.

SUMMARY AND CONCLUSIONS

During the 1980s and early 1990s, the growth in the volume of derivatives trading increased very rapidly, both on exchanges and in over-the-counter markets. Plain vanilla derivatives such as forwards, futures, and options contracts and interest rate and currency swaps were used as part of risk management strategies by corporations, banks, and governmental entities. Exotic derivatives were created by financial engineers trained in finance and mathematics for the purpose of hedging very specific risks which were so customized that these instruments could not be traded in a marketplace with any degree of liquidity. In fact, some of these "xotics" may have had a shelf life of less than one hour.

Several losses were announced stemming from the use of derivatives, although most or all of these instances were cases of the use of so-called plain vanilla derivatives, e.g., forwards, futures, options, or swaps. Some losses were attributed to derivatives in cases where derivatives were not used. Exotic derivatives, although not understood by many who used them, did not appear to be the cause of any of the losses incurred by companies such as Procter & Gamble, Gibson Greetings, Metallgesellschaft, or government entities such as the Treasurers Office of Orange County, California. Many corporate and banking officials appeared to understand neither derivatives in general nor exotic derivatives specifically.

By the early 1990s, central bank regulators and other national bank supervisory agencies began to clamor for new and stronger standards in dealing with derivatives. Some of this fervor was strongest among U.S. bank regulators whose motive was to cover their backs because several of the losses from derivatives were by American companies and the 1980s was a period in which several banks and savings and loan associations failed, many as a result of lax supervision.[46]

Some of the fear of derivatives stemmed from political motivations. Some of the concern about the use of these financial instruments was the result of fear of systemic risk—that one or two large banking firms might fail and lead to the failure of many others around the world. The Basle Committee added derivatives to its list of balance sheet assets for which more capital needed to be maintained by banks.

Many reports were published dealing with derivatives markets activity during the past decade. Many of these reports contained nothing new. Many were self-serving documents published by firms or groups with vested interests in the derivatives markets activity. Most stressed the one common sense recommendation which was very obvious in the Barings Bank case. When dealing with financial instruments which are in the derivatives category, firms and banks should implement controls which will deal with any issues which arise from the use of derivatives financial instruments. The first step in a workable control system is to be completely familiar and knowledgeable with that which is being utilized.

NOTES

1. Lee Berton, "Understanding the Complex World of Derivatives," *The Wall Street Journal*, June 14, 1994, p. C1.

2. Ibid.

3. Ibid.

4. James C. Baker, *International Finance: Management, Markets, and Institutions* (Upper Saddle River, NJ: Prentice Hall, 1998), pp. 366–368.

5. K. Michael Fraser, "What It Takes To Excel In Exotics," *Global Finance*, Vol. 7 (March 1993), p. 44.

6. Caren Chesler-Marsh, "Nightmare on Wall Street," *Euromoney*, February 1992, p. 26.

7. James C. Baker, *International Finance: Management, Markets, and Institutions*, pp. 370–371.

8. Peter Lee, "How to Exorcise Your Derivatives Demons," *Euromoney*, September 1992, p. 37.

9. K. Michael Fraser, "What It Takes To Excel In Exotics," *Global Finance*, p. 47.

10. Ibid.

11. Lisa N. Galaif, "Index Amortizing Rate Swaps," *Federal Reserve Bank of New York Quarterly Review*, Vol. 18 (Winter 1993–1994), p. 63.

12. Miriam Bensman, "Tailor Your Trade with Exotics," *Future: The Magazine of Commodities and Options*, Vol. 23, No. 8 (August 1994), p. 43.

13. K. Michael Fraser, "A Hot Combination," *Global Finance*, Vol. 8 (February 1994), p. 78.

14. Chase Securities Inc., "Mundane Problems, Exotic Solutions," *Euromoney*, August 1992, p. 42.

15. Ibid., pp. 42–48.

16. Fraser, "A Hot Combination," *Global Finance*, p. 45.

17. "Signs of Global Economic Slowdown Cast Shadow over International Markets," *IMF Survey*, Vol. 30 (March 19, 2001), p. 95.

18. Ibrahim Warde, "Crony Capitalism: The Banking System in Turmoil," *Le Monde Diplomatique*, November 1998, p. 3, found on the Internet at http://www.monde-diplomatique.fr.

19. Michelle Celarier, "New Catastrophe Scenarios Bedevil Derivatives," *Global Finance*, Vol. 7 (October 1993), p. 60.

20. Paula Dwyer, et al., "The Lesson from Barings' Straits," *Business Week*, March 13, 1995, p. 31.

21. James C. Baker, *International Finance: Management, Markets, and Institutions*, pp. 325–326.

22. Ibid., p. 326.

23. Ibid., pp. 380–381.

24. George Melloan, "Leeson's Law: Too Much Leverage Can Wreck a Bank," *The Wall Street Journal*, March 6, 1995, p. A15.

25. Michelle Celarier, "New Catastrophe Secenarios Bedevil Derivatives," *Global Finance*, Vol. 7 (October 1993), pp. 60–65.

26. Melvyn Westlake, "Into Basle's Inner Sanctum," *The Banker*, Vol. 144 (March 1994), p. 15.

27. Bank for International Settlements, *64th Annual Report* (Basle, Switzerland: Bank for International Settlements, 13th June 1994), p. 118.

28. Charles A.E. Goodhart, "Introductory Remarks: The Role of Clearing Houses," in Board of Governors of the Federal Reserve System, *Symposium Proceedings: International Symposium on Banking and Payment Services* (Washington, D.C.: Board of Governors of the Federal Reserve System, 1994), p. 150.

29. Bank for International Settlements, *63rd Annual Report* (Basle, Switzerland: Bank for International Settlements, 14th June 1993), pp. 123–128.

30. "Derivatives Bother Basle," *The Banker*, Vol. 144 (July 1994), p. 29.

31. Bank for International Settlements, *64th Annual Report* (Basle, Switzerland: Bank for International Settlements, 13th June 1994), p. 118.

32. "Derivatives Bother Basle," *The Banker*, p. 29.

33. Bank for International Settlements, "Proposals for Improving Global Derivatives Market Statistics," found at http://www.bis.org/publ/ecsc06.htm, March 6, 2001, p. 1.

34. Ibid.

35. "Recent Trends in Foreign Exchange, Derivatives Markets Detailed in New Study," *IMF Survey*, Vol. 28 (May 24, 1999), p. 176.

36. *G10 Approve Regular Collection of Derivatives Market Statistics* from BIS Press Release found at http://www.bis.org., January 27, 1997.

37. William J. McDonough, "The Global Derivatives Market," *Federal Reserve Bank of New York Quarterly Review*, Vol 18 (Autumn 1993), pp. 1–5.

38. Joan Ogden, "The 'D' Word: A User's Update," *Global Finance*, Vol. 9 (June 1995), p. 62.

39. Ibid., p. 61.

40. Charles M. Seeger, "How to Prevent Future Nick Leesons," *The Wall Street Journal*, August 8, 1995, p. A13.

41. "The Complacent Derivatives Industry," *Euromoney*, August 1993, p. 5.

42. Ibid.

43. Ibid., pp. 5–6.

44. Ibid., p. 6.

45. Chicago Mercantile Exchange, "Dealing with Myths about Derivatives," (Summer 1995), pp. 1–4.

46. Peter Lee, "How to Exorcise Your Derivatives Demons," *Euromoney*, p. 46.

CHAPTER 7

Payment and Settlement Systems and the Bank for International Settlements

INTRODUCTION

During the past 20 years, the volume of international trade and investment has increased rapidly. International commerce and banking have benefited from this growth. Cross-border financial transactions have grown commensurately. Today, average daily global volume in the foreign exchange markets amounts to US $1.5 trillion. Global custody has become a major function by leading international banks.

Financial risks have increased greatly in this world of global trade and investment. Two major financial risks are constantly present in these transactions. They are credit and liquidity risk. Credit risk is the risk that one party will not settle an obligation for full value, either when due or at any time afterwards. Liquidity risk is the risk that a counterparty to a transaction will not settle an obligation for full value when due, but will do so on some unspecified day afterwards. Before the performance of such an obligation, it may not be possible to know whether the failure to settle an obligation for full value when due represents liquidity risk or credit risk.

These two financial risks are the components of settlement risk. This is the risk incurred when one party to a transaction does not fulfill his/her financial obligation. It has been referred to as Herstatt risk, or cross-currency principal risk. Thus, multinational companies (MNCs) and banks are constantly exposed to settlement risk. Failure to cope with settlement risk can lead to other risks such as insolvency and thus, in the case of banks, systemic risk. Settlement risk is, therefore, a major concern for central bankers.

Other financial risks may result from the settlement of cross-border financial transactions.[1] Among these are replacement cost risk stemming from the loss of unrealized gains; principal risk, which is the risk of loss of the full value of securities or funds that one firm transfers to the defaulting counterparty where settlement is made prior to the default of the counterparty; operational risk, which results from some technical failure in equipment or procedures during trading and before settlement of a transaction; and systemic risk, which is the risk that a failure of some part of the transaction by one firm or bank will result in the failure of other firms or banks.

Major Payment Systems

In order to protect the firm or bank from these risks, payment systems must be established. Banks and non-bank commercial firms have utilized payment systems for many years. The major payment systems being used at the present time are: (1) Fedwire which connects the 12 U.S. Federal Reserve Banks, U.S. depository institutions, U.S. Treasury Department, and other U.S. government agencies; (2) CHIPS, the Clearing House Interbank Payments System, connecting nearly 150 U.S. and foreign banks; (3) CHAPS, the Clearing House Automated Payments System, owned and operated by a consortium of banks in the United Kingdom; (4) FX Net, a foreign exchange bilateral netting settlement system with more than 20 financial institutions as members; and (5) SWIFT, the Society for Worldwide Interbank Financial Telecommunications, a cooperative headquartered in Belgium which services some 2,000 bank and financial firm members by transferring the instructions in the form of standardized codes. These facilitate financial transactions through a computer network whose speed, accuracy, safety, and low cost makes the transfer of such information much more efficient than other systems, such as cable.

Other Systems. Canadian and U.S. banks are serviced by a settlement system developed by the International Clearing Systems, Inc. This is a bilateral netting system which is being upgraded to a multilateral netting arrangement. The European Clearing House Organisation established its ECHO system centered in London in 1994 which services 50 Organisation for Economic Cooperation and Development (OECD) banks and settles transactions in more than 20 currencies. The ECHO system was created by 15 major international banks from seven countries.[2] The International Swaps and Derivatives Association (ISDA) has begun a bilateral netting system for swaps transactions. In Hong Kong, financial transactions are settled by the Hong Kong & Shanghai Bank through CHATS, the Clearing House Automated Transfer System. The latter is provided a credit facility by the Hong Kong & Shanghai Bank but it could incur liquidity risk if it has insufficient funds to cover a deficit.[3]

Role of Central Banks in Payment Systems

Central banks play a key role in the global payment system. They maintain direct relationships with the clearing house and banks and indirect relationships with non-bank financial institutions. Central banks are usually responsible for a smoothly functioning payments system. In other countries, such as Sweden, they are required by law to maintain the payment system. In some countries, such as Italy, the central bank operates the clearing house. Some central banks may own, operate, audit, set, and enforce regulations with regard to the payments system in their country.

In the United States, the Federal Reserve System operates Fedwire which electronically connects the 12 U.S. Federal Reserve Banks, U.S. depository institutions, the U.S. Treasury Department, and other U.S. government agencies. This system was fully automated in 1973. The Clearing House Interbank Payments System (CHIPS) clears payments for 41 U.S. banks and 98 foreign banks operating in the United States. Its counterpart in Great Britain, the Clearing House Automated Payments System (CHAPS) is owned and operated by a consortium of British banks.

Banks' Role in Payment Systems

Banks also play a major role in national and international payment systems. They make up the membership in most of the important systems such as CHIPS, CHAPS, CHATS, and SWIFT. More than 90 percent of the foreign exchange market volume is traded by banks. Large international banks furnish most or all of the global custody services available for international business firms. Investment banks handle most of the merger and acquisition activity generated by international firms. A great deal of specialized, over-the-counter derivatives activity is written by major international banks.

THE BIS AND PAYMENT AND SETTLEMENT SYSTEMS

Global payment and settlement systems must be regulated and supervised. National central banks are generally overwhelmed by the complex, sophisticated activities necessary to operate a payment and settlement system designed for cross-border financial transactions. A multilateral, or international, agency must furnish the regulatory and oversight functions.

Thus, the BIS became involved in the development of a center for formulation of rules and standards dealing with international payment and settlement systems. Major financial crises such as the collapse of the Herstatt Bank in 1974 and the stock market crash in 1987 prompted the BIS to focus on these issues. The BIS formed a Group of Experts on Payment Systems in conjunction with the G10 central banks and this group met in Basle in mid-1988.

BIS Studies on Payment and Settlement Systems

The purpose of this meeting of the Group of Experts on Payments Systems was to study various types of financial netting arrangements as part of a larger payment and settlement system. Such systems were operating in several countries. The committee was chaired by Wayne D. Angell, a member at that time of the Federal Reserve Board of Governors. The report has come to be known as the Angell Report.

The Angell Report.[4] The major objective of the Angell Report, published in February 1989, was to assess arrangements which could be used to net out amounts due between banks arising from foreign exchange contracts or from the exchange of payment instructions. An underlying motive was the reduction of global foreign currency risk among international banks.

The conclusions reached by the Angell committee included the fact that banks have an incentive to reduce counterparty credit exposures as well as interbank payment flows. A better system of netting can achieve both of these goals. The conclusions also had monetary implications. It was found that most netting systems operate so that one financial obligation is exchanged for a similar, off-setting obligation, with only the net difference being settled in money. The report also analyzed the various financial risks incurred in the international financial system and the broader policy issues of netting systems were discussed.

The Lamfalussy Report.[5] The Angell Report was published in February 1989 and spurred the G10 central bankers to establish a high level, ad-hoc committee, the Committee on Interbank Netting Schemes, for the purpose of further analysis of the policy implications of cross-border and multi-currency netting arrangements which the Angell Report identified as being of concern to central bankers. This committee was chaired by M.A. Lamfalussy and, thus, the results of the study have come to be known as the Lamfalussy Report.

The Lamfalussy Report proposed a set of minimum standards by which netting schemes should operate as well as principles for cooperative central bank oversight. The study's objectives for analysis included the common policy objectives of central banks, such as the efficiency of interbank settlements and markets, the stability and containment of systemic risk, and the effectiveness of policy instruments used by central banks. In addition, the committee analyzed the impact of netting on credit, liquidity, and systemic risks including the effects on costs and the measurement of exposures, the importance of legal enforceability, and any systemic risks in multilateral netting systems. Finally, the broader implications of netting were examined by the committee, including the market implications of contract netting and implications for central banking and supervisory practices. These standards have become the key reference for commercial banks as well as central banks.

The Lamfalussy Report set forth six minimum standards for netting schemes. They are as follows:[6]

1. netting schemes should have a well-founded basis under all relevant jurisdictions;
2. netting scheme participants should have a clear understanding of the impact of the particular scheme on each of the financial risks affected by the netting process;
3. multilateral netting systems should have clearly-defined procedures for the management of credit and liquidity risks which specify the respective reponsibilities of the netting provider and the participants;

4. multilateral netting systems should, at a minimum, be capable of ensuring the timely completion of daily settlements in the event of an inability to settle by the participant with the largest single net-debit position;

5. multilateral netting systems should have objective and publicly-disclosed criteria for admission which permit fair and open access; and

6. all netting schemes should ensure the operational reliability of technical systems and the availability of back-up facilities capable of completing daily processing requirements.

The fourth standard above seems to be the key proposal in a multilateral netting system vis-à-vis risk.[7] Multilateral systems, where more than two parties have their balances netted out, will generally always be superior to bilateral netting systems, which are systems in which only two parties are involved.

In addition to these minimum standards proposed by the Lamfalussy Report, several principles were formulated to develop interbank payment and settlement systems which will facilitate more safely the cross-border and multi-currency netting systems since these arrangements have a great deal of influence on the overall credit structure of international financial markets. The major principles advanced in the Lamfalussy Report are as follows:[8]

1. netting systems should be subject to oversight by an authority that accepts primary responsibility to do so;

2. a presumption should exist that the host-country central bank will undertake this responsibility but that it could be mutually agreed that another authority might undertake the primary responsibility in some cases;

3. the responsible authority should review the design and operation of the system as a whole and consult with other central banks and supervisory authorities that may have an interest in the system's prudent operation;

4. determination of the adequacy of the settlement arrangements should be the joint responsibility of the central bank of issue and the authority with primary responsibility; and

5. in the absence of confidence in the soundness of the design or management of a cross-border or multi-currency netting or settlement system, a central bank should discourage use of the system by institutions subject to its authority.

Two initiatives which stemmed from the Lamfalussy Report were systems which embodied the principles advanced in the study. These were ECHO in Great Britain and Multinet in the United

States. Both of these systems are multilateral netting schemes for spot and forward foreign exchange transactions. Members who deal in several currencies and counterparties throughout the day now settle one position at the end of the day.

The ECHO system, as mentioned earlier, was created by 15 international banks from seven countries for the European Clearing House Organisation. It permits banks to net all their foreign currency contracts with other participants. A participant will need to make or receive only one payment in each currency during any one trading day by clearing through ECHO.[9]

Multinet is a system designed to clear and net foreign exchange transactions on a global basis. Several U.S. and Canadian banks established Multinet in collaboration with International Clearing Systems, a wholly-owned subsidiary of the Options Clearing Corporation of Chicago. Member banks include Bank of Montreal, Chase Manhattan, First National Bank of Chicago, Royal Bank of Canada, and Toronto-Dominion Bank. Currencies of seven major nations are cleared and netted by Multinet.[10]

With the minimum standards and principles for establishing efficient netting systems, the Lamfalussy Report moved the BIS/G10 central bankers in a more specific direction in the payment and settlement issue. The issue became one of what settlement method should be employed. As the world of cross-border financial transactions became more sophisticated and utilized more electronic equipment, commercial parties to international transactions began to demand faster and more efficient means for settling international commercial and financial transactions. The Lamfalussy Report gave the central and private banking community quite valuable minimum standards which the international financial system has broadly applied.[11]

Another positive result of the Lamfalussy Report was the change of attitude in the international banking community toward the need for loss-sharing arrangements in payment netting programs. Banks became aware of the fact that they were exposed to and responsible for potential losses from their netting schemes. Banks which did not have centralized risk control systems required some of them to sign loss-sharing agreements, much to their chagrin.[12]

Central banks play a crucial role in the formulation and implementation of netting arrangements. The large volume in cross-border financial transactions makes it mandatory that efficiency in interbank settlements and markets be maintained. Stability of financial markets can be maintained by central bank oversight in this area and systemic risk in the international financial system can be reduced.

In the meantime, the BIS changed the name of its lead committee in this area from the Group of Experts on Payment Systems to Committee on Payment and Settlement Systems (CPSS) with its secretariat located in Basle at the BIS headquarters. This change reflected a more general focus for the committee's studies and the possible admission that the committee may not have been so expert in their work.

The Parkinson Report.[13] The newly named Committee on Payment and Settlement Systems issued a report based on its study of a specific area involved in securities settlement systems, the delivery versus payment (DVP) methodology. The committee was chaired by Patrick Parkinson, a member of the U.S. Federal Reserve Board of Governors; thus, the study's results are referred to as the Parkinson Report.

This study was prompted by the October 1987 stock market crash. The settlement of securities transactions in such events could have disturbing effects—and it did in 1987—which could spread to payment systems and other financial markets. Central banks had already made recommendations to strengthen settlement systems for government securities. But volume in equities around the world was far greater than that for government securities and could have far greater consequences.

At their December 1990 meeting in Basle, the G10 central bankers had identified the need for a better understanding of the concept of delivery versus payment (DVP) and the implications for design of a DVP for credit and liquidity risks in securities settlements. The Parkinson Report includes a review of the design and operation of securities settlement systems in use in the G10 countries. Common approaches to DVP were identified and the implications of various approaches for central bank policy objectives concerning financial market stability and how systemic risk could be contained were evaluated.

The Parkinson Report concluded that the largest financial risk in securities clearance and settlement occurs during the settlement process, that is, settlement risk. This is analogous to Herstatt risk, the cross-currency settlement risk which occurred when the Herstatt Bank in Germany failed and did not settle its foreign exchange transactions with counterparties.

The settlement process is completed when the securities are transferred from seller to buyer, that is, delivery, and final transfer of funds is made from the buyer to the seller, that is, payment. In some markets, no mechanism exists to insure that delivery occurs only if payment occurs. Counterparties are exposed to settlement risk if no mechanism, that is, DVP, is required. Thus, the Parkinson committee set the objective of formulating a DVP for worldwide securities market transactions. The committee also confirmed the conclusions of the Angell and Lamfalussy Reports, discussed earlier, that the benefits of netting of foreign exchange contracts are applicable to netting of securities transactions.

The Parkinson study group proposed three models for achieving DVP.[14] They are as follows:

1. Model 1: systems that settle transfer instructions for both securities and funds on a trade-by-trade (gross) basis, with final (unconditional) transfer of securities from the seller to the buyer (delivery) occurring at the same time as final transfer of funds from the buyer to the seller (payment);

2. Model 2: systems that settle securities transfer instructions on a gross basis with final transfer of securities from the seller to the buyer (delivery) occurring throughout the processing cycle, but settle funds transfer instructions on a net basis, with final transfer of funds from the buyer to the seller (payment) occurring at the end of the processing cycle;

3. Model 3: systems that settle transfer instructions for both securities and funds on a net basis, with final transfers of both securities and funds occurring at the end of the processing cycle.

One of the key findings of this study was the recognition that credit and liquidity risks were more complex and were of longer duration in an environment of cross-border financial transactions. Counterparties are located in different time zones with different currencies and, thus, the gaps are larger in such transactions.[15]

In addition to BIS studies of this issue, the private sector also examined the problem of clearance, settlement, and custody of cross-border financial transactions especially with regard to securities market operations. The Breuer-Weatherstone group published a report of the fundamental issues about clearance and settlement in international securities markets.[16] The group, commissioned by Euroclear, the European securities clearing agency, was chaired by Dr. Rolf-Ernst Breuer, Chairman of the Board of Euroclear Clearance System, and a member of the Deutsche Bank Board of Managing Directors, and Dennis Weatherstone, Chairman of JP Morgan. This study group identified the best means of settlement infrastructure to facilitate the growth of transactions in international securities markets and the costs of infrastructure investments made by the securities industry.

The Noël Report. The CPSS under the chairmanship of Wayne D. Angell published a report entitled "Central Bank Payment and Settlement Services with Respect to Cross-Border and Multi-Currency Transactions" as a follow-up to the Lamfalussy Report. It has been referred to as the Noël Report for Tim E. Noël, a member of the committee and, then, Deputy Governor of the Bank of Canada. Its objective was to analyze the options which central banks could consider to reduce risk and increase efficiency of the settlement of cross-border and multi-currency interbank transactions. The committee analyzed the advantages and disadvantages of various payment and settlement schemes that central banks might promote to deal with the principal risk in foreign exchange transactions, often called Herstatt risk.[17]

Four options for central bank payment services were identified by this study. They were as follows:[18]

1. the provision of home-currency settlement accounts and credit transfer which could be finalized during normal business hours;
2. extension of the hours of operation of large-value transfer systems;
3. the establishment of bilateral or multilateral cross-border links built directly into large value transfer systems; and
4. provision of multi-currency payment and settlement services through one or more central banks or through an agent newly created by a central bank.

An analysis of the central bank service options was included in the Noël Report.[19] Each option was believed to have some potential effect on current monetary policy operational procedures in one or more countries. In addition, intraday final transfers between accounts at central banks which issue them might give financial institutions the technical ability to fund and discharge their settlement obligations in each currency during the day. In other words, private sector liquidity might be affected.

Systemic risk has been a primary concern of the BIS. The Noël Report held that a source of the systemic risk that can eminate from the settlement of cross-border and multi-currency obligations could be traced to the variety of home-currency payments systems then involved in the process.

Payment and settlement systems have legal implications. The Noël Report held that the laws and regulations of any country would need to be coordinated with the operational and accounting procedures of its home-country payments system for transfers between accounts at the cental bank to have intraday finality.

Competitive effects and cost-effectiveness were reviewed by the Noël Group. It believed the settlement of foreign exchange transactions could support settlement of a variety of domestic and international transactions. In addition, the development of large-value funds transfer systems whereby intraday final transfers were not available would require a large initial investment.

Further Studies of Payment Systems and Their Risks. In 1993, two more studies were published under the auspices of the BIS. These were a monograph about the nature and management of payment system risks and the second was a massive document containing a comparative analysis of the payment systems in the G10 countries. These studies are discussed in the remainder of this section.

The first of these studies was a BIS Economic Paper published in February 1993 which presented an international perspective of the nature and management of payment system risks.[20] This short monograph contained an analysis of the structure and evolution of payment systems, a discussion of the nature of payment system risks, and coverage of the management of payment system risks. The monograph contains good examples of various forms of interbank funds transfer systems.

The study was prompted by the spectacular increase in global financial activity and the concomitant rise in the volume and value of payment flows, both within nations and across national borders. With this increase, the total value of interbank funds transfers also became quite large. Liquidity and credit risks among institutions globally were affected and the effects were often adverse. This BIS-commissioned study recommended the introduction of appropriate liquidity-pooling and loss-sharing mechanisms to ensure settlement of transactions when a failure by one of the parties to fulfill his/her obligation occurs.[21] The study recognized that as markets continue to be internationalized, the safety and soundness of the international payment system will need to be strengthened by international cooperation.[22]

In December 1993, the BIS published the fourth edition of a reference work on payment systems in the G10 countries. This was prepared by the Committee on Payment and Settlement Systems under the direction of its chairman, Wayne Angell, then a member of the U.S. Federal Reserve System Board of Governors. This is the so-called Red Book—for the color of its cover—and is a massive tome which includes summary information for all G10 countries on payment media used by non-banks, a general overview and structure, operation, and administration of interbank exchange and settlement services, a discussion of the special use of interbank transfer systems for international and domestic financial transactions, and coverage of the role of the central bank in interbank payment systems.[23] The Red Book represents the best source on payment and settlement systems for any regional area of the world. It has become the key reference for any national agency wishing to implement a new system or update the country's existing system.

THE COMMITTEE ON PAYMENT AND SETTLEMENT SYSTEMS

The BIS is the host for meetings of the Committee on Payment and Settlement Systems (CPSS) and provides the secretariat of this committee. The CPSS along with its working groups is reponsible for analysis and research designed to improve the efficiency and stability of domestic and international payment and settlement systems. The forerunner of this committee was the Group of Experts on Payment Systems.

The CPSS and its predecessor have examined such issues as large-value funds transfer systems, foreign exchange settlement risk, securities settlement arrangements, and retail payment systems. Some of the more significant studies by the CPSS have involved the above-discussed publications including the Angell Report in which netting arrangements were assessed, the Lamfalussy Report which set minimum standards under which netting systems should operate, the Parkinson Report which proposed a delivery versus payment (DVP) methodology in securities settlement systems, and the Angell Red Book which contains a discussion of the G10 countries' payment systems.

This committee and its various groups cooperate with a number of other international organizations. Among them are the IMF, World Bank, and the International Organisation of Securities Commissions (IOSCO). During the late 1990s, the CPSS established an international task force to develop minimum standards for interbank settlements including improvements in trading foreign exchange, derivatives, and securities and to prepare a consultative report containing core principles for the most important payment systems where systemic risk might be involved.

Improvements in Foreign Exchange, Derivatives, and Securities Trading

The CPSS proposed improvements to trading in foreign exchange, derivatives, and securities in 1996 with the assistance of the advances in electronic technology.[24] At that time, clearing of trading in such financial instruments had usually been done at the end of the day. The Herstatt case in 1974 had demonstrated that time zone differences could create a problem between the time at which the buyer settled his/her account and the time at which the seller received the funds. The settlement risk involved could lead to a systemic risk in the system.

In March 1996, the CPSS published a report on Settlement Risk in Foreign Exchange Transactions in which a strategy for reducing foreign exchange settlement risk was presented. During the next two years, the G10 central banks implemented a three-track strategy. The first track was aimed at action by individual banks with recommendations for them to take immediate steps to apply a credit control process to their foreign exchange settlement exposures. Banks were directed to measure and manage their foreign exchange risk exposures. The second track was aimed at industry groups which were encouraged to develop multi-currency services whose objectives were to reduce the risk of individual banks. The third track requested central banks to encourage faster private sector progress by stimulating private sector action in its domestic market.[25]

The CPSS study moved the experts closer to a solution for this potential problem by utilizing existing electronic technology to move the international financial system toward one of real-time gross settlement (RTGS) in which all interbank transfers would take place automatically and at once. RTGS will be discussed in a later section in this chapter.

Core Principles for Payment Systems

The international Task Force appointed by the CPSS was assigned the duty of preparing a consultative report for the G10 central banks including the formulation of a set of 10 Core Principles for systemically important payment systems as well as responsibilities of central banks in the application of these principles. The Task Force was comprised of payment systems experts from 23 central banks as well as representatives from the IMF and the World Bank. Many central bank experts including those from LDCs were consulted for this study.

The first part of the report was released in December 1999. The consultation period expired in September 2000. The first part of the report set forth the 10 Core Principles and responsibilities for central banks and their application. The second part of the report offered guidance on how these principles might be interpreted.

The IOSCO had developed a set of objectives and principles of securities regulation in 1998. In 2001, the CPSS finalized its Core Principles for Systemically Important Payment Systems and has planned work with IOSCO in the development of recommendations for securities settlement systems. A Task Force on Securities Settlement Systems has been established for this purpose and is comprised of 28 central bankers and securities regulators from 18 countries.[26]

The consultative report on the design, operation and oversight of securities settlement systems contains minimum requirements for such systems with 18 recommendations for securities issued in both industrialized and developing nations and for securities trading in both domestic and cross-border trading. Public comments were solicited by the CPSS and IOSCO with the comment period to end in April 2001.

Real-Time Gross Settlement. During the 1990s, the BIS became concerned about the volume of cross-border financial transactions, especially in the settlement of foreign exchange, derivatives, and securities transactions. With more than US $1.5 trillion of daily trades in foreign currencies around the world, the old settlement systems were no longer adequate to handle this volume. New electronic technology dictated better, faster, and more efficient settlement and payment systems so that future Herstatts could be avoided.

A settlement system known as real-time gross settlement (RTGS) had been adopted by a number of central banks in order to decrease their exposure to settlement risk. As mentioned earlier, this is a system in which cross-border financial transactions are settled automatically and at once between counterparties. Essentially, processing and settlement of gross balances between parties to a transaction take place in real time. In other words, settlement is continuous rather than on a net basis at some specified period of time, usually at the end of the day. The CPSS took on the responsibility of analyzing RTGS and its benefits.[27]

In the traditional netting payment system, settlement does not occur until the end of the business day. Thus, no funds are transferred between banks until transactions are settled at closing. Each bank will have either a net credit or debit position at the end of the day and, thus, must settle accordingly. Each party to the transaction essentially grants credit to the other. One party may not fulfill its obligation and, thus, the exposure to settlement risk is present. Liquidity shortfalls or credit losses may be incurred by the other party.

An RTGS system handles the payment in such transactions in a more timely manner. Payment instructions are processed and settled on an individual basis immediately from accounts held at the central bank. Thus, the central bank plays a very important role in this system. Each customer of the central bank would have his/her transactions settled immediately from the central bank account as such transactions were performed. The system operates continuously throughout the day. If one party fails during the day under an RTGS system, counterparties are unaffected because transactions would have been settled.[28] Inherent settlement risk is virtually eliminated by an RTGS system. Banks can use funds from transactions immediately instead of waiting for a settlement at the end of the day.

RTGS has the potential to successfully deal with Herstatt risk. An RTGS system for one currency large value payments would probably be linked with similar systems in other countries, thus permitting simultaneous real time final settlement of both sides of a foreign exchange transaction. Principal risk would be eliminated assuming that both systems operated at the same time.[29]

Some banks may be deterred from using the RTGS system because of some of its costs.[30] A bank must have the necessary funds in its central bank account or must be granted credit by the central bank in order to settle each transaction. The opportunity costs to the commercial bank of holding these funds with the central bank might be quite significant. In addition, central banks have usually not offered cost-effective intraday credit to their customers. In addition to these financial costs, an RTGS system requires more effort on the part of management. Management must ensure that funds are always available to settle transactions during the day.

Despite these disadvantages, some central banks have implemented some form of RTGS system. Most G10 countries have an RTGS system in operation. Europe has initiated such a system and tied its central banks into a network called TARGET. This network supports the euro as a single currency. Other countries which have established some type of RTGS system include Hong Kong, Korea, and Thailand, with Australia, China, and New Zealand planning such a system in the future.[31]

Among the G10 countries, Fedwire in the United States was the first to use an RTGS system. All G10 countries except Canada have implemented an RTGS system. All G10 countries except Switzerland and Japan have intraday credit facilities provided by central banks. Intraday credit is extended through intraday overdraft facilities in Belgium, Germany, Italy, the Netherlands, Sweden, and the United States. All central banks except the U.S. Federal Reserve require some form of collateral to secure intraday overdrafts. The central banks in the United Kingdom and France provide intraday repurchase agreements instead of intraday overdraft facilities.[32]

In addition to these differences in G10 countries' RTGS systems, most are owned by the central bank in the individual country. The Belgian and English systems are co-owned by the central banks and companies whose members are direct participants. Access to the systems varies among the central banks as well. Some central banks require participants to have an account with them. Some permit indirect access by a third party institution. RTGS systems in some G10 countries can coexist with traditional net settlement systems, as in Germany, Japan, and the United States.[33]

In summary, the primary role played by the BIS in the utilization of RTGS systems is to furnish information about their use. The CPSS has researched the use of these systems and will continue to do so in the future in order to make improvements in this innovation designed to reduce settlement risk and make cross-border financial transactions more efficient. Many smaller countries, especially LDCs, cannot afford the research necessary to establish or improve an RTGS system. Thus, the BIS will need to provide such a service.

Recent Work of the CPSS

The CPSS has worked closely with other international agencies and the G10 central banks during the 1999–2000 period on a number of projects.[34] In December 1999, its Task Force on Payment System Principles and Practices formulated a consultative report on Core Principles for Systemically Important Payment Systems. The CPSS also created a joint Task Force of CPSS and the IOSCO at the end of 1999 to draft recommendations for securities settlement systems and to identify minimum requirements that such systems should meet to minimize systemic risks at both the domestic and international levels. A previous joint CPSS/IOSCO Working Group on Securities Lending published a report on Securities Lending Transactions: Market Development and Implications in July 1999. This report provided an overview of the dynamics of the securities lending market and addressed risks present in securities lending transactions and proposed practices for market participants to alleviate these risks.

The CPSS' Working Group on Retail Payment Systems produced two reports in the 1999–2000 period. The first of these reports identified and analyzed trends in the use of retail payment instruments. The second report analyzed clearing and settlement methods for retail payments.

SUMMARY AND CONCLUSIONS

During the 1980–2000 period, the volume of cross-border financial transactions increased greatly. Daily foreign exchange trading volume around the world grew to more than US $1.5 trillion. Innovations in electronic technology began to overwhelm international banking regulators. Payment and settlement systems became antiquated as commercial and investor interests demanded systems which could reduce settlement risk caused when one party to a transaction failed to perform his/her obligation. International banks were faced with systemic risks caused by the failure of individual companies to perform their financial obligations.

Part of the latter problem was alleviated by the BIS work discussed earlier with regard to strengthening the capital position banks had to maintain through the Basle Accord. The work of the BIS' Committee on Payment and Settlement Systems (CPSS), in conjunction with the International Organisation of Securities Commissions, and advances in electronic technology has slowly alleviated many of the other payments and settlement system problems.

The CPSS and its predecessor have studied several aspects of the international payment and settlement issue. These have included areas such as settlement of foreign exchange and securities trans-actions, delivery versus payment, and real-time gross settlement systems. A number of significant reports were issued by this com-mittee in the 1990s including the Angell, Lamfalussy, Noël, and Par-kinson Reports. A report presenting a discussion of the payment and settlement systems of the G10 countries was also published. Minimum standards and operational principles were formulated by this committee and its associated groups.

These reports published by the BIS and its research groups have resulted in improved payment and settlement systems. But such improvement can do little to alleviate direct credit exposures to a counterparty which fails. The systemic risk or risk of contagion which can result from credit and liquidity exposures from unfore-seen events can be reduced, if not eliminated. Capital losses from partly completed settlement of securities or foreign exchange counterparties can be reduced.[35]

One problem with the G10 central banks in dealing with the prin-ciples and recommendations formulated and promoted by the BIS in the area of payments and settlements is that the BIS has no en-forcement powers. The national governments in Europe and, partic-ularly in the European Community, have legislation and authority that is missing at the G10 level. The latter must rely on informality and voluntary agreement to implement their standards.[36]

The work of the BIS Committee on Payment and Settlement Sys-tems and its groups has been instrumental in improving the stabil-ity of the international financial system. The BIS has accepted the leadership role as a central bank for central banks to furnish the one service necessary to all national central banks with regard to the issue of payment and settlement of cross-border financial transac-tions: information. Without the proper information concerning what works and how to make it work more efficiently, the interna-tional financial system will become overwhelmed by the burgeoning volume of transactions.

Finally, domestic institutions compete internationally to imple-ment their payment and settlement systems. Some of these systems are compatible while others are not. The challenges of the cross-bor-der financial markets require that these payment and settlement systems be compatible and that they have smooth and interlocking interfaces. The BIS through the Committee on Payment and Settlement Systems is in a prime position to smooth out the inconsistencies and to assist central banks in implementing compatible systems for the international financial system of the 21st century.

NOTES

1. James C. Baker, *International Finance: Management, Markets, and Institutions* (Upper Saddle River, NJ: Prentice-Hall, 1998), pp. 492–493.

2. Graham M. Duncan, "Clearing House Arrangements in the Foreign Exchange Markets," *Proceedings of the International Symposium on Banking and Payments Services* (Washington, D.C.: Federal Reserve Board of Governors, 1994), pp. 168–174.

3. Mitsuo Yamaguchi, "An Assessment of Payment System Risk in Asia," *Payment Systems Worldwide*, Vol. 4 (Winter 1993–1994), p. 22.

4. Bank for International Settlements, *Report on Netting Schemes* (Basle, Switzerland: Group of Experts on Payments Systems, February 1989).

5. Bank for International Settlements, *Report of the Committee on Interbank Netting Schemes of the Central Banks of the Group of Ten Countries* (Basle, Switzerland: Committee on Interbank Netting Schemes, November 1990).

6. Ibid., p. 5.

7. Charles A.E. Goodhart, "Introductory Remarks: The Role of Clearing Houses," in Board of Governors of the Federal Reserve System, *Proceedings of the International Symposium on Banking and Payment Services* (Washington, D.C.: Federal Reserve Board of Governors, 1994), p. 149.

8. BIS *Report of the Committee on Interbank Netting Schemes of the Central Banks of the Group of Ten Countries*, p. 7.

9. Baker, *International Finance: Management, Markets, and Institutions*, p. 508.

10. Ibid., p. 507.

11. Wayne D. Angell, "Payment and Settlement Systems Policies and Incentives: A Proposal for Defining the Property Rights of Daylight Reserve Holders," *Proceedings of the International Symposium on Banking and Payment Services* (Washington, D.C.: Federal Reserve Board of Governors, 1994), p. 117.

12. Ibid.

13. Bank for International Settlements, *Delivery versus Payment in Securities Settlement Systems* (Basle, Switzerland: Committee on Payment and Settlement Systems, September 1992).

14. Ibid., p. 4.

15. Rolf E. Breur, "Risk Management in Cross-Border and Multi-Currency Securities Clearance and Settlement," *Proceedings of the International Symposium on Banking and Payment Services* (Washington, D.C.: Federal Reserve Board of Governors, 1994), p. 135.

16. Euroclear, *Cross-Border Clearance, Settlement, and Custody: Beyond the G30 Recommendations* (Brussels, Belgium: Morgan Guaranty Trust Company, June 1993).

17. Tim E. Noël, "Report on Central Bank Payment and Settlement Services with Respect to Cross-Border and Multi-Currency Transactions," *Proceedings of the International Symposium on Banking and Payment Services* (Washington, D.C.: Federal Reserve Board of Governors, 1994), p. 124.

18. Ibid., pp. 124–125.

19. Bank for International Settlements, *Central Bank Payment and Settlement Services with Respect to Cross-Border and Multi-Currency Transactions* (Basle, Switzerland: Committee on Payment and Settlement Systems, September 1993), pp. 27–34.

20. C.E.V. Borio and P. Van den Bergh, *The Nature and Management of Payment System Risks: An International Perspective* (Basle, Switzerland: Bank for International Settlements, February 1993).

21. Ibid., p. 64.

22. Ibid., p. 65.

23. Bank for International Settlements, *Payment Systems in the Group of Ten Countries* (Basle, Switzerland: Committee on Payment and Settlement Systems, December 1993).

24. Susan Strange, *Mad Money: When Markets Outgrow Governments* (Ann Arbor, Michigan: University of Michigan Press, 1998), pp. 162–163.

25. Bank for International Settlements, *66th Annual Report* (Basle, Switzerland: Bank for International Settlements, 10th June 1996), p. 174.

26. Tommaso Padoa-Schioppa, "Recommendations for Securities Settlement Systems," found at http://www.bis.org/publ/cpss42.htm, March 6, 2001, p. 1.

27. "Press Communique on Real-Time Gross Settlement Systems," online available from http://www.bis.org/press/index.htm, April 22, 1997.

28. Jeff Stehm, "Analyzing Alternative Intraday Credit Policies in Real-Time Gross Settlement Systems," *Journal of Money, Credit, and Banking*, Vol. 30 (1998), p. 833.

29. Eddie George, "International Banking, Payment Systems and Financial Crises," *Proceedings of the International Symposium on Banking and Payment Services* (Washington, DC: Federal Reserve Board of Governors, 1994), p. 78.

30. Stehm, "Analyzing Alternative Intraday Credit Policies in Real-Time Gross Settlement Systems," *Journal of Money, Credit, and Banking*, Vol. 30 (1998), p. 833.

31. "Press Communique on Real-Time Gross Settlement Systems," April 22, 1997.

32. "Report on Real-Time Gross Settlement Systems," online at http://www.bis.org/publ/index.htm, March 1997.

33. Ibid.

34. Bank for International Settlements, *70th Annual Report* (Basle, Switzerland, Bank for International Settlements, 2000), Section on Activities of the Bank, pp. 155–191.

35. Eddie George, "International Banking, Payment Systems, and Financial Crises," *Proceedings of the International Symposium on Banking and Payment Services*, pp. 76–77.

36. Tommaso Padoa-Schioppa, "Central Banking and Payment Systems in the European Community," *Proceedings of the International Symposium on Banking and Payment Services* (Washington, DC: Federal Reserve Board of Governors, 1994), p. 29.

CHAPTER 8

The Bank for International Settlements and Its Relations with Central Banks

INTRODUCTION

The BIS was established to be a bank for central banks, among other objectives, by helping these institutions manage and invest their currency reserves. From the very beginning, the major shareholders in the BIS were central banks. After its initial objective of facilitation of the German reparations settlements after World War I, its activities have focused on central banks and their major constituents, commercial banks around the world.

This chapter contains a discussion of the relationship the BIS has with central banks. The major functions the BIS performs for central banks are referred to as facilities and include taking deposits and making loans, swaps of currency for gold, credits advanced against a pledge of gold or marketable short-term securities, foreign exchange operations, acting for Latin American countries with regard to Brady bond operations, and other settlement and cooperative activities with central banks including the advancement of unsecured and standby credits. The BIS also carries out foreign exchange and gold transactions within the market.[1]

The confidentiality with which the BIS performs these functions is very important. If the BIS maintains as much confidentiality as possible in its dealings with central banks, it will retain the respect of these national agencies. That concept of confidentiality on the part of the BIS with regard to these transactions with central banks will also be discussed in this chapter.

The BIS contributes to central bank cooperation by organizing regular meetings of central bank governors and senior central bank officials as well as furnishing the secretariat for several committees which formulate and implement standards and principles dealing with the international banking system. The major meetings held by the BIS in the fulfillment of this function will also be discussed in this chapter.

Finally, the BIS must insure that its relationships with the central banks of the major industrialized nations will be as good as possible. This is especially so with regard to the U.S. Federal Reserve System and its Board of Governers. This relationship, strained at first during many years when the U.S. Federal Reserve was not a member of the BIS Board of Directors, will also be analyzed in this chapter.

BIS FUNCTIONS WITH CENTRAL BANKS

For most of its history, the BIS has been perceived as a European agency with primarily European members and with a major focus on the European members of the G10 countries. Such perception was one of the reasons the U.S. Federal Reserve System did not take its seat on the BIS Board of Directors until 1994.

The central banks of Belgium, France, Germany, Italy, Japan, and the United Kingdom were founders of the BIS when it was established in 1930. After a redistribution of shares, the central banks of Portugal, Iceland, Turkey, and Ireland joined the BIS in the early 1950s. Canada did not become a member until 1970 and the United States finally joined in 1994.

In the middle 1990s, the BIS began to invite central banks from other parts of the world to become members, including some from less-developed countries and other emerging nations. At the end of 2000, the BIS had 49 central bank members. Other central banks also attend the BIS Annual Meetings and other meetings as observing participants. For example, at the June 2000 Annual Meeting of the BIS in Basle, 99 central banks participated with governors of 76 of these in attendance.

Deposits and Loans

One of the major functions which the BIS offers central banks is the ability to borrow from the BIS or to deposit funds with the agency. These operations are carried out by the Banking Department of the BIS and the objective of this function is to assist central banks in their external reserves management.

The BIS bases these operations on the principle in Article 19 of its Statutes which is as follows: "The operations of the Bank shall be in conformity with the monetary policy of the central banks of the countries concerned." The BIS can only offer this service to central banks. It cannot lend to governments of open current accounts in a government's name.

Deposits. The deposit and loan function is offered to any central bank and not solely to members of the BIS. Nearly 120 central banks and international financial institutions currently have deposits with the BIS. Deposits made to the BIS amounted to US$128 billion as of March 2000[2] and represent approximately 7 percent of the world's foreign exchange reserves. The BIS must maintain a high degree of liquidity with these deposits since the central banks which have them on deposit may need them at a moment's notice. More than 95 percent of BIS liabilities are in the form of deposits held for central banks.

The BIS invests these deposit funds from central banks in high quality short-term government securities and in highly-rated commercial banks. The BIS also assists central banks in their longer-term reserve management by offering investment instruments with maturities up to five years and also custom designs portfolio management programs for central banks.

At the end of March 2000, deposits in the BIS by central banks rose from 54,016 million gold francs (US$104,791 million) to 60,667 gold francs (US$117,694 million) during the previous year. The value of a gold franc is the equivalent of US$1.94, based on a market price of fine gold of US$208 per ounce. The increase in these deposits by central banks reflected the BIS' role as a safe haven in an uncertain economic environment as well as the use of the BIS by central banks for their liquidity management.

Loans. The BIS offers credit facilities to other central banks in the form, for example, of short-term advances to central banks. One of the innovations created by the BIS in recent years is the bridge loan to less-developed countries (LDCs). The BIS makes bridge loans to

LDCs to assist the central banks in these countries with balance of payments problems. These are large-scale short-term loans and have been made to Latin American and East European nations. In the case of these countries, the loans were made to alleviate cash flow problems in those countries while they waited for the receipt of credits from the International Monetary Fund, i.e., bridge loans for interim relief.

These bridge loans are part of the BIS' function of lender of last resort. The objective of the BIS in the lending function is to assist central banks in sudden financial crises. The bridge loan is stop-gap financial assistance until more permanent financing is received from an international financial institution such as the IMF or the World Bank.[3]

In 1998, the BIS coordinated a Credit Facility for a maximum of US$13.28 billion in the favor of the Banco Central do Brasil, the central bank of Brazil. These funds were guaranteed by 19 participating central banks.[4] The drawings from this facility, supported by a parallel facility granted by the Japanese monetary authorities, were made under an IMF Supplemental Reserve Facility.

During its 70th fiscal year, the BIS also made several short-term advances to central banks on both an uncollateralized and collateralized basis. The Brazilian facilities were each drawn against twice and have since been terminated.

During the year ending March 2000, the BIS made several advances to central banks. These amounted to 1,941 million gold francs (US$3,765.54 million). Most of these loans were funds extended under the facility mentioned earlier to the Banco Central do Brasil.

Investment Services

The BIS works with central banks to improve the return on their foreign assets by offering them a number of investment services. Among these are financial products designed to help central banks more efficiently manage their liquidity positions. The BIS also offers investment instruments with maturities of up to five years for central banks in need of long-term reserve management. More custom-designed portfolio management instruments are also made available to central banks by the BIS.

Gold Operations

The BIS may take deposits of gold owned by central banks for safekeeping or to sell on the market. The BIS also may purchase gold on the world market for central banks. As of March 2000, the BIS held 192 tons of gold. Its assets in gold declined from 3,879 million gold francs (US$7,525 million) to 3,506 million gold francs (US$6,801 million) from March 1999 to March 2000. This decline was primarily the result of reductions in gold deposits received.[5]

Shareholder Central Banks

During the year ending March 2000, the BIS invited five non-G10 central banks to become members. These were the Banco Central de la República Argentina, the European Central Bank, Bank Indonesia, Bank Negara Malaysia, and the Bank of Thailand. These banks could pay for their shares in either gold or in a convertible currency the amount of which would be necessary to purchase the same weight of gold on the market on the value date of the payment. As of the end of March 2000, 49 central banks were members of the BIS. See Figure 2.1 for a listing of these central banks.

THE BIS AS A FORUM FOR CENTRAL BANKS

In the fulfillment of its objective of facilitating cooperation among central banks on policy issues concerning monetary and financial stability, the BIS provides a forum. Most of this activity is carried out by the Monetary and Economic Department of the BIS.

A major part of the work of the BIS with regard to central bank cooperative efforts is concerned with international banking statistics. This data-gathering function is primarily centered in the Monetary and Economic Department of the BIS. The major industrialized countries' central banks collect and share, with the BIS, comprehensive statistics on the cross-border and foreign currency business of their domestic banking systems. These statistics are collected in two parts: those dealing with locational banking data on a residence and nationality basis and those that are world-wide consolidated banking data. These data are major inputs into the cooperative exercise by the BIS, IMF, OECD, and World Bank to produce and disseminate creditor data on countries' international indebtedness.[6]

A major part of this function is the provision of a secretariat for various committees such as the Committee on Banking Supervision, Committee on Payment and Settlement Systems, and the Committee on the Global Financial System. The major work of some of these committees was discussed in earlier chapters.

Regular Consultations with Central Banks[7]

In addition to the work of the various BIS committees, regular meetings are held in Basle and other locations for the exchange of views and information and to identify issues and problems in the international monetary system. The BIS holds bi-monthly Board meetings. These meetings held during the year ending March 2000 were representative of such consultative meetings. During that period, the G10 central bankers met as one group while they and their counterparts from systemically significant emerging markets formed a second group and all governors of central banks which hold shares in the BIS formed a third group.

The meetings attended by only G10 central bank governors discussed several BIS committee reports and focused on issues dealing with the proposed revision of the 1988 Basle Capital Accord, the Y2K changeover and its related liquidity problems, and the management and prevention of financial crises.

The joint meetings of the G10 and emerging market economy central bankers focused on the exchange of views and information on the current condition of the international economy and financial markets. Potential medium-term problems were also identified.

Meetings of BIS shareholder central banks discussed a number of issues including the effects of the new capital adequacy regulations on the operations of rating agencies. Financial stability was a prime topic and the Long-Term Capital Management (LTCM) bailout was the focus in this area because of the possibility for hedge funds like LTCM to disrupt the operations of international financial markets. One of the major concerns with the LTCM case was the systemic risk threatened by the failure of such a large financial institution with significant ties to the rest of the financial world.

The conduct of monetary policy in a floating rate environment was the topic of several meetings. These topics included how to strengthen the Asian financial systems, the impact of the euro on financial markets and portfolio choices, and central bank independence, accountability, and transparency for appropriate decision-making.

In addition to these bimonthly meetings at the BIS, other regular meetings were also held. The Gold and Foreign Exchange Committee of the G10 central banks, whose secretariat is hosted by the BIS, held several meetings. The topics of these meetings included the euro, the growth of international financial markets and implications for monetary and financial stability, and the current state of the global economy.

Information Gathering and Analysis

The BIS served central banks by gathering statistical information about international financial market and banking activities and analyzing this data. This function was performed by the Central Bank Governance Steering Group. This group is comprised of central bank governors from both industrialized and developing countries. The objective of this group in fulfilling this function is to provide comparative information to assist central banks in their efforts to improve their operations. The relationship between central bank mandates in their respective countries and autonomy, transparency, and accountability was a major agenda item during the year ending March 2000.

Cooperative Efforts with LDCs

A number of meetings have been convened by the BIS which involved senior central bankers from LDCs. Two regional working groups were formed during the year ending March 2000 and held outside Basle. These focussed on strategic monetary policy issues. One was held in Brazil and co-hosted by the Banco Central de la República Argentina. Its discussion topic was monetary policy challenges in Latin America. The Bank of Korea co-hosted an Asian regional meeting and focused on the Asian monetary crisis. The BIS also convened a meeting of deputy governors of African central banks which dealt with the development finance sector in Africa.[8]

PERMANENT COMMITTEES

During the past three decades, the BIS has formed a number of permanent committees whose secretariats are located at the BIS in Basle. These were discussed in Chapter 3 and include the Committee on Banking Supervision, the Committee on the Global Financial

System, the Committee on Payment and Settlement Systems (CPSS), the Committee of Experts on Gold and Foreign Exchange, and the Euro-currency Standing Committee. The work of the first three committees was discussed in detail in Chapters 4, 5, and 7. These three committees established by the G10 central banks with BIS assistance have made the largest contribution during the past three decades.

Committee on Banking Supervision

The Committee on Banking Supervision has contributed to institutional soundness in the international banking system by formulating the Concordats of 1975 and 1983 and the Capital Accords of 1988 and 2001. The Committee on the Global Financial System has contributed to a more efficient functioning of the financial markets. The Committee on Payment and Settlement Systems has contributed to the financial system infrastructure in its research and analysis of netting, delivery versus payment, and reports on comparative netting systems in major countries.

Committee on Payment and Settlement Systems

The CPSS formed a Task Force on Payment System Principles and Practices in December 1999. This group was comprised of representatives of the G10 central banks and an equal number from non-G10 central banks as well as from the European Central Bank, the IMF, and the World Bank. The group formulated and published a consultative report on Core Principles for Systemically Important Payment Systems.

In addition, the CPSS worked with other committees or groups to formulate new guidelines or standards. It worked with the Committee on Banking Supervision to write guidelines for supervisors on foreign exchange settlement risk. The CPSS formed a Working Group on Securities Lending with the International Organisation of Securities Commissions (IOSCO) to publish a report entitled "Securities Lending Transactions: Market Development and Implications" in the summer of 1999.

Financial Stability Forum. Each of these committees participates in the work of the Financial Stability Forum at the BIS. Their joint efforts have strengthened global financial stability. The Committees on Banking Supervision and on Payment and Settlement Systems collaborated in the formulation of the IMF Code of Good Practices on Transparency in Monetary and Financial Policies.

Policy Papers. The Committee on Banking Supervision issued several policy papers during the 1999–2000 period. These subjects included corporate governance, credit risk, highly leveraged institutions, loan accounting transparency and disclosure, and the Y2K problem.

COOPERATION WITH REGIONAL CENTRAL BANKS

The BIS cooperated with central banks other than the G10 institutions. It and its committees worked with regional central banks to develop closer interaction with these banks coping with similar economic, financial, and political problems. This cooperation included meetings in which BIS representatives made addresses or participated in other ways.

Among the regional groupings with which the BIS maintained cooperative contacts, several were associations comprised of central banks from LDCs. These included the Arab Monetary Fund, the Centro de Estudios Monetarios Latinoamericanos, the Executive Meeting of East Asian and Pacific Central Banks, the Gulf Cooperation Council, the South Asian Association for Regional Cooperation, the Southern African Development Community, and the South-East Asian Central Banks.

Asian Consultative Council

One of the most recent regional groupings of central banks assisted by the BIS is the Asian Consultative Council (ACC). This group was established by the BIS on March 12, 2001 and is comprised of the governors of the BIS member central banks in the Asian/Pacific region. Its purpose is to furnish a means of communication between the Asian and Pacific members of the BIS and the BIS Board and Management on issues of concern to the Asian central banking community. Its first chairperson is Ian Macfarlane, Governor of the Reserve Bank of Australia. The BIS Representative Office in Hong Kong will be used for annual meetings of the ACC.

TECHNICAL ASSISTANCE

The BIS offers technical assistance to central banks. One example of this service is the BIS work with the central banks of central and eastern Europe, the Commonwealth of Independent States, and some Asian economies in transition.[9]

The BIS also offers technical assistance to central banks in industrialized nations. This assistance has been given to central banks in more than 20 countries. The BIS coordinates this assistance by means of a database and regular meetings that bring together officials of the donor and recipient central banks concerned along with officials from the IMF and other international financial institutions as well.

The BIS also participates in a training institution known as the Joint Vienna Institute. This was established in 1992 to offer courses primarily to officials of central banks and economic and financial authorities of the countries whose economies were formerly managed by central planning systems.

CONFIDENTIALITY OF BIS OPERATIONS

The BIS is considered by central banks to maintain a high degree of integrity and confidentiality in its dealings with them. Many, if not most, of the transactions carried out by the BIS on behalf of central banks require the utmost secrecy. Central banks must be very careful in their implementation of monetary policy in their home countries because of the possible adverse effects advance notice might have on their home country financial markets and economies.

Transparency of financial transactions by governments and corporations is an ideal, but in the real world of cross-border financial transactions, it is a principle much denied by the decision-makers at the highest levels. In fact, the culture of most countries, especially LDCs, does not openly espouse more than a modicum of transparency in domestic or international financial dealings.

Examples of speculation resulting from advanced leaks about major international financial decisions, e.g., gold transactions, devaluation of a currency, major equity or bond flotations, or changes in monetary policy, in some countries have resulted in stock or debt market selloffs, derivatives market collapses, and major declines in the price of precious metals such as gold.

The BIS offers central banks the highest discretion and confidentiality in the deposit, lending, gold, and foreign exchange operations it makes available. Among its customers are central banks which actively manage their reserves as well as institutions such as the IMF which do not manage their reserves. In addition to the expertise in these transactions, the BIS can offer confidentiality and secrecy which is higher than a triple-A rated bank.[10]

This secrecy can sometimes result in problems. Central banks work in as much secrecy as possible when implementing their policies. They organize their swaps and credits, for example, with a great deal of secrecy. When the public speculates that the central bankers are really quite worried behind their facade of secrecy, then this speculation can breed unfounded rumors about financial transactions which create instability in financial markets. The public can discern the general pattern of credits or interest rates, but the specific details of which central bank is drawing what amounts at a specific time are only known later—often much later when the consequences may have happened.[11] Usually transactions such as borrowing between or among central banks can be executed much more confidentially than, say, national government financial transactions.

At any rate, the relationship between the BIS and central banks has grown because of the confidentiality present in financial services offered by the BIS. It is apparent that this guiding principle practiced by the BIS has been quite successful both in fostering a favorable attitude toward the BIS on the part of central bankers as well as a characteristic which facilitates the lack of awareness by the general public about the work of the oldest international financial institution still operating.

THE BIS AND THE FED

The U.S. Federal Reserve System and its Federal Reserve Board is the most powerful central bank in the world. It has oversight responsibility granted by U.S. Congressional legislation over Federal Reserve member banks, U.S. banking operations in foreign countries, and foreign banks operating in the United States. The Chairman of the Federal Reserve Board is generally one of the most powerful men in the United States, if not the most powerful. The last two such chairmen, Paul Volcker and Alan Greenspan, certainly fit that description.

Thus, the relationship between the BIS and the U.S. Federal Reserve System is certainly one of the most important international relationships at the present time. The United States central bank was eligible for BIS Board membership from the inception of the institution. However, the U.S. Federal Reserve System (Fed) did not become a member until 1994. The reasons for this delay in accepting membership were discussed in Chapter 2. This section contains a discussion of the current relationship between the BIS and the Fed.

The Fed and the G10

The G10 central bank governors have met informally since 1961. These are the central bank governors from the ten major free market countries.[12] These countries are Belgium, Canada, France, Germany, Italy, Japan, the Netherlands, Sweden, the United Kingdom, and the United States. Switzerland's central bank is an 11th member of the group.

During the time the G10 central bankers have met, the Fed has played an active role in these meetings, as well as those of the group's subsidiary committees and other specialized meetings of central bankers held at the BIS.[13] Until 1994, the United States was the only country whose central bank had the right to be represented on the BIS' Board of Directors but which had not chosen to be represented. The reasons for this were discussed in Chapter 2. The Fed finally decided that the positive reasons for being represented on the BIS Board offset the negative reasons and the Fed took its seat on the Board.

Before 1994 when the Fed finally joined the Board, its major impetus in BIS/G10 policy stemmed from the Fed's cooperative effort in the formulation of the Capital Accord by the Committee on Banking Supervision. The Fed probably instigated the move by the Basle Committee to draft a risk-based capital adequacy standard into the Accord. The Fed had promoted capital maintenance by banks based on a measurement of the riskiness of their assets. This became a significant factor in the Basle Capital Accord.

The Fed was also instrumental, along with the Bank of England and other major industrialized nations' central banks, in closing down the global operations of the Bank for Commerce and Credit International (BCCI), the criminal banking institution whose case was discussed in Chapters 1 and 4.

A number of the reports written by the Committee on Banking Supervision and the Committee on Payment and Settlement Systems (CPSS) were chaired by Federal Reserve officials. For example, Wayne D. Angell chaired the CPSS which was instrumental in its studies of netting. The so-called "Red Book," a comparative analysis of the payment and settlement systems in the G10 countries, was written by a group chaired by Angell, then a member of the Federal Reserve Board of Governors. Patrick Parkinson was another Governor of the Fed when he chaired the group which formulated a report on the delivery versus payment system, known as the Parkinson Report. These reports were discussed in detail in Chapter 7.

SUMMARY AND CONCLUSIONS

The BIS has maintained excellent relations with central banks around the world. Its primary cooperative efforts have been with the G10 central banks, both before and after the U.S. Federal Reserve System became represented on the BIS Board of Directors.

The special committees such as the Committee on Banking Supervision and the Committee on Payments and Settlement Systems were actually formed by the G10 central banks but have their secretariats in Basle at the BIS. Their reports and analyses have increased the stability of the international financial system and have made it more efficient.

The BIS has increased the number of central banks which are members in recent years. Its focus has drastically moved from solely European to a much wider scope. Central banks from LDCs have been admitted to membership in the BIS and the institution has carried out cooperative efforts with a number of central bank groupings from the emerging nations.

One of the most important central banks is the U.S. Federal Reserve System. When the BIS was established in 1930, the Federal Reserve was eligible to join the BIS Board of Directors. For several reasons, this did not happen until 1994. During that year, the United States finally became represented on the BIS Board. The U.S. central bank had participated in and cooperated with numerous projects formulated and implemented by the BIS, the G10 committees, and their specific project groups. Federal Reserve Governors served on major BIS/G10 committees and chaired some of the most important studies, including the Angell and Parkinson Reports.

The Federal Reserve participated in the formulation of the Basle Concordats and Basle Capital Accords as well as the work of the Committee on Payment and Settlement Systems, including studies on netting and other systems such as the delivery versus payment methodology. The risk-based capital adequacy rules of the Basle Accord were instigated by the U.S. Federal Reserve position. In short, the relationship between the U.S. Federal Reserve System and the BIS has resulted in a more efficient and stable international monetary system and in better regulation and supervision of international banks.

The BIS offers a number of services to central banks. It accepts deposits in foreign exchange and gold from central banks which are either members or non-members. It makes loans or advances to these central banks to assist them in the short-term management of their reserves. It offers short- and medium-term investments to central banks for the purpose of facilitating their liquidity management. The BIS carries on foreign exchange or gold transactions for central banks for a variety of objectives.

The key factor in all of these services is the very discrete relationship fostered by the BIS toward its central bank clients. Much of these operations must be transacted in a cloak of secrecy. The confidentiality offered by the BIS in these financial operations with central banks has given it a reputation unequaled among the world's international financial institutions. The lack of transparency in many of these BIS transactions may be helpful for central banking operations but the populist political movement around the world may lead to a different style of operations by the BIS in the future. The issues raised in Chapter 12 were kept relatively secret for more than 50 years. Declassification of documents and a search for the truth in cases which may involve illegal or unethical operations will probably change the way many international organizations, including the BIS, do business.

If one area of BIS/central bank cooperative efforts can be faulted, it may be BIS operations with central banks in Asia. The economic problems in Japan are almost completely centered in the banking system. Yet, the Bank of Japan has had minimal effect in correcting problems among Japanese banks. The BIS has exercised little influence over the Bank of Japan and its control over Japanese banks. In the Asian countries affected by the currency crisis of the late 1990s, many of the economic problems remain unresolved. Again the banking systems in these countries have been part of the problem. And again the BIS has played a relatively small role in the alleviation of any banking problems in these countries, except for Basle Concordat and Basle Accord rules applied to banks in the area.

Because of these reasons, the BIS established the Asian Consultative Council in March 2001. This Council is comprised of the BIS member central banks of the Asian/Pacific region. The relationships to be formed between the BIS and the Asian/Pacific central bank governors in Hong Kong meetings one or more times each year should furnish the platform for discussion of proposals to alleviate most or all of these problems.

The BIS has reached out during the past decade to increase its focus to central banks other than the G10 countries. The new relationship with the U.S. Federal Reserve Board and the new Asian Consultative Council should spread the work of the Basle Committee and other BIS groups to regulation and supervision of banking and financial markets throughout the world. It is a form of leadership in these areas long needed and overdue. These relationships should bring added stability to the international financial and monetary system.

NOTES

1. Ray August, *International Business Law: Text, Cases, and Readings* (Englewood Cliffs, NJ: Prentice Hall, 1993), pp. 396–397.

2. See http://www.bis.org/about/profil2001.htm, March 6, 2001, p. 5.

3. Linda Allen, *Capital Markets and Institutions: A Global View* (New York: John Wiley & Sons, 1997), p. 60.

4. Bank for International Settlements, *70th Annual Report* (Basle, Switzerland: Bank for International Settlements, 2000), "Activities of the Bank," p. 15.

5. Ibid., p. 17.

6. "Forum for Central Banks—Other Activities," found on the Internet at http://www.bis.org/forum/others.htm, March 21, 2001, p. 1.

7. Ibid., p. 2.

8. Ibid., p. 3.

9. Frank Smets, *Measuring Monetary Policy Shocks in France, Germany, and Italy* (Basle, Switzerland: Bank for International Settlements, 1997), p. 7.

10. Melvyn Westlake, "Into Basle's Inner Sanctum," *The Banker*, Vol. 144 (March 1994), p. 19.

11. Paul Ferris, *The Money Men of Europe* (New York: Macmillan, 1968), pp. 257–258.

12. Ray August, *International Business Law: Text, Cases, and Readings*, p. 397.

13. Charles J. Siegman, "The Bank for International Settlements and the Federal Reserve," *Federal Reserve Bulletin*, Vol. 80 (October 1994), p. 901.

CHAPTER 9

The Bank for International Settlements and Other International Financial Institutions

INTRODUCTION

The BIS has maintained a strong relationship with central banks around the world, as discussed in the preceding chapter. The organization also maintains close working relationships with international financial institutions. These include the International Monetary Fund (IMF), World Bank, and regional development banks such as the Inter-American Development Bank, Asian Development Bank, African Development Bank, and the European Bank for Reconstruction and Development. The relatively new European Central Bank, the central bank whose jurisdiction includes the European Union countries, should also be included among those international institutions with which the BIS maintains a cooperative relationship. These relationships and their implications are the focal subjects of this chapter.

The cooperative efforts of the major international financial institutions have included the formulation of international standards in several areas in which the international financial system is concerned. These include: (1) data dissemination; (2) fiscal, monetary, and financial policy transparency; (3) banking regulation and supervision; (4) securities and insurance regulation; (5) accounting, auditing, and bankruptcy; and (6) corporate governance.

The Basle Committee on Banking and Supervision, headquartered at the BIS, has issued a number of principles. These have included the Basle Capital Accord, the Core Principles for Effective Banking Supervision, Sound Practices for Banks' Interactions with Highly Leveraged Institutions, and the Supervision of Cross-Border Banking. These standards were discussed in Chapters 4 and 5.

The International Organisation of Securities Commissions (IOSCO), also closely allied with the BIS, has issued standards for the securities industry. These have included a Supervisory Framework for Markets and Objectives and Principles of Securities Regulation. The BIS has recognized that securities markets are becoming more correlated as global cross-border financial transactions continue to increase, especially in the area of financial markets operations. As these activities continue to increase and as securities transactions become a way of life in the emerging markets and transition economies, these financial markets will require more regulation and supervision by national authorities. The BIS and its work with IOSCO will be at the forefront in the future development of global securities regulatory and supervisory standards.

The International Association of Insurance Supervisors (IAIS) has its secretariat at the BIS and works closely with BIS committees and special groups. The IAIS has formulated several standards for supervision of the international insurance industry. These have included the Insurance Supervisory Principles. Insurance business has grown significantly in its global outreach in the last few decades. The industry has extended its markets into the emerging markets and transition economies. Many of its activities need tighter supervision but the predominant means of regulation and supervision of this industry is at the state level in the United States or at the national level in foreign countries. As the industry becomes more complex and more and more integrated with banking and other financial institutions and markets, demands will increase for Federal regulation and supervision in the United States and some form of international supervision at the global level.

The coordination and cooperative efforts made by the major international financial institutions including the BIS, its committees, and special groups has been very beneficial in making the international financial and monetary system more efficient. Their work has alleviated the problem of asymmetric information in financial markets whereby investors must make decisions based on inadequate information. Often this leads to financial market panics, currency crises, and other economic problems, especially in the emerging markets. The implementation of standards and principles in the operations of banking, insurance, and securities business can reduce financial instability in the international financial system. Thus, the remainder of this chapter is devoted to a discussion of the cooperative efforts between the BIS and the other major international financial institutions.

THE INTERNATIONAL MONETARY FUND AND THE WORLD BANK

The BIS has developed a working relationship with other international financial institutions since World War II. The two most important of these are the International Monetary Fund (IMF) and the World Bank. These relationships are discussed in the following sections.

The BIS and the IMF

The IMF was established at the end of World War II at the Bretton Woods, New Hampshire, conference at which the World Bank was also formed. The primary objective of the IMF is to assist countries with short-term balance of payments problems by making short-term loans to these governments from a fund subscribed to the IMF by member countries. The IMF had the responsibility at the time of its inception for setting par values of all member countries' currencies and, in some minor way, assisting these countries in the management of their currencies under the fixed rate international monetary regime in effect until 1973.

During the past few decades, the IMF has taken on other responsibilities. These include attempts to alleviate regional or national currency crises such as the those in South America, Mexico, Russia, Europe, and Asia which have occurred during the last 10–15 years. The IMF has drafted plans for many of these nations to improve their economies and currencies. Thus, the IMF will necessarily deal with the international banking system.

In preceding chapters, major functions of the BIS, in cooperation with the G10 central banks, have been discussed. These have included analysis of the growth of the Eurocurrency markets, payment and settlement systems, acting as agent for the private ECU Clearing and Settlement System, and facilitation of the settlement system for the European Payments Union from 1950–1958. The

ECU is the European currency unit in which many European financial instruments were denominated before the advent of the Euro. Critics of the BIS have held that much of this work could have been done by other international financial institutions including the IMF or the Organisation for Economic Cooperation and Development (OECD), an international organization headquartered in Paris.[1]

However, the BIS deals primarily with central banks. The IMF deals with national governments, primarily of its member countries. Thus, the IMF has a broader focus while the BIS narrowly focuses on central banking operations, although its studies have implications for entire governments or for financial institutions such as commercial banks. In order for the IMF to have an impact on national central banks, the BIS must inevitably have a presence in whatever the endeavor. One such enterprise during the past two years was the joint effort between the IMF and the BIS in working with a representative group of central banks, financial agencies, and banks to create a Code of Good Practices on Transparency in Monetary and Financial Policies. This code can be found on the Internet at the IMF web site, www.imf.org.

The BIS and the World Bank

The World Bank, technically the International Bank for Reconstruction and Development, was established at the same Bretton Woods conference as the IMF. Its primary original objective was to assist the reconstruction of war-torn countries and development of emerging countries. It now concentrates solely on the latter objective. Its member countries subscribe to its capital and it makes loans to member countries which are for social infrastructure projects and must be guaranteed by the government receiving the funds. The World Bank's loans are made to LDCs with per capita incomes usually above US$1,000 while its sister agency, the International Development Association (IDA) makes non-interest bearing loans to countries with incomes under the US$1,000 amount. Another affiliated multilateral international financial institution, the International Finance Corporation (IFC) makes investments in business enterprise projects in LDCs, but without government guarantee.[2] The BIS has little or no cooperative contact with the IFC.

In addition to IDA and IFC, the World Bank has two other affiliates whose functions are designed to facilitate the flow of private foreign investment into LDCs. These are MIGA, the Multinational

Investment Guarantee Agency, and ICSID, the International Centre for Settlement of Investment Disputes.[3] The latter institution assists in the settlement of contract disputes between foreign investors from signatory member countries and host state governments which are also signatory member countries. The BIS and its related institutions would have little to do with ICSID.

On the other hand, MIGA's primary function might be of interest to the BIS and its relationship with IAIS. MIGA guarantees foreign direct investments by investors from MIGA member countries where the investment is made in a MIGA member country which is an LDC. The investments are guaranteed against political risks such as expropriation, contract interference, violence from local disturbances, and currency inconvertibility. MIGA cooperates with international insurance companies in the coverage of some of these guarantees and also reinsures some of its coverage with leading reinsurers. At some time in the future, the proposed standards formulated by the IAIS may have some significance to the work implemented by MIGA. In addition, foreign insurance companies planning investments in emerging market countries might consider obtaining investment guarantees from MIGA.

Both the IMF and the World Bank are usually represented at the major meetings held by the BIS, including those of its G10 committees when they deliberate major rules such as the Basle Concordats and Capital Accords, and the work on payment and settlement systems. Some of the international development banks have also attended these meetings.

Another area in which the BIS cooperates with the IMF, World Bank, and other multilateral financial institutions is in the gathering of financial statistics. For example, external debt statistics are gathered and disseminated by the BIS, IMF, World Bank, and the OECD. These data are collected primarily from creditor and market sources.

Currency Crises

The BIS has cooperated with the IMF, World Bank, and other regional development banks in attempts to alleviate currency crises. The Asian currency crisis in the late 1990s is an example of such cooperative effort.[4] This crisis, centered primarily in Indonesia, Korea, Malaysia, and Thailand, was caused by a large amount of credit growth in the area, as well as an over-excessive expansion of capital stock, poor banking supervision, asset price bubbles, very tight foreign exchange rates, and political cronyism.

Another example of economic problems caused by a currency crisis occurred in Latin America in the mid-1990s. The financial crisis there caused much investor anxiety but a very tight monetary policy, advised by BIS and IMF officials, alleviated the problem. During this crisis, Brazil's economy suffered greatly. The BIS put together a US$13.3 billion credit facility which was supported by central banks from 19 industrialized nations. Other international financial institutions also made funds available in this bailout of the Brazilian economy. These included the IMF, the World Bank, the Inter-American Development Bank, as well as Japanese authorities.

Problems with the Brazil Package. During the period July 1998 to January 1999, US$50 billion of foreign currency reserves were appropriated from Brazil by private financial institutions. These reserves were mostly transacted with options and futures contracts. Most of these funds which had left Brazil by capital flight were then loaned back to the country in the form of a US$41.5 billion financial package. The package was put together by the IMF and the U.S. Treasury Department with assistance from the World Bank, the Inter-American Development Bank, and the BIS. The IMF imposed an economic program on the Brazilian Government in return for the financial assistance which included reforms of the country's social security, public administration, public expenditure management, tax policy, and revenue sharing programs. The financial assistance program was criticized as a plan to aid Wall Street financiers who had been involved in a speculative plot against the Brazilian real.[5]

The US$41.5 billion package was intended to instill confidence in the Brazilian economy. However, the IMF-sponsored assistance only accelerated the outflow of monetary wealth from Brazil. Another US$20 billion left Brazil in the two months after the package was approved. The problem was one of moral hazard. The financial assistance put money back into the Brazilian economy only to be taken out by banks, hedge funds, and institutional investors. If the money was there, it could be taken, that is, a form of moral hazard was created by the financial aid. The Brazilian central bank reserves fell from US$75 billion in July 1998 to US$27 billion in January 1999.[6] Financial assistance, facilitated by the efforts of the BIS, only financed further capital flight.

The aid has been referred to as an IMF-sponsored scam. It was co-financed by the monetary authorities of the G7 countries (Canada, France, Germany, Great Britain, Italy, Japan, and the United States) and central banks of 14 other nations. The BIS facilitated the funds transfers by its operations with the central banks which were involved in the bailout.

The Basle Committee on Banking Supervision announced formal recommendations for the Central Bank of Brazil at the September 1997 Annual Meetings of the IMF and the World Bank. These recommendations outlined 25 basic principles designed to improve the efficiency of banking supervision and reduce the risk of a financial crisis in Brazil.

Regular meetings of the BIS with governors of the IMF and G10 country presidents have been held to discuss the problems and implications of these currency crises. Several financial issues have been discussed in these meetings including monetary policy, foreign exchange reserves, and currency problems.

Moral Hazard and the BIS. In addition to the moral hazard involved in the bailout of the Brazilian economy, other examples of moral hazard can be found in cooperative efforts in which the BIS and other international financial institutions were involved. The Mexican Government had to be bailed out when its bonds began to fail in 1994. In 1997, the Thai baht collapsed. This was followed by the Russian default in 1998. The effects of the latter problem began to spread into the U.S. financial markets. The U.S. Federal Reserve Board of Governors eased monetary policy in late 1998 in a form of lender-of-last-resort action. The added liquidity was intended to avoid the failure of U.S. financial institutions.

The liquidity furnished to Mexico, Thailand, and Russia was followed by the Long-Term Capital Management (LTCM) case. The near bankruptcy and bailout of LTCM was discussed in detail in Chapter 4. This bailout was sponsored by the Federal Reserve Board of Governors and added moral hazard to the previous cases in the 1990s. One might argue that problems for which moral hazard was increased were caused by mismanagement by institutions such as the IMF and the U.S. Treasury Department.[7]

The Basle Capital Accord and the IMF

The Capital Accord formulated by the Basle Committee on Banking Supervision and the BIS is an area which has implications for the international financial institutions such as the IMF. The use of internal and external ratings will require bank management and banking supervisors who are experts in their field and will require an improvement in the quality of these managers and supervisors. The new system, revised in 2001 to be effective in 2004, suggests more transparency of banking operations. Individual countries will need to invest greater resources in staff, training, and information technology systems to implement the new Accord rules. LDCs will be hardpressed to invest the needed resources. The IMF will be pressed to furnish assistance in training bankers and supervisors and implementation of the Basle Core Principles which support the new Accord.[8]

Financial Stability Forum

Another vehicle in which the BIS cooperates and works with international financial institutions is the Financial Stability Forum (FSF). The FSF was formed in February 1999 at the instigation of the G7 finance ministers and central bank governors. The G7 countries are Canada, France, Germany, Great Britain, Italy, Japan, and the United States.

These countries are represented by 35 high-level officials from national and international financial agencies. These officials include representatives from each of the G7 nations' finance ministries and central banks as well as from the IMF, World Bank, International Organisation of Securities Commissions, International Association of Insurance Supervisors, Organisation for Economic Cooperation and Development, and the BIS/G10 committees: the Basle Committee on Banking Supervision, the Committee on Payment and Settlement Systems, and the Committee on the Global Financial System.

The FSF has cooperated with major international financial institutions in the formulation of guidelines and standards for increasing the stability of financial systems in emerging markets. The group collaborated with the IMF and the World Bank to formulate guidelines on sovereign debt management and the production of a handbook on developing domestic public debt markets. The FSF objective for these products was to furnish tools to alleviate problems arising from volatile capital flows. The FSF also cooperated in the IMF-World Bank Financial Sector Assessment Program which is used to assess financial weaknesses in emerging markets including aggregate and key sectoral exposures.

The FSF was established to strengthen international cooperation and coordination in financial market supervision and surveillance. It meets regularly to discuss issues and problems which affect the international financial system and to identify the means to address these problems. Among the issues discussed by the FSF have been developments in e-finance for regulators and supervisors, the new Basle Capital Accord, and accounting and provisioning issues for financial institutions. To facilitate its work, the FSF has developed a website which contains a directory of global training opportunities in the field of financial supervision. This is a joint project with the IMF, the World Bank, and the BIS. The FSF is discussed in more detail in Chapter 11.

THE BIS AND THE EUROPEAN CENTRAL BANK

On January 1, 1999, all but four of the 15 EU countries took the first major step for a European Monetary Union (EMU) when they adopted the euro as a single currency for the group. The EMU is an economic bloc with a single currency, the euro, which will go into full circulation in 2002. The group will also have a single monetary policy to be formulated by a single central bank, the European Central Bank (ECB). Three EU countries, Great Britain, Denmark, and Sweden, opted not to join the EMU, at least not at first. Greece has not yet met the economic criteria for membership in the EMU.

The ECB formulates monetary policy for the European Union. Its management of interest rates is one of the major parts of its monetary policy. The euro will be the single currency used in its policy-making for all the EU members except Denmark and Great Britain, countries which, for now, have opted to keep their own currencies.

The BIS has worked with the EU in its monetary policy. Until the end of 1993, the BIS hosted various central bank committees which provided the institutional framework for monetary policy cooperative efforts in the EU. After that, the BIS hosted the European Monetary Institute until the organization was transferred to Frankfurt, Germany, where it was then transformed into the European Central Bank.

JOINT VIENNA INSTITUTE

The Joint Vienna Institute was formed in September 1992. This group was established to offer courses for officials of central banks and economic and financial authorities of countries whose economies were formerly under the control of central planning, that is, East European and former Union of Soviet Socialist Republic countries. The BIS participates in the Institute along with the European Bank for Reconstruction and Development, the World Bank, IMF, OECD, and the World Trade Organisation.

Other Relationships

From 1964 until the end of 1993, the BIS hosted the secretariat of the Committee of Governors of the Central Banks of the Member States of the European Union (Committee of Governors), then known as the European Community. This secretariat also serves the Board of Governors of the European Monetary Cooperation Fund (EMCF) and the BIS acted as agent for this organization. The Committee of Governors and the EMCF provided the institutional framework for monetary cooperation in the European Union until they were replaced in 1994 by the European Monetary Institute, the forerunner of the European Central Bank

From October 1986 until the end of 1998, the BIS served as agent for the private ECU Clearing and Settlement System. This relationship was implemented in accordance with the provisions of agreements between the Euro Banking Association, formerly the ECU Banking Association of Paris, and the BIS.

SUMMARY AND CONCLUSIONS

The BIS has maintained working relationships with several international financial institutions and other international organizations. It has worked with the IMF in a number of areas including the analysis of the growth of the Eurocurrency market, payment and settlement systems, as agent for the private ECU clearing system, and the facilitation of a settlement system for the European Payments Union in the 1950s, among other areas in the international financial system.

It has coordinated activities with the IMF and the World Bank in a number of national or regional currency crises. These have included the Asian currency crisis in the late 1990s as well as currency problems in Brazil, Mexico, and Russia. In most of these cases, of the contributing factors to the currency crises were the operations of banks in those countries. Bank supervision can be identified as a problem in nearly every case. Political cronyism, coupled with weak bank supervisory agencies, led in many cases to bad loans made by banks which maintained inadequate capital to support these risky loans. Central banks in these countries had a major responsibility to ensure a stable banking environment. In many cases they did not do so. The BIS cooperative efforts in some of these cases was not effective in alleviation of these banking problems and lack of sound supervisory standards.

The BIS initiated the Financial Stability Forum with G7 countries, the IMF, World Bank, the International Association of Insurance Supervisors, the International Organisation of Securities Commissions, and the OECD. The Financial Stability Institute emerged from this Forum. Although this group meets regularly and has produced some workable principles, it has not operated long enough to furnish an in-depth evaluation.

The BIS has also kept a relationship with the European Central Bank. This is the central bank formed to maintain monetary policy and manage the euro as the single central bank for the European Union countries. The BIS has hosted central banks from the EU countries as well as the European Monetary Institute, the forerunner of the European Central Bank. Thus far, the performance of the ECB has been cloudy with regard to its support of the euro during the past two years. The euro has fallen consistently against the US dollar. However, this result may have been caused more by the strong dollar than by anything the ECB may have done, as well as the fact that the U.S. economy has been relatively stronger than the EU economy. However, it has been quite reluctant to cut interest rates in the face of a weak European economy and has begun to do so for the first time in Spring 2001. The BIS has given few guidelines to the ECB to alleviate this situation. The BIS seems to be more interested in the supervisory side of banking authority than in the regulation of monetary policy.

These relationships with other international financial institutions have had a positive effect on the stability of the international monetary and financial system. The discretion with which the BIS fulfills its functions with central banks is used in these relationships and the skills of its senior officials have resulted in efficient coordination of the efforts to solve currency crises and international monetary issues.

The BIS has worked with the IMF in attempts to end the Asian currency crisis of the late 1990s. Some of the problems in those countries remain unresolved. It appears that BIS efforts to alleviate some of the economic problems of that geographic region have not been overly successful, if at all.

Although the international financial system seems more stable now and central banks, the insurance industry, and securities firms have a number of coordinating and cooperative platforms on which to air the issues of financial system supervision, the world still needs stronger efforts by the IMF, World Bank, BIS, and other agencies to end currency crises which may lead to systemic risk in the global financial and monetary environment. The fact that these agencies do not have legal authority to enforce their promulgations may be the weak link in the international system.

NOTES

1. Melvyn Westlake, "Into Basle's Inner Sanctum," *The Banker*, Vol. 144 (March 1994), p. 17.

2. See James C. Baker, *International Business Expansion into Less-Developed Countries: The International Finance Corporation and Its Operations* (Binghamton, NY: The Haworth Press, Inc., 1993) for detailed coverage of the IFC and some comments about the World Bank and IDA.

3. See James C. Baker, *Foreign Direct Investment in Less Developed Countries: The Role of ICSID and MIGA* (Westport, CT: Quorum Books, 1999)

4. Matthew Montago-Pollak, "The Revolution Gets Rolling," *Asian Business*, September 1995, pp. 58–63.

5. Michel Chossudovsky, "Brazil's IMF Sponsored Economic Disaster," *Heise Online*, April 25, 2001, p. 5, found online at http://www.heise.de/tp/english/special/eco/6373/1.html.

6. Ibid., p. 6.

7. Robert L. Bartley, "The Moral-Hazard Bubble," *The Wall Street Journal*, April 9, 2001, p. A29.

8. Jan van der Vossen, "Basel Committee Presents Proposals for New Capital Adequacy Standards for Banks," *IMF Survey*, Vol. 30 (February 5, 2001), p. 40.

CHAPTER 10

The Bank for International Settlements and Insurance Supervisors

INTRODUCTION

The relationship between the BIS and central banks and international financial institutions has been discussed in the preceding two chapters. Another area in which the BIS has taken an interest during the past decade has been the insurance industry. Insurance has increasingly become a global business. It also has been characterized as a financial business which, if regulated at all, the regulation and its concomitant supervision has been local, either state by state in the United States or merely nationally in other countries. Internationally recognized rules by which global insurance companies must operate have been largely absent.

Thus, the BIS has become more and more interested in developing standards for global supervision of insurance. Insurance is, after all, becoming more and more a part of the banking business. The BIS has been concerned with increasing the stability of the international banking system and reducing the riskiness of this industry. The insurance side of financial commerce is just another sub-set of the international financial community and, thus, needs attention from an international financial institution such as the BIS.

Regulatory and Supervisory Problems in the Insurance Industry

As mentioned above, the insurance industry, particularly the international insurance industry, is not regulated to the extent, for example, that the banking industry is. The classic theory of regulation holds that regulation is only necessary if market failures exist, such failures result in meaningful economic inefficiency or inequities, and government action could alleviate such inefficiency or inequity.[1] Market failures have occurred in the insurance business, especially in international insurance where, for example, explicit or implicit collusion resulted in price distortions. National tax treatment of insurers differs from country to country and may distort the price of the insurance product. Barriers to entry exist in many countries and government intervention has distorted competition with the application of anti-concentration and anti-trust rules. In the United States, insurance is regulated from state to state and an insurer must obtain a license from each individual state in which it wishes to operate.[2]

Insurers may differentiate their products. Price discrimination is often practiced and, if unjustified, is usually prohibited by insurance regulators. Predatory pricing is not often practiced in the insurance business. If done internationally, it is referred to as "dumping." However, it is practiced by some insurers.

Information, or the lack thereof, is one of the major problems in the insurance industry. Until the advent of Internet web sites, which permit the consumer to compare insurance products and which offer the consumer the best product for the lowest price, the consumer has not been well informed about the alternative insurance products. The problem is one of asymmetric information. The consumer is at a disadvantage with regard to the product. The insurer is able to take advantage of the consumer's lack of knowledge about the product.[3]

These problems all exist in both domestic and international insurance markets. Market distortions do exist. Asymmetric information is present. Inefficiencies and inequities are inherent in the industry. This is especially true of the international aspects of this business. Rules and standards are needed and these need to be formulated and implemented by a multilateral organization. The International Association of Insurance Supervisors (IAIS) was established for these reasons. Its work is discussed in the following sections.

As financial service customers become more aware of the costs and benefits of insurance products, they will demand more transparency on the part of the insurance industry in order to reduce the asymmetric information issue and more supervisory authority from government. National laws have been passed in Australia, the United Kingdom, and the United States to increase disclosure of company information and to prohibit misrepresentation by insurance companies.[4]

The regulation of insurance companies has been haphazard. However, since they sell promises of future delivery, they should be regulated in every national market. It has been suggested that regulators should be aware of at least six issues in the regulation of the insurance industry. These issues are listed in Figure 10.1.

Capital Adequacy Standards. The sixth issue concerns the solvency of the insurer. Some countries have addressed the capital adequacy of insurance companies. In the United States, the National Association of Insurance Commissioners (NAIC) developed risk-based capital standards for life-health insurers which were adopted in December 1992. A property-liability insurer risk-based capital formula was adopted in 1993 and became effective the following year.

The NAIC capital model uses a formula to derive implied capital needed by an insurer to safely support the risk inherent in its assets, liabilities, and premium writings.[5] This standard is similar in

Figure 10.1
Issues of Insurance Regulation

---

1. The role of government as a supplier of insurance products.
2. The qualifications for admission into the insurance market.
3. Balancing the role and benefits of competition among insurers versus the need to protect consumers.
4. How to regulate solvency of insurance companies.
5. What response should be taken to assist insurers in financial difficulty.
6. How to protect insured consumers against the insolvency of an insurer.

Source: Harold D. Skipper, Jr., "The Nature of Government Intervention into Insurance Markets: Regulation," in Harold D. Skipper, Jr., *International Risk and Insurance: An Environmental-Managerial Approach* (Burr Ridge, IL: Irwin McGraw-Hall, 1998), pp. 268–269.

concept to the Basle Accord developed in 1988 with changes proposed in 2001 for commercial banks, the topic of Chapter 5.

The NAIC risk-based capital requirements utilize four major risk classifications, as follows:[6]

1. underwriting risk for losses incurred on insurance policies that exceed premiums collected;
2. asset risk determined by the credit risk and price risk of the insurance company's portfolio;
3. credit risk on reinsurance and other receivables, accounting for approximately 5 percent of capital requirements; and
4. off-balance sheet risk, which includes a measure of growth risk.

In terms of the first classification, this loss reserve requirement is the most significant part of risk-based capital and is calculated using loss ratios for the worst year in the past 10 years. The second classification above represents approximately 20 percent of property-liability insurer risk-based capital requirements. As with Basle Accord capital requirements, interest rate risk is not considered.

Insurance companies under the supervisory jurisdiction of the NAIC must file a detailed Regulation 126 report which examines the risk exposure of the asset and liability portfolios of the firm under various interest rate scenarios. Well-capitalized insurance companies are exempt from filing a Regulation 126 report. The exemption scenarios are shown in Figure 10.2.

The European Union (EU) issued recommendations for insurance intermediaries in 1991.[7] These recommendations address: (1) the establishment of general professional standards for insurance intermediaries throughout the EU and the registration of these intermediaries; (2) a distinction between insurance agents and brokers and disclosure of this distinction to the customer; (3) possession by insurance intermediaries of general, commercial, and professional knowledge and ability; (4) establishment of a central registry of all qualified insurance intermediaries and distinction between agents and brokers; and (5) sanctions issued by member states to prevent unregistered persons from acting as insurance intermediaries.[8]

Mergers and Acquisitions. During the past decade, the financial services industry has been deregulated in many areas. In the United States, the Glass-Steagall Act, which separated commercial and investment banking activities and prohibited U.S. banks from doing business in some insurance and real estate areas, was abolished

Figure 10.2
Exemptions from Insurance Company Regulatory Reporting Requirements

Asset Range	Capital/ Assets	Liabilities/ Assets	Noninvestment Grade Bonds/ Capital
To Be Exempt from Regulation 126 Reporting Requirements:			
If assets < 20m	≥ = 10%	< 30%	< 50%
If assets $20–100m	≥ = 7%	< 40%	< 50%
If assets $100–500m	≥ = 5%	< 50%	< 50%
If assets > $500m	No exemption		

Source: Linda Allen, *Capital Markets and Institutions: A Global View* (New York: John Wiley, 1997), p. 133.

and replaced by the Financial Services Reform Act of 1998. This act permits U.S. banks to engage in investment, insurance, and real estate activities to some extent.

In short, the act permits banks to establish financial holding companies for providing financial services previously prohibited under U.S. Federal law. With regard to the insurance business, the new law requires a bank that wants to sell insurance to set up an affiliate insurance company within a holding company structure. The bank then will have to transfer capital to its affiliate and, thus, drain bank resources. Revenue generated from the nonfinancial activities cannot exceed 5 percent of the company's total revenue. The bill still does not place insurance regulation under Federal control. Such regulation is still left to states.

Merger and acquisition (M & A) activity in the insurance industry has increased in recent years as a means to facilitate the holding company problem. In order to counter low organic growth rates in the industry, two distinct trends in M & A exist among insurance companies.[9] Insurers have either divested noncore operations and specialized in some area of insurance or they have built and diversified their operations through acquisitions. One major case which can be offered as an example of this movement is the merger of Citibank with the Travelers Company to form Citigroup.

Citigroup. As a result of the liberalization of banking operations in the United States and elsewhere, mergers between, for example, banking and insurance firms as well as investment firms has been taking place on an increasing scale. In 1998, the Travelers' Group, an insurance company, and Citibank, a commercial bank, merged to form Citigroup. This was done in anticipation that the Glass-Steagall Act would be abolished. This merger resulted in a firm with more than US$650 billion in assets. Travelers had just acquired Salomon Brothers, the investment firm, only the year before the announced merger with Citibank. Thus, this conglomerate will combine banking, securities, and insurance businesses.

The Citigroup merger of Citibank and Travelers is a very good case example for stronger regulatory and supervisory authority. An analysis of the operations of each company in the merger demonstrates the need for more efficient supervision. On the Citibank side, it manages more than US$100 billion for private investors. It has thousands of branches around the world to serve consumers' banking needs. It has more than 36 million credit card customers. Its corporate banking division derives most of its US$2.2 billion in profits from emerging markets. On the Travelers side, its consumer finance division has more than two million customers. Its life insurance business generated US$850 million in net income in 1997. Its property and casualty insurance business generated US$957 million in net profits in 1997. Its securities business is performed by its Salomon Smith Barney division which had more than a billion dollars of net income in 1997.[10] In addition, Travelers announced an extensive partnership in the securities business with the Japanese giant securities firm, Nikko Securities.[11] Travelers invested US$1.6 billion to acquire about 25 percent of Nikko Securities, the third largest securities firm in Japan.

Regulations have been relaxed on cross-sector mergers such as the Citibank-Travelers combination. BB&T Corportation is one of the leading banks in the United States (16th largest) and it operates the largest insurance agency in the Carolinas. Banks are interested in this merger activity because they can capture insurance company underwriting profits. Consolidations are also occurring in the insurance industry itself. The St. Paul Companies sold most of their personal life insurance operations to MetLife Inc. in 1999 and then sold its nonstandard auto insurance business to Prudential Insurance Company of America later that year.

These cross-sector mergers, reconsolidations, and sales of insurance company divisions, coupled with cross-border strategic alliances of banks and insurance companies, will create large business entities with monopolistic powers. These organizations will need more supervision than the state or national authorities can offer in order to protect consumers from the marketing problems discussed earlier. Thus, more national supervisory authority in the major industrialized nations will be needed. This, in turn, will require stronger international regulation and supervision of the insurance industry.

The Financial Services Act of 1998. In 1998, H.R. 10, entitled the Financial Services Act of 1998, was debated in the U.S. Congress. This bill, enacted into law in 1999, essentially abolished the Glass-Steagall Act which had been in effect since 1933 and which prohibited commercial banks from doing investment, insurance, and other business. The new act permits banks to establish financial holding companies to provide financial services which had been prohibited by Federal law. The law permits banks to do insurance business but instead of doing this in an operating subsidiary, banks must set up an affiliate insurance company within a holding company structure. Banks which desire to sell insurance products must transfer capital to the affiliate. Thus, the bank's capital would be diminished instead of setting up the insurance subsidiary with its own equity. The new law allows U.S. banks to carry out insurance business but creates a problem in the funding of the operation with bank capital.

The preceding discussion has focused on the current state of regulation and supervision of insurance firms. For the most part, this oversight function is performed at the national level, if at all. The reasons for continued and broader regulation and supervision of the insurance industry were included in the discussion as well as examples of selected national oversight programs. What may be needed is an international supervisory and regulatory authority for the insurance industry given the cross-border expansion of the insurance business and the blending of banking and insurance operations into the same financial service provider. Such an institution is the subject of the following section.

The Influence of the World Trade Organisation. The World Trade Organisation (WTO) members have formulated an agreement to expand world trade. The WTO is the only global international organization that deals with rules of trade between nations. The organization is headquartered in Geneva, Switzerland. It has 140 member countries and its Secretariat has a staff of 500. Mike Moore is the Director General. The agreement recently negotiated includes the financial services industry, including insurers. A globalization issue has arisen whereby a global capital market is being created by the WTO move, especially in the services sector. As mentioned above, the merger and acquisitions activity among financial services firms, including insurers, has increased significantly in recent years. The large U.S. insurers want access to European markets but the European Union has its own set of rules for insurance firms. Many European insurers have actually acquired many large U.S. insurers recently. In many countries, state-owned insurance firms are dominant. For example, in China, the People's Insurance Company has dominated the field. But as China becomes a working member of the WTO, it must open its borders to competition in the field. These are all areas which will need some type of international oversight. The BIS and the IAIS are the appropriate agencies to accomplish such improvement in the supervision of global insurers.

Captive Offshore Insurers. Captive insurance companies are firms that underwrite the risks of their owners. During the last few decades, captive insurance business has grown significantly from more than 300 firms in 1974 to more than 3,500 around the world in 1996. These firms are closely-held companies whose business is supplied by their owners and whose principal beneficiaries are the original insureds.[12] They play little or no role in the management of their owners. They are found in many nations but primarily in those countries with less active regulation and lower tax rates. These countries are often referred to as tax havens because they have relatively low corporate tax rates or no such taxes at all. Bermuda accounts for more than one-third of all captive insurance firms.

Captive insurance firms have both advantages and disadvantages. They can reduce their parents' risk costs. They offer direct access to reinsurance. They can facilitate payment plans which increase cash flows to the parent firms. They can offer tax advantages to the parent firms because of their operations in tax haven countries. They can operate as a risk management tool for the parent firms. On the other hand, they do not guarantee successful risk financing to the parent firm. Their operating costs as well as travel costs for staff can be quite high. They require up-front investments of capital and surplus. Their management can become obsessed with the mechanics of the insurance business when their objectives are really to assess the parent's risk and assist in the management of that risk.

Since they operate in many tax haven countries, the regulation and oversight responsibility is usually quite lax in such countries, if it exists at all. Several issues may arise in the operation of offshore captive insurers. These include asymmetric information for investors and consumers, lack of transparency in their financial transactions, and possible tax evasion. They are a large part of the rationale for tighter regulation and supervisory oversight of international insurance operations.

Major International Supervisory Organizations

The insurance industry, as discussed earlier, does not have a well-defined supervisory authority organization, at least not on an international basis. International insurance supervisory organizations have only begun to develop in the 1990s and have very limited activities and authority. Those now operating exist primarily to exchange information and to furnish a forum to discuss and propose new industry rules and standards. Only the United States and the EU have insurance supervisory authorities which can affect industry policies. In the United States, this function is performed by the National Association of Insurance Commissioners (NAIC).

The NAIC is comprised of insurance regulators from all 50 states, as well as the District of Columbia and four territories.[13] This organization monitors non-U.S. insurers which write insurance policies in the United States. It develops model rules and industry standards which the states may choose to adopt. However, it has no enforcement powers. The states still regulate the insurance business within each state, if they regulate at all.

Other Supervisory Agencies

Regional insurance supervisory associations can be found in Africa, Asia, the Caribbean, Eastern Europe, and other regions. Two of the more significant of these are the Association of Insurance Superintendents of Latin America (ASSAL) and the Offshore Group of Insurance Supervisors (OGIS). ASSAL was formed in 1979 because of the growth of the insurance industry in Latin America. This group promotes cooperation among the Latin American country insurance supervisors and is a conduit for the exchange of information aimed at the maintenance of capital adequacy and strengthening of the industry. ASSAL also engages in educational and training services for members. OGIS was formed in 1993 because of the global concerns of supervisory authorities and the state of the industry's business in offshore locations such as Bermuda. Its primary objective is to raise the standards of the insurance business in offshore jurisdictions.[14]

INTERNATIONAL ASSOCIATION OF INSURANCE SUPERVISORS

Establishment and Operations

The IAIS was founded in 1993 at a Chicago, Illinois, meeting of insurance supervisory officials from 53 countries. The new organization began operations in 1994 and now has 80 members from 70 countries.[15] The IAIS was established for the purposes of (1) ensuring improved supervision of the insurance industry, (2) formulation of practical standards for the supervision of insurance operations, and (3) the provision of mutual assistance and exchange of information to promote the development of domestic insurance markets. The BIS has hosted the secretariat of the IAIS since the beginning of 1998.[16]

The IAIS has issued several international insurance supervisory principles, standards, and guidance papers. Among these pronouncements have been: (1) Insurance Core Principles, (2) the Insurance Concordat, (3) Principles for the Conduct of Insurance Business, (4) Guidance on Insurance Regulation and Supervision for Emerging Market Economies, (5) Supervisory Standard on Licensing, and (6) Supervisory Standard on Derivatives.[17] These are discussed in the following sections.

Insurance Core Principles. The IAIS formulated its Insurance Core Principles in 1997 and revised them in October 2000. These principles present a framework for insurance supervision and they identify subject areas that should be addressed in legislation or regulation in every jurisdiction. They also give the IAIS a framework for the development of international standards.

Insurance Concordat. The Insurance Concordat is a set of principles whose objective is to improve the supervision of international insurance companies and states that all insurance firms should be subject to effective supervision. Any cross-border activities should be subject to consultation between the relevant supervisors. In addition, provision should be made for external audits and information sharing with other supervisors. This standard was adopted in September 1997 and revised two years later.

Principles for the Conduct of Insurance Business. In December 1999, the IAIS developed a set of principles whose objective was to improve the relationship among insurers, financial intermediaries, and consumers. These principles should strengthen consumer confidence in the insurance industry.

Guidance on Insurance Regulation and Supervision for Emerging Market Economies. In September 1997, the IAIS formulated a paper, "Guidance on Insurance Regulation and Supervision for Emerging Market Economies." It was designed to encourage insurance supervisors in emerging and transition economies to conform to the principles outlined in the Insurance Supervisory Principles paper.

Supervisory Standard on Licensing. In October 1998, the IAIS developed a Supervisory Standard on Licensing. Licensing is an important function in the insurance industry. This standard is aimed at the prudential aspects of licensing and contains requirements for an insurer seeking a license. The principles apply to the licensing procedure as well as a review of changes in the control of a licensed insurance company. Licensing is a legal procedure whereby a firm (licensor) licenses another firm, perhaps in a foreign country (licensee), to make and sell a product which is owned by the licensor. A manufacturing company licensor usually permits the licensee to use patents, formulae, registered trademarks, or other intangible property rights to facilitate manufacture and sale of the product by the licensee. The licensee then reimburses the licensor with a percentage of the sales of the product in the form of a royalty.

Supervisory Standard on Derivatives. In October 1998, the IAIS adopted a Supervisory Standard on Derivatives. This standard gives supervisors guidance in assessing how insurers control risks when they employ derivatives for hedging purposes. The standard presents risk management controls for insurers that are active in the use of derivatives. It also offers a reporting framework which companies can use for a full range of derivatives activities.

Supervisory Standard on Group Coordination. This IAIS standard builds on the Joint Forum Coordination paper establishing general principles regarding the supervision of financial conglomerates with the objective of development of coordination and information sharing agreements between supervisors of international insurance groups and other international financial groups which have a large involvement in the insurance industry.

Supervisory Standard on On-site Inspections. This IAIS standard sets forth objectives of on-site inspection and its procedure and organization. It was developed in 1998 and is closely related to the on-going oversight process.

In 1997, the IAIS issued its first paper, "Insurance Supervisory Principles: Guidance on Insurance Regulation and Supervision for Emerging Economies." This report was comparable to the Basle Concordat and was considered a model memorandum of under-standing to be used by insurance supervisors to improve the ex-change of information and to facilitate cooperation.

The IAIS held its fifth annual conference in Cancún, Mexico, in October 1998. At that conference, three new standards on insur-ance supervision were approved by the organization's members. The standards covered licensing of insurance companies, on-site in-spections, and the use of derivatives. The primary objective of these standards is improved supervision of the insurance industry at both international and domestic levels. The three standards are shown in Figure 10.3.

Figure 10.3
Insurance Supervision Standards of the IAIS (October 1998)

1. Supervisory Standard on Licensing	Identifies requirements which should be met by an insurance company seeking a license and covers the standards which apply to the licensing procedure itself.
2. Standards on On-Site Inspections	Procedures and standards for the organization of on-site inspections which will give supervisors reliable data and information in order to assess a company's current and prospective solvency.
3. Supervisory Standard on Derivatives	Provides guidance to supervisors in assessing how insurers control risks in derivatives.

Source: Bank for International Settlements Press Release, "The International Association of Insurance Supervisors (IAIS) Fifth Annual Conference: New Global Insurance Standards Adopted," October 6, 1998, pp. 1–2.

BIS and the IAIS

The BIS provides support in technical and administrative matters at the IAIS secretariat in Basle. The IAIS works in close cooperation with the Basle Committee on Banking Supervision because of the overlap in matters concerning financial stability as differences between financial institutions and sectors such as banking and insurance are diminished. The IAIS combined with the Basle Committee and the International Organisation of Securities Commissions (IOSCO) in a Joint Forum on Financial Conglomerates for the purpose of issuing a report in 1995 on the supervision of financial conglomerates. During the late 1990s, the United States and other nations have liberalized the financial industry to permit commercial banking, insurance, and investment banking activities to be carried out by the same financial institution.

The documents developed in this joint forum dealt with four matters and were published in 1999.[18] They are as follows:

1. techniques for the assessment of capital adequacy of conglomerates including the detection of excessive gearing, or leverage;
2. the facilitation of the exchange of information among supervisors;
3. coordination among supervisors;
4. testing of the fitness and propriety of managers, directors, and major shareholders of conglomerates.

The Financial Conglomerates Forum held a meeting in June 2000. The group discussed existing coordination arrangements with regard to international insurance groups and financial conglomerates. A proposal was formulated to develop a model agreement for the exchange of information between supervisors of different financial sectors.

One of the concerns of regulators has been whether a financial conglomerate has adequate capital for its varied activities, which may include banking, insurance, and securities. The report issued in 1999 by this joint effort concluded that more cooperation is needed among supervisory authorities, that these authorities need to consider the conglomerate as a whole when measuring its capital adequacy, and that appropriate techniques are needed to assess capital adequacy.[19]

In addition to the work concerning the capital adequacy of financial conglomerates, the IAIS, with the assistance of the BIS, reported that it will create, by Fall 2002, a global standard or standards which cover solvency requirements for insurance firms. The solvency standard will differentiate between life and non-life companies as well as reinsurers. This work will have similar objectives for the insurance industry as does the Basle Accord for the banking industry.

The IAIS is in the process of expanding its focus and mission. It has proposed that its charter be amended to make the organization the international agency for insurance supervision just as the Basle Committee is for banking supervision and the IOSCO is for securities supervision. In the meantime, the three groups under the aegis of the BIS, the host of the secretariats of the three groups, will maintain their cooperative efforts in their supervisory work and formulation of standards whose objectives are stability and efficiency in the international financial system.[20]

Joint Year 2000 Council

Another area in which the BIS has cooperated with the IAIS was the Joint Year 2000 Council. In 1998, a Round Table on the year 2000 was held at the BIS. The Council included representatives from the Basle Committee on Banking Supervision and the Committee on Payment and Settlement Systems, as well as the IAIS and the IOSCO.

The Council was formed for a number of purposes. Among them were: to ensure a high profile for the Year 2000 computer challenge within the international financial supervisory community, to share information on regulatory and supervisory strategies and approaches, to discuss contingency measures, and to serve as a point of contact with national and international private sector initiatives.

IAIS Training Programs

The IAIS has facilitated a number of training programs and developed training materials for insurance supervisors in recent years. In 1999, the IAIS organized regional training seminars for insurance supervisors in Asia (held in Singapore), in Latin America (held in Argentina), in Central and Eastern Europe (held in Poland), in Africa (held in South Africa), for all emerging markets (held in Tokyo), and for offshore jurisdictions (held in Aruba).

SUMMARY AND CONCLUSIONS

The insurance industry is a part of commerce and finance that has been loosely supervised and regulated. Much of domestic insurance activities are regulated and supervised, if at all, by the states in which they operate. This is especially true of the United States where insurance business operations are not supervised at the Federal level. This function is left to the states to manage, even though much of the operations of insurance companies are interstate in nature and should receive some type of Federal oversight.

Bank regulation and supervision has generally been more strict both nationally and internationally than has the regulation and supervision of the insurance industry. While banking supervisors are more concerned with macro-economic issues and the stability of the financial system, insurance regulators have been more concerned with product and marketing issues. As more cross-product mergers and consolidations occur between banking and insurance firms, the regulation and supervision of these business entities may converge in terms of the focus of such oversight.

International insurance activities are not regulated or supervised by some multilateral agency but by national authorities, if they are supervised at all. The focus of the International Association of Insurance Supervisors (IAIS), a relatively new organization, is on the promulgation and implementation of internationally accepted standards for the supervision of international insurance operations.

The BIS was instrumental in the establishment of the IAIS and hosts the organization at its Basle headquarters. The IAIS coordinates activities with the major G10 committees of the BIS, as well as the International Organisation of Securities Commissions. One of the concerns of the IAIS is the capital adequacy of insurance conglomerates, especially those which operate internationally. Thus, it has worked with the Basle Committee in adapting the Basle Capital Accord to the international insurance industry. These activities with the BIS and its constituent committees and groups may be the first steps toward appropriate supervision of insurance firms. The beneficiaries will be the consumers of insurance products around the world.

It stands to reason that, as more and more insurance companies form relationships with banking organizations in a world of consolidated financial services, national banking supervisory authorities will become more interested in the supervision of insurance operations and will apply banking-type supervisory standards to this industry.

NOTES

1. Harold D. Skipper, Jr., "Rationales for Government Intervention into Insurance Markets," in Harold D. Skipper, Jr., *International Risk and Insurance: An Environmental-Managerial Approach* (Burr Ridge, IL: Irwin McGraw-Hill, 1998), p. 243.

2. Ibid., pp. 244–245.

3. Ibid., pp. 250–251.

4. Andrew F. Giffin and Bryan Clontz, "Integration and Globalization of Financial Services," in Harold D. Skipper, Jr., *International Risk and Insurance: An Environmental-Managerial Approach* (Burr Ridge, IL: Irwin McGraw-Hill, 1998), p. 179.

5. Harold D. Skipper, Jr., "The Nature of Government Intervention into Insurance Markets: Regulation," in Harold D. Skipper, Jr., *International Risk and Insurance: An Environmental-Managerial Approach* (Burr Ridge, IL: Irwin McGraw-Hill, 1998), p. 279.

6. Linda Allen, *Capital Markets and Institutions: A Global View* (New York: John Wiley, 1997), p. 127.

7. Harold D. Skipper, Jr., "The Nature of Government Intervention into Insurance Markets: Regulation," pp. 284–285.

8. Ibid., p. 285.

9. "SNL's Analysis of Insurance M&A," found on the Internet at http://www.snl.com/mergers/insurance/analysis_overview.html, April 16, 2001, p. 1.

10. Anthony Saunders, *Financial Institutions Management* (Burr Ridge, IL: Irwin McGraw-Hill, 2000), p. 478.

11. Ibid., p 538.

12. H. Felix Kloman, "Captive Insurance Companies," in Harold Skipper, Jr., *International Risk and Insurance: An Environmental-Managerial Approach* (Burr Ridge, IL: Irwin McGraw-Hill 1998), pp. 659, 661.

13. M. Bruce McAdam, "Important Intergovernmental Organizations Involved in Insurance," in Harold D. Skipper, Jr., *International Risk and Insurance: An Environmental-Managerial Approach* (Burr Ridge, IL: Irwin McGraw-Hill, 1998), p. 330.

14. Ibid., p. 332.

15. Ibid., p. 331.

16. "Bank for International Settlements Profile," found on the Internet at http://www.bis.org/about/profil2000.htm, January 8, 2001, p. 3.

17. Financial Stability Forum, "Compendium of Standards," found at http://www.fsforum.org/Standards/BodyIAIS.html, April 16, 2001, pp. 1–3.

18. International Association of Insurance Supervisors Press Statement, February 18, 1999.

19. Ibid.

20. Ibid.

CHAPTER 11

Research and Miscellaneous Activities

INTRODUCTION

In the preceding chapters, the special committees whose secretariats are located at the BIS have been discussed and their work analyzed. The relationships between the BIS and central banks and between the BIS and other international organizations also have been topics of discussion and analysis. The BIS has another important function which will be discussed in this chapter. This is compilation and analysis of monetary and economic data, work done by the Centre for Monetary and Economic Research (hereafter the Centre), a part of the BIS' Monetary and Economic Department, and which will be discussed in this chapter.

In addition, the BIS has performed other activities, some of which are related to its research and analysis function. Among these, the most significant was the Y2K work carried out during the latter part of the 1990s. Y2K refers to the Year 2000. The BIS study was concerned with problems stemming from computer system configurations which control the date function. The business world, including the international banking community, believed that problems would occur when computers turned over the date at January 1, 2000. It was thought that computers would not be able to recognize the year 2000 because of the configuration of 1–1–00. The computer might think this date to be 1–1–1900, or some other similar date. The BIS carried out extensive research about the Y2K issue and this work will be discussed in this chapter.

Monetary and Economic Research

The Centre conducts research on monetary and financial issues. These studies are designed to support the activities of the various committees and groups at the BIS. It also gathers data which are used by contributing central banks on an intra-bank basis.

Three major types of reports are published by the Centre. These are the *Quarterly Review*, the *Annual Report*, and other publications which deal with monetary and financial issues and which are disseminated in a variety of outlets. These will be discussed in the following sections.

Quarterly Review

The BIS publishes a *Quarterly Review* which provides a detailed commentary on financial market developments. Much of the statistical data collected by the BIS is included in the *Quarterly Review*. The *Quarterly Review* published in March 2001 by the BIS contained a discussion of international banking and financial market developments.

Annual Report

The BIS publishes an *Annual Report* which is one of most highly sought documents in the area of international finance. The *Annual Report* is published in several languages. It is very difficult to get on the BIS' mailing list for the document because of its popularity. The information contained in the BIS *Annual Report* has become available in recent years on the BIS web site at www.bis.org.

The *Annual Report* contains a number of specific analyses about various aspects of the international financial system and is a review of international economic and financial developments during the preceding BIS fiscal year. These include developments in the world economy, international trade, monetary policy in industrialized countries, activities in international bond markets, foreign exchange market activity, financial flows into LDCs, an analysis of international financial markets in general including derivatives, and specific activities of the BIS. Its statistical data on these markets is always a good start for researchers working on international finance projects.

Other Reports and Data Gathering

BIS Conference and Policy Papers. The BIS publishes its own research findings in its conference and policy papers. These papers also include papers submitted by constituent central banks.

A list of these papers can be found on the BIS web site. Among them, for example, is the paper, "Banking Crises in Emerging Economies: Origins and Policy Options," by Goldstein and Turner.[1] This paper contains a discussion of banking crises during the past few decades, their causes, and suggested policy options for strengthening banking systems. It is aimed at bank supervisory authorities and its objective is to strengthen the international banking system.

Another example of a paper published by the Monetary and Economic Department of the BIS is the study "Capital Flows in the 1980s: A Survey of Major Trends" by Philip Turner.[2] This report is an overview of the major characteristics of capital flows during the 1980s. Turner examines the behavior of the principle components of these flows and draws implications.

These papers are representative of the policy papers published by the Centre. Nearly 100 BIS working papers are also available on a vast array of topics. These cover subjects as diverse as money and inflation in the Euro area, corporate hedging using derivatives, reserve currency allocation, the pricing of bank lending and borrowing, monetary policy in industrialized countries, and exchange rate regimes in sub-Saharan Africa.

Data for Central Banks. The BIS compiles and analyzes data concerning activities in international banking and securities markets. The most important part of these data is international banking statistics. These data examine the international business of banks and its recent growth. Such data are used by national governments in the compilation of their balance of payments statistics.

As part of this data gathering function, the BIS collects aggregate loan volume data for countries, primarily for their central banks. One of the problems with this type of data is that it is often more than six months old when published. For example, Citigroup may know its current loan volume position with, say, Thailand. But the banking/insurance group may not know with any accuracy Thailand's outstanding external loans and debt with any other lender in the world.[3] This may be a general problem with international financial and monetary data in that it is often obsolete by the time it is published. But it may be the only data for policy decision-makers to utilize.

Foreign Exchange and Derivatives Data. The discussion in preceding chapters about BIS committee work showed that some of these committees have mandated the BIS to construct databases on activity in international debt markets in addition to exchange-traded and over-the-counter derivatives activity. The BIS, for example, publishes a *Central Bank Survey of Foreign Exchange and Derivatives Market Activity.*

Other Reports. The BIS, as mentioned earlier, manages an intra-central bank statistical database to which central banks which contribute to it have automated access. The BIS also contributes to a joint BIS–IMF–OECD–World Bank publication of external debt statistics on the Internet. In fact, the BIS has produced a very comprehensive web site at www.bis.org.

THE Y2K PROBLEM

The Year 2000 problem, or Y2K as it has been called, has to do with the way in which many personal computers (PCs) and mainframe computers, together with electronic clock and timer-based appliances including bank automatic teller machines, have kept track of years in their internal clocks. They usually use the abbreviation "99" for "1999." This is an acceptable usage but it was found that not all systems realize that the year "00" was supposed to mean "2000" when the millennium arrived. It was speculated that some computers might revert back to the date 1980 and others might revert back to the year 1900. It was also believed that those computers which would recognize the date 2000 might not realize that it would be a leap year.

For most computers manufactured before 1997, this posed a problem. A software application, the date and time is utilized through five connected layers of hardware and software. These include the hardware, the operating system, the software program, data, and date sharing. It was believed that the Y2K problem could affect PCs and mainframes across all five of these layers. Computers and computer networks, it was feared, might simply stop working on January 1, 2000, as dates and date cross-checking would become ambiguous and confused. Programs might fail to work correctly or produce serious errors that would become immediately apparent.

The BIS and Y2K

In September 1997, the BIS published a report, *The Year 2000, A Challenge for Financial Institutions and Bank Supervisors*, through the Basle Committee on Banking Supervision. This report was followed up by the Round Table on the Year 2000 held at the BIS on April 8, 1998, at which a Joint Year 2000 Council (Y2K Council) was established. Senior officials of the Basle Committee on Banking Supervision, the Committee on Payment and Settlement Systems (CPSS), the International Association of Insurance Supervisors (IAIS), and the International Organisation of Securities Commissions (IOSCO) were members of this council. With the advent of the Y2K Council, the BIS stated that it would raise awareness of the Y2K problem by fostering international cooperation and coordination and by maintaining a high awareness of the issue within the supervisory community.

The Y2K Council met in early 1998 and again in summer 1999 to review reports and hear comments of guest analysts on the problem. At one of these gatherings, the Gartner Group, an international information technology research firm, estimated that Y2K problems would affect 50 million computer devices around the world. British Telecommunications reported they would need 1,000 additional staff to check and correct more than 300 million lines of computer code.

The Y2K Council agreed on a range of initiatives in order to promote attention within the global financial supervisory community to the Y2K computer problem. It shared information on regulatory and supervisory strategies and approaches, discussed contingency measures, and served as a central point of contact with national and international private sector initiatives.

The Y2K Council met in London in May 1998 during which meeting the G7 finance ministers gave a mandate to the Council and its sponsoring committees to monitor the global Y2K problem and take any steps to encourage readiness to meet any potential consumer panic or real problems which might affect the international financial system.

The Y2K Council met in July 1999 and formulated a number of initiatives to raise general awareness of the Y2K problem. Some of these initiatives included policy issues such as testing, information sharing and contingency planning; the estabishment of a global database of key Y2K contacts; the organization of regional meetings; and the distribution of a regular newsletter to financial market authorities worldwide.[4]

The Y2K Council established a number of goals. These included the following:

1. promotion of a high level of awareness of the Y2K computer challenge within the global financial supervisory community;
2. the sharing of information on regulatory and supervisory strategies and approaches;
3. discussion of possible contingency measures; and
4. service as a point of contact with national and international private sector initiatives dealing with the Y2K problem.

The Y2K Council designated several projects to be implemented during the last two years of the decade. These included:

1. provision of a forum for the disclosure of the status of global financial market preparations for Y2K;
2. encouragement of all payment and settlement systems, clearing houses, exchanges, and other parts of the global financial market infrastructure to make publicly available information on their preparatory efforts and testing programs;
3. regular meetings with an external consultative committee comprised of organizations or associations with an international perspective on Y2K preparations;
4. development of a global supervisory contact list for the Y2K challenge that included a coordinating contact covering as many countries as possible;
5. support, co-sponsoring, and provision of assistance in planning further conferences and roundtables on the Y2K challenge in different regions of the world;
6. facilitation of exchanges of information related to Y2K testing programs within the international financial system;
7. encouragement of coordinated cross-border testing to the maximum extent possible;
8. development of a series of publicly available working papers on different aspects of the Y2K issue.

Problems with the BIS Y2K Work. The major problem with the BIS Y2K function was the limited means available to the BIS and the Y2K Council. The Y2K Council was criticized for being a loosely organized body which did not have the authority to enforce its Y2K promulgations as did the U.S. Federal Reserve System and the U.S. Federal Deposit Insurance Corporation.[5] The Y2K Council relied primarily on the media and its contacts with financial institutions to enforce its findings. The Council regarded the fostering of cooperation as its major objective.

The end of the decade neared and the outlook seemed gloomy for the international financial and banking community. Credit and swaps spreads rose in anticipation of the closing of global financial markets in December 1999. Borrowers and bankers became nervous about anticipated liquidity and short-term funding shortages. Central banks went on standby as lenders-of-last-resort. The financial community came to believe that contingency plans formulated by banks and businesses were more dangerous than the computer problem.[6]

The Y2K problem came and went. Very few significant disruptions to domestic or international commerce or banking occurred. The major cost was incurred in the plans and staffing developed during the last few years of the 1990s to alleviate the Y2K problem. It remains unclear to what extent the BIS was instrumental in the avoidance of a major global disaster from the effects of the Y2K problem. The work of the BIS and its Y2K Council did help central banks and the international bank supervisory authorities to prepare for the direst of contingencies. Historians may, in years to come, conclude that no serious problem was ever present and that the paranoia may have been worse than the supposed problem. At any rate, the downturn in profits and stock market prices of the computer, semiconductor, and computer chip manufacturers in 2001 probably stemmed from the advanced purchase of new equipment in the latter part of the 20th century. This overkill in purchasing by high-tech users no doubt led to an oversupply of everything from servers to computers to chips. The BIS did little to predict this phenomenon.

OTHER BIS ACTIVITIES

The BIS activities include a variety of miscellaneous meetings and other groups which have been established for specific reasons. These include meetings with G10 central bank governors and other officials and the work of the Financial Stability Institute, the Financial Stability Forum, and the Joint Forum. These activities are discussed in the following sections.

Miscellaneous Meetings and Activities

Since the relationship with the G10 central banks was initiated by the BIS, meetings of various types have been hosted by the BIS in Basle. For example, in the 1960s and early 1970s, the currency markets underwent a great deal of turbulence when the pound sterling and the U.S. dollar were devalued. The G10 governors met at the BIS on Sundays in what were referred to as "Basle weekends." The news media covered these meetings intensively during a time when the BIS received more publicity than at any time in its history.[7]

The BIS has been involved in other activities aside from the research and data analysis function which have broadened its focus on cooperative efforts to the maintainence of international financial stability. In 1994, the BIS organized periodic meetings of central bankers on the subjects of financial and exchange market volatility, inflation risks in the economic boom of that period, and the impact of financial structure on the methodology for transmitting monetary policy. The BIS has hosted meetings of this type throughout the past few decades.

The Financial Stability Institute. The BIS established the Financial Stability Institute (FSI). One of the major functions to be performed by this group is the training of bank supervisors for national banking authorities. The FSI will continuously update the training of these banking supervisors.

The Financial Stability Forum. The Financial Stability Forum was founded in February 1999.[8] This international cooperative platform was proposed by the G7 finance ministers and central banks. It furnishes a means for discussion at regular meetings to appraise issues which affect the international financial system and to present solutions to these problems. The Forum is comprised of 35 high-level officials from national and international financial institutions. Among its members are top officials from the IAIS, the major subject of Chapter 10.

The Financial Stability Forum was established to strengthen international cooperation and coordination in financial market supervision and surveillance. The 35 members are from G7 finance ministries, central banks, and supervisory authorities, the IMF, the

World Bank, the Basle Committee on Bank Supervision, the Organisation for Economic Cooperation and Development, the CPSS, IOSCO, and the Committee on the Global Financial System. The General Manager of the BIS chairs the group.

The Joint Forum. The Joint Forum was established in 1996 as a platform for discussion of supervisory issues which stem from the emergence of financial conglomerates and the blurring of distinctions among the banking, securities, and insurance sectors. Its secretariat is located at the BIS and is comprised of senior insurance, banking, and securities supervisors representing each supervisory constituency. Representatives come from 13 countries including Australia, Belgium, Canada, France, Germany, Italy, Japan, the Netherlands, Spain, Sweden, Switzerland, the United Kingdom, and the United States. It is essentially a forum for coordination of information sharing among the three major BIS groups: the Basle Committee on Bank Supervision, the IAIS, and IOSCO.[9]

The Joint Forum has discussed a number of supervisory issues in its short life. Its members have examined a means to exchange information between supervisors within their own sector and between supervisors in different sectors. It has investigated legal and other barriers which impede the exchange of information between supervisors within and between different sectors. The Joint Forum has formulated principles for more effective supervision of regulated firms within financial conglomerates. It has focused on large-scale financial conglomerates with international operations but its findings have general application to small companies which only operate nationally.[10]

During 1999, the Joint Forum produced a number of documents for supervisory authorities. Among these were: (1) a note on intra-group transactions and exposures and risk concentrations principles; (2) a paper on intra-group transactions and exposures principles; and (3) risk concentrations principles.[11]

SUMMARY AND CONCLUSIONS

The BIS has furnished the international financial system with monetary and financial data in many forms for the past several decades. Its Monetary and Economic Department is responsible for the compilation and analysis of this data. In addition, the BIS has taken on other issues with the objectives of alleviation or solution of a potential problem which might affect the stability of the international banking system. The Y2K issue was one of those problems for which the BIS took a leadership position.

The BIS *Annual Report* is the major product of this research process. The international banking and financial community awaits its annual publication with a great deal of anticipation. Published in many languages, it presents data and analysis of international financial operations by national governments and the international financial markets, including those for debt instruments, foreign exchange, and derivatives.

BIS Economic Papers are published by the BIS or in research journals and other outlets. These papers are aimed at central bankers, national bank supervisory officials, bank management, as well as academicians. They have contributed to national policy making with regard to banking and financial market activities.

The BIS has developed a variety of databases for monetary and financial data. Some of these have been mandated by the BIS/G10 committees and they cover a variety of issues. Those concerned with foreign exchange and derivatives activities are valuable resources for central bank officials, bank management, and academicians in the formulation of monetary and financial policy and the implementation of research projects in these areas.

The data and papers published by the BIS and its constituent committees is quite easy to access. In addition to their depth, the products published by the BIS Monetary and Economic Department can be found, in most cases, on the BIS web site. The contributions produced by this function may be the most underrated part of the activities of the BIS.

In a specific issue area, the Y2K problem was feared by governments and banking supervisory authorities to disrupt the international financial system and result in possible severe losses for the global economy. The BIS formed a Joint 2000 Council to deal with the problem from the viewpoint of central banks and bank supervisory authorities.

This council was comprised of senior officials from the Basle Committee on Banking Supervision, the Committee on Payment and Settlement Systems, the International Association of Insurance Supervisors, and the International Organisation of Securities Commissions. This cooperative effort resulted in meetings, reports, objectives, and the formulation of a strategy to deal with any Y2K contingencies.

The Y2K problem did not materialize into a disruption of the international financial system or lead to noticeable instability among financial institutions and markets, domestically or internationally. However, this favorable result to the speculated problems might have been the result of the work of many international and national governmental institutions and agencies as well as private companies in their formulation of objectives, plans, and strategies with which to cope with this issue. The BIS and the Joint 2000 Council certainly contributed in a positive way to a solution to this once-in-a-century problem. Without the planning recommended by these groups and by central banks and other institutions around the world, the international information technology system might have incurred a serious breakdown.

NOTES

1. Morris Goldstein and Philip Turner, "Banking Crises in Emerging Economies: Origins and Policy Options," BIS Economic Papers, No. 46, October 1996, pp. 1–67.

2. "Global Capital Markets Might Behave Differently in the 1990s, Says BIS Study," IMF Survey, Vol. 20 (June 24, 1991), p. 198.

3. Anthony Saunders, Financial Institutions Management (Burr Ridge, IL: Irwin McGraw-Hill, 2000), p. 339.

4. Bank for International Settlements, "Press Release for the Joint Year 2000 Council's Round Table Meeting," July 1, 1999.

5. Marius Meland, "Y2K: Foreign Banks Lag," at http://www.forbes.com/1999/03/11/mu9.html.

6. Marcus Walker, "Nothing to Fear but Fear Itself," Euromoney, September 1999, pp. 34–38.

7. Melvyn Westlake, "Into Basle's Inner Sanctum," The Banker, Vol. 144 (March 1994), p. 16.

8. "Financial Stability Forum," found at http://www.iaisweb.org/1/inter/061.html, April 16, 2001, p. 1.

9. "The Joint Forum," found at http://www.iaisweb.org/1/inter/062.html, April 16, 2001, pp. 1–4.

10. Ibid.

11. Ibid., p. 2.

CHAPTER 12

Nazi Gold, the Bank for International Settlements, and Central Banks

INTRODUCTION

During the 1930s preceding World War II, the BIS operated according to its principal objectives: (1) to promote central bank cooperation; (2) to provide additional facilities for international financial operations; and (3) to act as trustee or agent with regard to international financial settlements, including the facilitation of reparations payments by Germany. After the international financial crisis of 1931 and the advent of world depression, the German reparation payments were suspended.

In the years leading up to World War II, the BIS focused on its promotion of central bank cooperation and the provision of banking facilities to its member central banks. The latter function included a wide variety of banking services for central banks. These operations included the following: (1) management and investment of the BIS' resources; (2) receipt of interest on these investments and payment of interest to central banks on their deposits with the BIS; (3) grants of monetary and commercial credits to central banks; (4) foreign exchange operations for central banks; (5) gold transactions for central banks; (6) settlement of international postal payments; and (7) payment of dividends to its shareholders.

Gold transactions mentioned above was the area in which the BIS performed what some claim were illegal or, at the least, unethical operations. The BIS offices in Basle did not have the facilities to store and handle gold. Its central deposits permitted the BIS to carry out numerous gold transactions for its customers. These transactions included sales, purchases, exchanges, and transportation of gold in and between various gold markets. The BIS would occasionally organize the physical transportation of gold from one depository to another. The BIS shipped much of this gold from Europe to New York during the years leading up to the war for safekeeping purposes. Shipments to New York were made by the BIS on behalf of the central banks of Belgium, Estonia, France, the Netherlands, Norway, Poland, Switzerland, and the United Kingdom. Thus, these were the type of gold transactions executed by the BIS during the 1930s.

EUROPEAN CENTRAL BANKS AND THE NAZI REGIME

Central banks from neutral countries entered into business transactions with the Nazi regime during World War II. These included Switzerland, Sweden, Spain, Portugal, and Turkey, among others. These activities will be discussed in the following sections.

Swiss Banking Crisis

In 1997, the Swiss banking industry in cooperation with the World Jewish Council and the U.S. Government publicly announced what many had suspected. Switzerland has always maintained a high level of neutrality with other nations, particularly European countries. Geography contributed to this perception of neutrality in the form of the mountain range separating Switzerland from the rest of Europe. In addition, the country had prided itself in having a strong military force. These factors seemed to have protected Switzerland from World War II, although it appears plausible that the German military machine could have overrun Switzerland just as it did Poland and Czechoslovakia.

However, financial collaboration with the Nazi government ruling Germany may have been a more significant protectant. The Swiss banking industry publicly admitted the confiscation of accounts opened by German Jews prior to the war. The industry also acknowledged its participation in the handling and re-smelting of gold that had been received from Germany after allegedly being stolen from other countries or from victims of the Holocaust.

Much of this gold had been melted down and made into new bars of gold with incorrect stampings from mints of the countries that the Nazi regime had already captured. Swiss so-called neutral banks as well as the BIS permitted the German regime to reprocess gold that it had stolen from other governments or, at least, they overlooked the practice. It is also alleged that at the end of the war, gold stolen from Holocaust victims was melted down, mixed with other less tainted gold, and formed into new bars of gold.

The Allies contributed to the crisis. In the shipping process, the Allies combined the two types of gold, that is, official or "purer" gold and that which had been mixed containing victims' gold. The Allies neglected to perform the work of separating the "purer" gold from the victims' gold. Some gold bars in circulation today may still contain a mixture of victims' gold. The victims' gold would have contained gold from dental fillings, wedding rings, and personal property.

The BIS did not knowingly, it was presumed, perform this function for the Nazi government. It was expected to be a neutral forum for international financial and banking firms in the execution of its gold transactions as a cooperative international financial institution working within its by-laws. To knowingly assist the Nazis in these transactions would have undermined the financial security of its member central banks. However, as declassified documentation has been released in later years, the presumption of innocence seems somewhat strained.

In December 1939 after the outbreak of the war in Europe, the BIS issued a document which was essentially a code of conduct for the institution for the duration of the war. It stated that the BIS would only do those activities which were above reproach by either belligerents or neutrals. In fact, the BIS had suspended meetings of its governors during this period.[1]

The code of conduct stated that the BIS would not carry out any transaction for the central bank of a belligerent country with another country with which the belligerent was at war. In addition, the document stated that the BIS would abstain from holding, in its own name, gold for the account of the central bank of a belligerent country that was earmarked for the latter's use or other assets on the market of another nation with which the belligerent country was at war. Thus, the BIS supposedly was to carry on no banking operations involving the central banks or financial markets of countries at war with one another. It was to reduce its operations to only those which would safeguard the pre-war financial interests of its members in its capacity as a neutral institution.

Swedish Central Banks

During World War II, Sweden was classified as a neutral country. However, the nation carried on trade with Nazi Germany until the late stages of the war. According to Stuart Eizenstat in his on-the-record briefing at the release of a U.S. Department of State report,[2] Sweden furnished most of Germany's iron ore requirements, especially high-grade iron ore for steelmaking. Sweden also furnished much of Germany's ball bearings supply.

By early 1943, Ivar Rooth, Head of the Swedish Central Bank, 1929–1948, and also a BIS Board member, became concerned that the gold transferred to Sweden by the Nazis to pay for iron ore and other goods was stolen gold. The Foreign Ministry informed Rooth that Emil Puhl, the Nazi official at the BIS, had guaranteed that all gold sold by Germany to Sweden was of pre-war origin. As will be discussed later, the Nazis were experts at melting stolen gold into new bars with pre-war stampings. Thus, Rooth, as well as Dag Hammarskjöld, then Swedish secretary of state in the finance ministry, Chariman of the Central Bank executive board, and later United Nations Secretary-General, used the Puhl statement throughout the war to justify Sweden's gold transactions with the Nazis. The Swedish Central Bank did not refuse Nazi gold because it was used to regulate the clearing balance between the two countries.[3]

By the beginning of 1944, the Swedish Central Bank must have suspected the institution was dealing with looted gold. For example, Rooth knew that 288,000 kilos of gold had been sent to Berlin from the French colony of Senegal. Various central banks including Belgium had deposited gold with the French national bank. Before the French collapse in 1940, the gold had been shipped to Senegal. The Nazis pressured the Vichy French to send the gold to Berlin where it was remolded into new ingots with pre-war stamps and certificates of authenticity. Of this, 20,000 kilos were considered at risk for being stolen by the Nazis.[4]

After the Tripartite Gold Commission investigation of 1946, Sweden was pressured into returning 7,152 kilos of gold to the Belgian national bank. German documents showed that the Nazis had stolen 32,000 kilos of Dutch gold florins. This was part of the gold shipped to Sweden. Sweden later repaid 6,000 kilos of gold to the Netherlands. These repayments represent only 65 percent of the 20,000 kilos of gold at maximum risk of being stolen.[5]

The Swedes just kept buying Nazi gold and did not ask whether it had been stolen. The important question is whether the Swedish Central Bank acted in good faith during the war or was it aware that it was buying stolen gold? Circumstantial evidence points to illegal activities by a sovereign neutral in this case.

Other Neutrals' Activities[6]

Other so-called neutrals carried out trade with the Nazis in return for looted gold. Turkey, for example, furnished much of Germany's needs in chromate, used to harden steel for armor. In 1943, 100 percent of Germany's chromate was obtained from Turkey in return for gold.

Germany obtained wolfram, from which tungsten is produced and which is used to harden steel, from Spain and Portugal. From 50 to 100 percent of Germany's wolfram supplies came from these two countries.

In addition to these shipments of manufacturing inputs, these neutrals also acted in other questionable ways. For example, Spain furnished troops to fight with the German Wehrmacht on the Russian front. On the other hand, Spain offered refuge to Jews fleeing Nazi persecution. Portugal granted use of the Azores islands to the Allies for air bases. Sweden allowed German troops to regularly move through its countryside.

Again officials of these countries rationalized their trade with the Nazis as self-protection. If they did not deal with the Nazis, they feared being occupied. On the other hand, the several investigations discussed in this chapter show that these countries did not cooperate very well after the war to find the looted assets and make restitution. It seems that they did so only under extreme pressure and the overall restitution has fallen far short of the magnitude of the Nazi looting.

BIS GOLD OPERATIONS DURING WORLD WAR II

The BIS continued to execute gold transactions for its members during World War II but on a reduced scale. Between September 1,

1939, and May 8, 1945, the BIS reported that it purchased 71,205 kilograms of fine gold from 16 different central banks or international institutions and sold 60,096 kilograms of fine gold to 13 different central banks or international institutions.[7] Many of these nations were, according to their governments, acknowledged neutral countries although they traded with the Nazis with gold transferred by the BIS. These nations included Sweden, Spain, Portugal, Argentina, Turkey, France, Great Britain, Poland, Hungary, and the United States. Some of these countries were belligerents.[8]

After 1942, the BIS reported significantly diminished transactions in gold. Of the gold transactions reported above, the BIS data reports that 5,480 kilograms of fine gold was sold to the German Reichsbank and 9,142 kilograms of fine gold was purchased by the BIS from the German Reichsbank.[9]

Thus, the BIS did enter into gold and currency transactions with Nazi Germany through its participation with the Reichsbank. Did it knowingly violate both its stated neutrality as well as its own published code of conduct? The answer to this question remains for historians to decide. Some speculative opinions will be offered later in this chapter.

It may be more important at this time to review the unconditional surrender of Germany after World War I and the agreement to the Treaty of Versailles which the country signed. Germany was committed to large war reparations—the settlement of which was facilitated by the BIS—and agreed to possess no arms except those necessary to maintain order within the country. From the beginning, the Nazis in Germany disregarded the peace agreements. An official of that country who became influential in the purchase of armaments with credit arrangements was Hjamnar Schacht, who also completely supported the establishment of the BIS. He would become economic minister at the beginning of the Nazi political reign in Germany.

Schacht created two sets of books in the 1930s. One would be accurate and the other would hide the fact that Germany had begun to rebuild its gold reserves, a violation of the Treaty of Versailles. By 1939, he had become instrumental in placing high-ranking Nazi officials and foreign collaborators on the BIS Board of Directors. Much of this early history of the BIS comes close to the inference that the German government planned to use a BIS-type institution for its financial transactions from the very beginning. Thus far, no direct evidence has been found to suggest that the Germans had such a plan in 1930.

Thomas McKittrick was a U.S. citizen, Harvard University graduate, and President of the BIS during the war years. His friends on the BIS Board included Emil Puhl, a Nazi, and Per Jacobssen, a Swede from a neutral country and who would later become head of the IMF.[10] McKittrick was suspected by Allied authorities of helping Axis countries acquire funds the U.S. government had tried to freeze. He maintained the BIS was neutral and that no looted gold was held by the BIS. The U.S. Office of Strategic Services, the forerunner of the Central Intelligence Agency, had found evidence that McKittrick had collaborated with the Nazis.[11] A report given to President Bill Clinton alleged that the Axis powers had virtually taken over the BIS.[12]

McKittrick's friends also had interesting backgrounds. Puhl was Deputy Head of the Reichsbank from 1939 to 1945 and was jailed for five years after the war for his role in the theft of valuables from Holocaust victims. He served only six months of the sentence and then took a job in a Hamburg bank. Jacobssen worked for the League of Nations as a financial expert during 1920–1928 and then for the BIS for period 1931–1956. He also served as head of the IMF from 1956–1963.

The U.S. government tried to close the BIS in 1944 as a result of McKittrick's behavior. At that time, among the BIS' leading customers were the Reichsbank and Portuguese government representatives. Gold was transferred by the BIS from the former to the latter which furnished war materiel to the Nazis.[13]

After the war, McKittrick was appointed to a high level position at Chase Manhattan Bank. Jacobssen, as mentioned above, became head of the IMF. And for nearly 50 years, the operations involving the BIS and Swiss banks and looted assets by the Nazis were hidden in classified documents.

The fact that Nazi officials were members of the BIS Board has never been related with any gold or currency transactions between the BIS and Nazi Germany. The United States monitored Swiss involvement with the Nazi government from the beginning of the war. The U.S. Treasury Department tracked Nazi gold as it moved in and out of the BIS. Several of these transactions were found to have occurred between the BIS and major Swiss banks. From these Swiss banks, money was used by the Nazis to purchase war materiel or was wired to accounts in Spain, Argentina, and the Middle East.

During World War II, the German Reichsbank often deposited new gold with the BIS. Before 1940, the deposits were either done on the Reichsbank's earmarked gold or gold sight account with the BIS which was held at the Swiss National Bank in Berne, Switzerland. These transactions occurred in two steps. First, the gold was sent by the Reichsbank to its own gold account held with the Swiss National Bank in Berne. Second, by order of the Reichsbank, it was transferred to the gold accounts held with the BIS. On one occasion, a deposit of new gold received by the BIS from the Reichsbank was made in 1945 near the end of the war. The deposit amounted to 1,525 kilograms of fine gold at the disposal of the BIS at the Reichsbankknebenstelle in Konstanz, Germany. The shipment was comprised of gold bars and coins. The Swiss authorities refused the physical transport of the gold from Germany to Switzerland but it was held under earmark in the name of the BIS and remained blocked in Konstanz until after the war.

The Reichsbank also participated in the international postal payments system through gold sight accounts held with the BIS by central banks. The Reichsbank also held a gold sight account with the BIS in London in 1939. This account was transferred to the Swiss National Bank in Berne later that year. During the war, the Reichsbank's gold sight account for international postal settlements was credited with gold transfers from the central banks of Argentina, Denmark, Estonia, Finland, Hungary, and Norway.

During the war, the BIS sold gold to the Reichsbank on a number of occasions. Overall, the BIS sold a total of 5,479 kilograms of fine gold to the Reichsbank. New deposits of fine gold totaling 13,542 kilograms were received from the Reichsbank. Of this, 9,649 kilograms was transferred by the BIS in various amounts to the National Banks of Romania, Yugoslavia, Bulgaria, Portugal, and the Swiss National Bank. The remaining 3,893 kilograms remained in the possession of the BIS at the end of World War II.

After the War

After the war ended, the Allies determined that the Germans had begun the war with a gold reserve amounting to US$120 million and had seized in excess of US$600 million in gold from occupied countries. In other words, this was primarily looted gold. Neutral countries such as Switzerland had accepted looted gold from the Nazis.[14] Allies estimated that the Germans had sold US$300 million in gold to Swiss banks and had laundered some US$140 million through Swiss banks for payment of goods from Portugal and Spain.

A reparation conference was held in Paris in late 1945. At this conference, the Allies established procedures for the restitution of gold looted by the Germans from European central banks. An international refugee organization established procedures for the restitution of non-monetary gold items such as watches and rings to individuals and groups of individuals. The identification of the victims of this looting was very difficult since many of these people died in the death camps.

The Tripartite Gold Commission

A Tripartite Gold Commission was established in September 1946 in accordance with the decisions of the Paris Reparations Agreement of January 1946. This body was located in Brussels, Belgium, and was authorized to review and settle claims from governments for the restitution of looted monetary gold recovered in Germany or acquired from the neutral countries in their negotiations with the Allies. Representatives from the United States, Great Britain, and France made up the Commission. Claims from 10 nations were received by the Commission. They were Albania, Austria, Belgium, Czechoslovakia, Greece, Italy, Luxembourg, the Netherlands, Poland, and Yugoslavia.

The BIS opened its books to the Commission after the war for the restitution of monetary gold. Of the 13,542 kilograms of fine gold delivered by the Reichsbank to the BIS during the war, captured records of the Reichsbank and the Prussian Mint showed that 3,740 kilograms of this had been looted by the Germans from the central banks of the Netherlands, Belgium, and Italy. Much of this had been resmelted and stamped with pre-war dates at the Prussian Mint. The BIS agreed to make restitution for this gold, worth about US $39 million today, to the Tripartite Gold Commission.

Commission's First Distribution. The Commission made its first distribution in 1947 with payments totaling US$143 million to Belgium, France, Luxembourg, and the Netherlands. In 1948, a second round of payments was made to Austria, Czechoslovakia, Italy, and Yugoslavia. Some US$550 million of looted gold was estimated to be owed to claimants. Of this, only US$78 million was turned over to the monetary gold pool at the Tripartite Gold Commission. Germany also held external assets in Switzerland, Spain, Portugal, and Sweden at the end of the war. Only US$128 million of this was liquidated for the Allies and war reconstuction in Europe.[15]

As recently as 1996, a payment was made to Albania. A total of US$380 million has been made to claimant nations. This is worth about US$44 billion in today's prices. It has been estimated that claimant countries have received about 65 percent of their original claims, since claims have exceeded the recovered looted gold. The Commission still controls about US$70 million at today's gold prices in the Federal Reserve Bank of New York and the Bank of England.

Disclosure Decree

In 1962, the Swiss Federal Council passed a bill referred to as the Disclosure Decree. It mandated a search for Holocaust victims' assets in Swiss banks and other fiduciaries, insurance companies, and related enterprises.[16] The goal of this decree was to find accounts for which nothing had been heard from depositors since May 9, 1945. Claimants had five years to submit a claim and the entire process would last ten years. Only 26 of 500 Swiss banks responded to the search. The process found only US$7 million.[17] Paul Volcker, former Chairman of the U.S. Federal Reserve Board, stated that auditors had found that Swiss banks had not been truthful with Swiss government investigators during the 1962 search.[18] The search process had been administered by the same banks which may have hidden looted assets. At any rate, the process was later considered a sham.

Further Developments

Two further developments concerning transactions in Nazi gold during World War II occurred in the late 1990s and shed further light on what really happened during that time. These were a conference convened in Washington, D.C., whose major topic was Holocaust-era assets and a Swiss commission chaired by a Swiss citizen, Professor Jean-François Bergier. The highlights from these events are discussed in the following sections.

Washington Conference on Holocaust-Era Assets. U.S. Senator Alfonse d'Amato of New York discussed the problem of Nazi looting of Holocaust victims with the head of the World Jewish Congress in 1996. His contention was that Switzerland did not return all of the money it held during the war belonging to Jews who died during the Holocaust. This meeting was followed by international pressure which led to an internal investigation. Banks then discovered another US$37 million in dormant accounts held since the end of the war. This finding resulted in a renewal of interest in German looted gold and the assets of Holocaust victims.

The U.S. Department of State and the United States Holocaust Memorial Museum co-hosted an Organizing Seminar to prepare for the Washington Conference on Holocaust-Era Assets. This conference was held in late 1998 at the Department of State. The goals of the conference organizers was to provide a forum so the global community could seek a consensus on the methodology of examining Nazi-era injustices as they related to specific asset categories.[19] These asset categories included gold, art, insurance, and other assets such as archives and libraries, bonds, securities, and communal property.

The Organizing Seminar summarized each asset category in terms of the activities around the world. This record is shown in Figure 12.1.

In Switzerland, an Independent Commission estimated that US$444 million (US$4 billion in today's dollars) in looted gold was transferred to or through Switzerland during the war years. This report further estimated that US$82 million of that was taken from individuals including US$2.9 million from Nazi victims. Reports from Portuguese, Spanish, Swedish, as well as U.S., British, and Swiss institutions fully established the role of Swiss financial institutions, particularly the Swiss National Bank, in financing and facilitating wartime commerce in Europe by receiving Nazi-looted gold and converting it into hard currencies. Switzerland seemed to be at the heart of the gold transactions.[20]

Bergier Commission. An Independent Commission of Experts: Switzerland—Second World War was commissioned in 1998 in Switzerland.[21] It was referred to as the Bergier Commission for its chairperson, Jean-François Bergier. This group investigated the Swiss role in transactions with the Nazis. The group released a report on gold activities on May 25, 1998.[22] The Bergier Commission report went further than U.S. estimates about the amount of gold transferred by the Nazis to the Swiss National Bank.

The report stated that evidence showed the governing board of the Swiss National Bank knew they were dealing in looted gold at an early point in the war. The Bergier Report estimated that US$440 million gold went to Switzerland, higher than the U.S. estimate of US$414 million of total looted and non-looted gold. Of the US$440

Figure 12.1
**Asset-by-Asset Activities Organizing Seminar, Washington
Conference on Holocaust-Era Assets (June 30, 1998)**

Gold

1) Italy established a commission to investigate wartime banking activities

2) Greece announced the opening of the archives of its Finance Ministry

3) Several delegations called for an opening of Vatican archives

4) Attention was given to the Romani community which had suffered from Nazi atrocities

5) Norway pledged US$60 million for a Holocaust victims restitution fund

6) A move was made to consolidate the Swiss Bergier Commission and U.S. gold reports

7) Creation of a central web site was proposed to link the sites of individual countries

Art

1) Less than half of the 220,000 works of art stolen during World War II were recovered and restituted

2) Association of Art Museum Directors announced guidelines for Nazi-confiscated art

3) Lithuania asked the Council of Europe to create similar guidelines

Insurance

1) Officials of the National Association of Insurance Commissioners discussed the complexities surrounding the investigation of insurance policies purchased before World War II

2) Germany announced its own investigation of wartime and post-war insurance activities

3) Allianz Insurance Company officials discussed their internal records investigation

Other Assets

1) Belgian investigation of gems

2) Delegates ask for investigation of communal property

3) Germany asked to do research of and make restitution of savings to slave laborers

4) Investigation suggested of theft and sales of victims' clothing and other personal belongings

Source: "Summary of the Organizing Seminar for the Washington Conference on Holocaust-Era Assets, Appendix A," June 30, 1998, pp. 913–914.

million estimated by the Bergier Commission, US$316 million was estimated to have been stolen gold.

The Bergier Commission recorded the gold movements of the Reichsbank including those to the Swiss National Bank, gold sales and purchases of the Swiss National Bank, and gold shipped to Swiss commercial banks by the Reichsbank. These data are found in Tables 12.1, 12.2, 12.3, 12.4, and 12.5.

How Nazis Laundered Gold

It has been alleged that the Nazis laundered gold looted from central banks and individuals during World War II. Investigative efforts by the Allies and other groups have speculated about how this occurred. After the annexation of Austria in 1938, the Nazi government confiscated the Austrian gold reserves and transferred them to the Reichsbank. The gold was then deposited in the German account at BIS. Gold stolen from Czechoslovakia was obtained in a more creative manner. This gold was deposited in Czechoslovakia's account in the Bank of England, supposedly to protect it from the war. Several days later, the Czech government sent a request to the Bank of England to transfer the gold to Germany's account. No one at the Bank of England apparently challenged this decision. At the time, the Bank of England was managed by a Nazi sympathizer, Montagu Norman, who had been a member of the BIS Board.

In addition to these transactions, the BIS allowed Nazi Germany to use this gold to make payments on loans it had obtained from the BIS. Thus, Germany was able to avoid defaulting on their loans and actually maintained the only financially stable European government during World War II.

Nazi Rationale. German rationalization for the gold transactions in Switzerland was voiced at the Nuremberg war crimes trial by Walther Funk, former member of the BIS Board and former President of the Reichsbank, who said that countries with which the Germans had done business introduced gold embargoes. Sweden refused to accept gold at all. Switzerland was the only country with which the Germans could change gold into foreign currency.[23]

However, several post-war commissions have demonstrated a more vicious reason for the behavior of the Nazi regime. That government used the looted gold and funds to "deliberately and ruthlessly" finance its war machine.[24] Without these funds, Nazi

Table 12.1

Gold Transactions of the Reichsbank (September 1, 1939–June 30, 1945) (in US$ millions)

I.	Initial Holdings	
Published Reserves		31.1
Secret Reserves		82.7
Other German Bank Notes		12.1
Austrian Gold Reserves		99.0
Czechoslovak Gold Reserves		33.8
Total		*258.7*

II. Gold from other Central Banks

National Bank of Netherlands	137.2
National Bank of Belgium	225.9
National Bank of Luxembourg	4.8
National Bank of Hungary	32.2
National Bank of Italy	64.8
Other Central Banks	10.1
Total	*475.0*

III. Gold from Individuals

Four-Year-Plan Activity	71.8
"Melmer-Gold"	2.5
Other Private Holdings	71.7
Total	*146.0*

IV. Purchases of Gold Abroad

Soviet Union	23.0
Japan	4.2
Bank for Int'l Settlements	2.3
Total	*29.5*

Total	**909.2**

V. Holdings at the End of the War

Gold Recovered in Germany	198.0
Gold from Italy	64.8
Gold from Hungary	32.2
Total	*295.0*

VI. Gold Shipped Abroad

Swiss National Bank	389.2
Swiss Commercial Banks	61.2
Other Foreign Banks:	
National Bank of Belgium	9.1
National Bank of Netherlands	2.2
Swedish Riksbank	4.6
National Bank of the USSR	7.0
Central Bank of the Turkish Republic	5.7
Consorzio Italiano Estero Aero	5.6
National Bank of Italy	3.6
National Bank of Croatia	0.4
National Bank of Romania	54.2
Reichsbank Branches Abroad	51.5
Total	*594.3*

VII. Domestic Commercial Use

Degussa	3.3
Sponholz & Co.	3.4
Deutsche Bank	3.6
Dresdner Bank	3.9
Total	*14.2*

VIII. Government Use

Auswaertiges Amt	3.1
Amtsgruppe Ausland Abwehr	2.2
Reichssicherheitshauptamt	0.1
Wehrmacht	0.3
Total	*5.7*

Total	**909.2**

Source: Independent Commission of Experts Switzerland—Second World War, *Gold Transactions in the Second World War: Statistical Review with Commentary* (Berne, Switzerland: Bergier Commission, December 1997), p. 5.

Table 12.2
Gold Transfers of the Reichsbank to the Swiss National Bank (1939–1945) (in millions of Swiss francs)

Year	Reichsbank to Switzerland (Reichsbank) (1)	Swiss Trade Statistics (supplemented) (2)	Swiss Trade Statistics (Rings) (3)	Shipments from Reichsbank to depot at Swiss National Bank in Berne (SNB figures) (4)
1939	0	17.1	16.8	0
1940	222.0	126.3	125.9	103.2
1941	349.9	279.4	268.9	192.9
1942	493.2	474.6	458.4	497.5
1943	609.3	596.9	588.9	588.0
1944	275.4	258.2	258.2	257.3
1945	0	15.8	15.8	15.7
Total only 1940–1945	1,949.8	1,751.2	1,716.1	1,654.6

(1) Shipments from Constance in Spring 1945 have not been recorded here.
(2) Column (3) supplemented by industrial gold (excluding 1944 and 1945).
(3) Only gold for banking transactions 1940–1945 according to Rings 1996 provided by the Swiss Federal Archives.
(4) Incoming transfers from Berlin according to a press documentation of the Swiss National Bank.

Source: Independent Commission of Experts Switzerland—Second World War, *Gold Transactions in the Second World War: Statistical Review with Commentary* (Berne, Switzerland: Bergier Commission, December 4, 1997), p. 12.

Table 12.3
Gold Sales and Purchases of the Swiss National Bank (September 1, 1939–June 30, 1945) (thousands of Sfr and US$)

	Sfr Purchases	$Purchase	Sfr Sales	$ Sales
I. Gold Reserves (September 1, 1939)				
	Sfr2,860,224	$660,758	Sfr4,626,300	$1,068,750
II. Axis				
Germany	1,231,850	284,577	19,495	4,504
Italy	150,036	34,661	0	0
Japan	0	0	4,956	1,145
Total	*1,381,886*	*319,238*	*24,451*	*5,649*
III. Allies				
United States	2,242,917	518,150	706,055	163,110
Great Britain	668,454	154,424	0	0
Canada	65,283	15,081	0	0
Total	*2,976,654*	*687,655*	*706,055*	*163,110*
IV. Other countries purchasing gold				
Portugal	85,101	19,660	536,601	123,964
Spain	0	0	185,149	42,772
Rumania	9,757	2,254	112,093	25,895
Hungary	0	0	16,740	3,867
Slovakia	0	0	11,254	2,600
Turkey	0	0	14,847	3,430
Total	*94,857*	*21,914*	*876,684*	*202,528*
V. Other countries selling gold				
Argentina	33,585	7,759	0	0
France	193,261	44,646	0	0
Greece	486	112	0	0
Sweden	94,520	21,836	20,009	4,622
Total	*321,851*	*74,353*	*20,009*	*4,622*
VI. Various				
BIS	61,508	14,209	18,201	4,205
Swiss Banks, industrial & other clients	71,206	16,450	701,198	161,988

Swiss Confederation	269,305	62,214	1,087,873	251,316
Swiss Mint	42,150	9,737	45,794	10,579
Total	*444,168*	*102,610*	*1,853,065*	*428,088*
VII. Corrections				
Correction in sale of gold on the market	39,085	9,029	0	0
Differences in weight	3	1	87	20
Revaluation transactions Sep 1, 1939–Dec 31, 1939	0	0	8,729	2,017
Other differences	0	0	3,350	774
Total	*39,088*	*9,030*	*12,166*	*2,811*
Total Purchases and Sales	5,258,504	1,214,800	3,492,431	806,808
Total	**8,118,728**	**1,875,558**	**8,118,731**	**1,875,558**

Source: Independent Commission of Experts Switzerland—Second World War, *Gold Transactions in the Second World War: Statistical Review with Commentary* (Berne, Switzerland: Bergier Commission, December 4, 1997), p. 14.

Table 12.4
Gold Transactions of the Reichsbank via the Swiss National Bank
(1940–1945) (millions of Swiss francs)

Inflows	1940	1941	1942	1943	1944	1945	Total
Transfers from Berlin	103.2	192.9	497.5	588.0	257.3	15.7	1,654.6
Turkish Central Bank	0	0	0	15.0	0	0	15.0
Outflows							
Swiss Nat'l Bank	67.1	142.7	428.4	374.2	182.1	29.8	1,224.2
Portuguese Central Bank	0	0	42.0	197.6	34.9	0	214.6
Swedish Central Bank	0	6.9	19.7	56.7	4.9	0	88.2
BIS	20.3	6.4	5.4	13.3	13.6	0	59.1
Rumanian Central Bank	0	0	0	0	51.1	0	51.1
Slovakian Central Bank	0	7.9	0	0	15.7	0	23.6
Spanish Central Bank	0	0	0	7.1	0	0	7.1
Various	-3.8	0	-0.1	5.7	0	0	1.7

Source: Independent Commission of Experts Switzerland—Second World War, *Gold Transactions in the Second World War: Statistical Review with Commentary* (Berne, Switzerland: Bergier Commission, December 4, 1997), p. 17.

Table 12.5
Gold Shipped to Swiss Commercial Banks by the German
Reichsbank (1940–1941) (millions of Swiss francs)

Bank	Swiss Francs	US Dollars	Refined Gold in Kilograms
Swiss Bank Corp.	158.6	36.6	32,571
Bank Leu & Co.	51.9	12.0	10,660
Union Bank of Switz.	37.0	8.5	7,593
Basler Handelsbank	9.5	2.2	1,946
Credit Suisse	7.7	1.8	1,573
Eidgenössische Bank	0.1	0.03	26
Total	**264.8**	**61.13**	**54,369**

Source: Independent Commission of Experts Switzerland—Second World War, *Gold Transactions in the Second World War: Statistical Review with Commentary* (Berne, Switzerland: Bergier Commission, December 4, 1997), p. 18.

Germany would have been unable to generate the war machine it used during World War II.

Swiss Rationale. History shows that the BIS did, in fact, enter into illegal transactions in gold. Why did this supposedly neutral institution violate its code of conduct and charter? The Swiss banking system should be examined before answering that question. Several reasons exist to explain the behavior of Swiss bankers during the war. Human frailty may explain much of the activities of Swiss bankers. Their banks were run by humans with human fears, desires, and prejudices. But the burning question remaining is why these banks resorted to illegal activities such as gold and money laundering which still has ramifications for the global economy 50 years later.

The fear factor may be an overriding rationale. Switzerland was bordered on all sides by the Nazis. The Swiss saw what the Germans had done to the citizens of other countries in the region. A Swiss revolt against the Germans would not have been any more successful than revolution was in Poland.

Switzerland also is a landlocked nation and must rely on its neighbors for access to shipping routes and the sea and to the acquisition of raw materials. Germany recognized the fact that Swiss neutrality would serve them well since they could continue to deal in financial matters with the Swiss. If the Germans occupied Switzerland, the Allies would cut off all economic contact with the country and Germany would lose its world banker.

A more significant motivation may be greed. The Swiss money machine has always operated on a principle of profits first, everything else second. The Swiss bankers made large profits from their money and gold laundering operations with the Germans. U.S. authorities estimated that the Swiss National Bank made US$20 million from commissions on laundered gold transactions during the 1939–1945 period which, in 1997 dollars, would be US$200 million.

Finally, the Swiss have had a history of anti-Semitic behavior. Not all Swiss were anti-Semitic since many Swiss citizens assisted Jewish refugees. But the Swiss government certainly appeared to be less than pure on this issue. In 1942, Switzerland declared a decree that forbade political asylum for persons who were refugees based only on racial grounds. The Swiss seemed to overlook cruel treatment of the Jews, but so did the Allied governments including the United States. The Swiss initiated the practice of stamping a "J" on all Jewish passports to make them easier to identify as Jewish. The Swiss willingly rounded up refugees who arrived at their borders and turned them over to the German Gestapo. Many of these refugees were sent to concentration camps. It was estimated that the Swiss sent more than 30,000 refugees back to Germany. When this fact was revealed, the Swiss countered with the statement that they had also admitted 28,000 Jews. But they also charged the Swiss Jewish community and other organizations for the cost of their support.[25]

The issue of the BIS operations is not one of human emotions or of human rights. The concept of anti-Semitism in Switzerland is incorporated as background material in order to understand how so-called neutral Swiss democracy could be compromised to meet the needs of the Nazi regime. The issue is complex and may never be answered completely. World War II and its prosecution was a complex conflict. The answer will have to be left to the historians.

Implications of the Nazi Gold Transactions. The fact is clear that the Germans laundered gold, much of it looted, but how significant was this activity in World War II? U.S. government officials estimated that Germany had gold reserves totaling US$150 million at the beginning of the war. Assuming that the Nazi regime laundered

US$621 million, the Germans, therefore, had more than US$750 million with which to buy war materiel. In 1997 dollars, this is US$7.5 billion. The Nazis also profited from currency speculation and the expropriation of factories and industries in the occupied countries, not to mention the slave labor made up of Jews and other minority groups.

Assistance for Nazi Refugees after World War II. A further interesting question concerns the transactions carried out by the BIS and Swiss banks during the final stages of the war and afterwards. If the Swiss were afraid of the Nazis, it stands to reason that when the war appeared to be lost by the Germans and, particularly, after the war, transactions with the Nazi leaders would have subsided or ended. In the early 1940s, Nazi officals deposited large sums of money in secret accounts in Switzerland. Near the end of the war, many of these account balances were transferred to banks in Argentina where many of the Nazi officials emigrated. In fact, the practice of money transfers to Argentina became so active that U.S. intelligence officials were sent to Argentina to investigate the large amount of money transfers from Switzerland.

Why Restitution Took So Long

Some ask why restitution to the victims of the money and gold laundering scheme took 50 years to begin. Some political scientists place the blame on Communism. After the end of World War II, the Cold War began. The free world became afraid of Communism. This was especially true of the European countries.

The Swiss banking stucture was considered instrumental in facilitating the reconstruction of war-torn Europe. The United States appropriated funds in the form of Marshall Plan aid to Europe in general and anti-Communist assistance to countries such as Greece and Turkey. Allied governments did not want to anger Switzerland fearing such would result in a Swiss/Soviet alliance. They did not want to upset the Swiss Government or the Swiss banking system.

The Washington Accord. The Washington Accord between the Allied Governments and Switzerland was signed on May 13, 1948, in order to appease the Swiss and keep them in the western camp. This Accord required the Swiss Government to: (1) give the Allies US$58.1 million in gold. The Swiss agreed to divide the liquid German assets 50/50 with the Allies; (2) make a contribution of 250

million Swiss francs to the International Refugee Organization; and
(3) attempt to return what they could of unclaimed Holocaust victim
deposits. The Allies would then release the Swiss from further liability in connection with stolen gold and other property. The United
States would also unfreeze assets that had been transferred to the
United States for safekeeping during the war. The Accord also required the BIS to relinquish some of its stores of looted gold. The BIS
transferred nearly 4,000 kilograms of gold to the Allies in 1946. This
covered the 3,740 kilograms of looted gold which the Tripartite Gold
Commission found the BIS to be holding and which was discussed
earlier in this chapter.

After the Washington Accord was signed, the 1,525 kilograms of
fine gold which had been blocked at the Reichsbank depot in
Konstanz was released to the BIS.[26] After being blocked at
Konstanz, the gold had been transferred to the gold depot of the
Banque de France in Strasbourg in March 1948. U.S. and French
authorities stated at that time that they had no further claims on the
Konstanz gold. It is possible that some of this gold had been looted
by the Nazis. However, the issue is by now forever moot.

The Washington Accord had many critics. Some believed it was
too lenient on the so-called neutral Swiss government. Switzerland
did not completely fulfill its part of the agreement. However, the
United States had, by that time, already unfrozen the Swiss assets
and democratic governments were not eager to anger the Swiss. So
the lack of cooperation by the Swiss was ignored in many circles.

By the time the investigation over Nazi gold and Swiss/BIS activities resurfaced in 1996, relevant documents had been declassified.
In the early 1980s, a report was issued which questioned the Swiss
assets. This report did not elicit the media attention given to the
claims raised in the mid-1990s. The Union Bank of Switzerland was
accused of destroying pertinent documents relating to the case after
the Swiss government had declared that all documentation was to
be preserved for the investigation.[27] Public opinion had damaged
the Swiss image of neutrality and, under the threat of economic boy-
cott by the United States, they created a fund for Holocaust survivors. By the end of 1997, the fund amounted to at least US$191
million.

Edgar Bronfman, Sr., estimated that the Swiss government owed
Jewish people US$7 billion for its part in the collaboration with the
Nazis.[28] Bronfman was President of the World Jewish Congress and
was also President of Joseph E. Seagram & Sons, Inc. He was instru-

mental in meeting with then U.S. Senator Alfonse M. D'Amato and others in December 1995 to initiate the latest round of investigations about the role of the Swiss in the victimization of Jewish people by the Nazis during World War II.[29]

The World Jewish Congress also recently released declassified documents revealing that the Allies had found bags of gold tooth fillings and Passover goblets along with a cache of Reichsbank gold valued at US$293 million in western Germany shortly after V-E Day in May 1945. That find was turned over to the Tripartite Gold Commission and has never been fully accounted for since then.[30]

Other countries that had filed claims on the looted gold relinquished their claims. They requested that their portion of the gold be used to assist Holocaust survivors. The investigation still continues but the identification of victims as well as survivors is a difficult task.

The Postwar German Contribution

German documentation of Reichsbank activities has been very scant if available at all. It seems that the political and historical significance of these documents was not understood and they were destroyed. Or the Germans very well understood the significance of these documents. According to Tono Eitel, head of the German delegation at the 1998 Washington Conference on Holocaust-Era Assets, Germany had made compensation payments totaling DM100 billion and continued to make annual payments of DM1.7 billion.[31] This compensation would seem adequate when Edgar Bronfman's estimate of US$7 billion owed by the Nazis to the Jewish community alone is considered. However, the reserves of several occupied countries along with more than 200,000 works of art and other assets were stolen by the Nazis. When all is considered, the German compensation may be only a pittance of the amount actually owed.

SUMMARY AND CONCLUSIONS

The preceding chapters have contained a discussion of the positive operations of the BIS and its committees and special groups. These activities have included the Basle Concordats and the Basle Accord on Bank Capital as well as studies dealing with derivatives, payment and settlement systems, and the Y2K problem. The international monetary and financial system has been made more stable by the work of the BIS in these areas. The economic and monetary data which is compiled and analyzed by the BIS has assisted central banks and other international financial institutions around the world. The cooperative efforts of the BIS with other international financial institutions and with such bodies as the International Association of Insurance Supervisors and the International Organisation of Securities Commissions has strengthened supervision and regulation of insurance companies and financial markets and has been instrumental in the coordination of facilitation of economic assistance to developing countries suffering from currency crises.

However, much of the good work of the BIS may have been offset by its operations during a short six year period of its existence. During the 1939–1945 period and, perhaps, for awhile afterward, the BIS ignored its neutrality when it knowingly and flagrantly mishandled gold and currency reserves looted by the Nazis from occupied countries and victims of the Holocaust. It appears that the BIS acted in its own interests and in the interests of the Swiss government rather than remaining neutral in these operations. These operations have been the topic of this chapter. It should also be noted that all of the data on BIS gold transactions is information made available by the BIS. The historian and analyst of the BIS gold transactions with the Nazis must rely on these data even though their validity may be in question.

In addition, this chapter contains information about many different amounts of gold, money, and other assets stolen by the Nazis, transferred from the BIS to one central bank or another, and eventually either found or lost. Some of this information has become available from the BIS and central banks which actually collaborated with the Nazis. Some data comes from representatives of Holocaust victims, some of whom may have a very sharp axe to grind. Some come from German documents and some were found in Allied files which have been declassified. The amounts are confusing at the least. However, these data do make the point that vast sums were stolen by the Nazis to finance their war machine. Vast sums have been found. Vast sums have been restituted to victims. But vast sums have disappeared. The final chapter on this horrible crime may never be written.

BIS operations carried out for high-ranking German officials during the last year of the war and afterwards raises the perception that the collaboration continued even after the Nazis lost the war. The transfers of funds from Swiss banks to Argentine banks and the facilitation of these and gold transactions by the BIS seem to confirm this suspicion.

To further compound the problem, the BIS did not open its archives until the 1990s. The pressures of global public opinion and high level investigations prompted the BIS and Swiss banks to cooperate with the search for looted funds. The fact that Swiss and BIS officials may have feared Communism after the war should not have precluded neutral operations by the BIS and an attempt to return to each country whatever portion of the stolen gold that could be identified. The human frailty mentioned above as one possible cause for the behavior of BIS and Swiss banking officials may have limited them from their function of remaining neutral in financial affairs during World War II.

The fact that Nazi sympathizers as well as actual Nazis were top officials of the BIS during the period in question further clouds the role of the BIS. More than human frailty and bottom-line profits may have motivated the BIS to operate as it did during World War II. Future historians must also examine the very establishment of the BIS to answer the question of whether it was formed as an instrument of the Germans from the very beginning.

The entire matter of the commercial transactions between the BIS and the Nazi regime may never be known. Investigations by the Tripartite Gold Commission shortly after the war ended were unable to completely uncover the mystery. The Allied governments acquiesced to what was offered by the BIS and the Swiss banks. The Allied powers possessed a large amount of information with regard to illegal financial transactions. International political motivations at that time suppressed the publication of a great deal of this documentation. After all, bankers and industrialists in the Allied countries also maintained a collaborative relationship with the Nazis. Documentation has revealed the investments in Nazi Germany made by U.S. companies such as the Ford Motor Company and IBM. But these investments are the subject of another study.

It remains for bodies such as the World Jewish Council and its cooperative groups to continue the research about this issue which was renewed in the 1990s. As time goes by, more and more documents will be declassified. This will happen as the men who made the decisions to violate neutrality and collaborate with the Nazis pass from the scene.

NOTES

1. Alan Cowell, "Global Central Bank Says It Held Gold Looted by Nazis," *New York Times*, May 13, 1997, p. A8.

2. Stuart Eizenstat, "U.S. and Allied Wartime and Postwar Relations and Negotiations with Argentina, Portugal, Spain, Sweden, and Turkey on Looted Gold and German External Assets and U.S. Concerns About the Fate of the Wartime Ustasha Treasury," (Washington, DC: U.S. Department of State, June 2, 1998), p. 2.

3. Swen Fredrik Hedin and Göran Elgemyr, "Sweden Swapped Iron for Looted Gold," *Dagens Nyheter*, January 21, 1997, pp. 3–4.

4. Ibid., p. 7.

5. Ibid.

6. Ibid., pp. 2–4.

7. Bank for International Settlements, "Introductory Note on the Bank for International Settlements, 1930–1945," May 12, 1997, p. 5, found on the BIS web site at http://www.bis.org.

8. Gregg J. Rickman, *Swiss Banks and Jewish Souls* (New Brunswick, NJ: Transaction Publishers, 1999), p. xvi.

9. Ibid.

10. Michael Hirsh, "Nazi Gold: The Untold Story," *Newsweek*, November 4, 1996, p. 47.

11. Alan Cowell, "Global Central Bank Held Gold Looted by Nazis," *New York Times*, May 13, 1997, p. A8.

12. Ibid.

13. Hirsh, "Nazi Gold: The Untold Story," *Newsweek*, November 4, 1996, p. 48.

14. Richard Z. Chesnoff, "Banks Profited from Nazi Gold," *U.S. News & World Report*, May 19, 1997, p. 43; for a detailed analysis of the Swiss connection, see Gregg J. Rickman, *Swiss Banks and Jewish Souls* (New Brunswick, NJ: Transaction Publishers, 1999).

15. Stuart E. Eizenstat, "Review of Gold Issues, Research and Resolution," (Washington, DC: U.S. Department of State, 1997), p. 61.

16. Rickman, *Swiss Banks and Jewish Souls*, p. 31.

17. Thomas Sancton, "A Painful History," *Time*, February 24, 1997, p. 41.

18. Rickman, *Swiss Banks and Jewish Souls*, p. 110.

19. Washington Conference on Holocaust-Era Assets, "Appendix A: Summary of the Organizing Seminar for the Washington Conference on Holocaust-Era Assets," June 30, 1998, p. 911.

20. Eizenstat, "Review of Gold Issues, Research and Resolution," p. 60.

21. See Independent Commission of Experts Switzerland—Second World War, *Switzerland and Gold Transactions in the Second World War: Interim Report* (Berne, Switzerland: Independent Commission of Experts Switzerland—Second World War, July 1998).

22. Eizenstat, "U.S. and Allied Wartime and Postwar Relations and Negotiations With Argentina, Portugal, Spain, Sweden, and Turkey on Looted Gold and German External Assets and U.S. Concerns About the Fate of the Wartime Ustasha Treasury," p. 1.

23. See Isabel Vincent, *Hitler's Silent Partners: Swiss Banks, Nazi Gold, and the Pursuit of Justice* (New York: William Morrow and Company, 1997) for a discussion of the Swiss banking system of the 1930s and 1940s.

24. Eizenstat, "Review of Gold Issues, Research and Resolution," p. 60.

25. Thomas Sancton, "A Painful History," *Time*, February 24, 1997, p. 41.

26. Bank for International Settlements, "Note on Gold Operations Involving the Bank for International Settlements and the German Reichsbank, 1st September 1939—8th May 1945" (Basle, Switzerland: Bank for International Settlements, 12th May 1997), p. 12.

27. Gregg J. Rickman, *Swiss Banks and Jewish Souls*, pp. 121–123.

28. Ibid., p. 231.

29. Ibid., p. 40.

30. Michael Hirsh, "Nazi gold: The Untold Story," *Newsweek*, November 4, 1996, p. 48.

31. Tono Eitel, "Concluding Statement: Germany," *Washington Conference on Holocaust-Era Assets*, December 1, 1998, p. 102.

CHAPTER 13

Evaluation and Conclusions

INTRODUCTION

The Bank for International Settlements was established in 1930 by a handful of central banks and a few U.S. private banks. Thus, it is the oldest existing international financial institution. It was established primarily to facilitate the reparations payments by Germany and Austria after the first World War. Shortly after its inception, reparation payments were suspended and, since 1932, the BIS has not dealt with its major objective.

The BIS then moved to its new modus operandi, that of being a bank to central banks, principally the central banks of the G10 countries and Switzerland. These operations include foreign exchange and gold transactions for these central banks as well as financial assistance with their asset/liability management. To accomplish this service, the BIS offers short- and medium-term debt instruments to these central banks as well as other member central banks. These operations have remained a major part of the BIS work since its establishment.

During the 1932–1975 period, the BIS limited its operations to these central bank relationships. On more than one occasion, the BIS appeared to be on the brink of abolition as an unnecessary institution. Until the 1990s, it was perceived as an institution concerned primarily with European central banks. Its members and Board of Directors were comprised primarily of representatives of European central banks. The U.S. central bank authority, the Federal Reserve Board, was not a member of the BIS Board although its representatives were present at BIS meetings.

The Federal Reserve Board gave several reasons for its absence on the BIS Board. The establishment of the International Monetary Fund in 1946 made the BIS superfluous, according to Fed officials. Conflict over gold policies dealing with South Africa made Fed membership on the BIS Board a sensitive issue. Fed officials thought that the European influence by the BIS made it a regional institution. The Fed finally joined the BIS Board in 1994 after the BIS had proved its significance in a number of areas of standard-setting with regard to bank supervision and regulation.

Although the BIS concentrated its focus on the G10 central banks, the institution invited several central banks to be members during the 1990s. Its outreach is now global even though its most important meetings are held with the G10 central bank governors. Any banking standards or monetary rulings formulated during these meetings are generalized to and may be accepted by central banks around the world.

The 1970s

During the 1970s, two large banks with extensive international operations failed. Franklin National Bank of New York and Bankhaus Herstatt in Germany failed after managerial ineptitude or fraud in foreign exchange dealings. The BIS took the leadership in making bank supervisory authorities stronger in their response to such bank failures and the possible systemic risk they might cause. It formed the Basle Committee on Banking Supervision (Basle Committee) with a secretariat at the BIS headquarters in Basle, Switzerland. Peter Cooke of the Bank of England was its first chairperson and, thus, it was referred to as the Cooke Committee.

The Cooke Committee drafted the first major rule aimed at the central bank authority when a foreign unit of a major bank fails. The first such document was the Basle Concordat of 1975. Its vagueness and other problems caused it to fail when its first real test occurred. This test was made manifest in the 1982 failure of the Luxembourg holding company of the Banco Ambrosiano, a large Italian bank.

The 1980s

Because of the Banco Ambrosiano case, the Basle Committee had to return to the drawing board and the result was the Basle Concordat of 1983. The new rule placed responsibility for the failure of a foreign subsidiary with the bank supervisory authority in the country in which the subsidiary was chartered. If the foreign unit is a branch, the supervisory responsibility now lies with the bank supervisory authority of the parent bank's home country. So far the 1983 Concordat has not been tested but major country bank supervisory authorities seem to have accepted it.

The Basle Committee then turned its focus to another serious problem facing the international banking system. Most large banks held inadequate capital funds to back their assets, especially loans and certain investments. The riskiness of these assets had not been fully considered and many banks failed during the 1980s because of insolvency. In 1988, the Basle Committee formulated the Basle Accord, a set of rules which incorporated the riskiness of a bank's assets in the determination of a minimum adequate amount of capital to be held. The U.S. and British central banks actually promoted this risk-based capital adequacy standard at first and forced the BIS through its Basle Committee to adopt the new rules. This 1988 standard did increase the stability of the international banking system but did not trickle down to the small bank or the banking systems in most emerging market or transition economy countries.

The 1990s

During the early part of the 1990s, the BIS shifted its attention to the innovations from financial engineering, especially derivatives used to hedge prices of foreign currencies and other assets. A number of well-publicized incidents in which major losses were incurred by companies, banks, and government agencies created strong concerns among bank supervisory authorities in many countries. The BIS began to perform research and compile statistics about derivatives trading, especially over-the-counter derivatives. The concern also included so-called exotic derivatives, some of which had a shelf life of 15 minutes and whose price had to be determined by experts with doctoral degrees in finance and mathematics, even though most of the incidents in which large losses had been incurred were of the plain vanilla variety of derivatives—ordinary futures, forward, options, and swap contracts.

A number of reports and studies were published by BIS committees and related groups on the use and control of derivatives. The BIS began to compile statistics on derivatives transactions and include it along with market analysis in its annual report. The BIS and its committees carried on joint efforts with other national central banks and international financial institutions on the problems underlying derivatives and their riskiness when used by banks.

During the 1990s, the BIS also became concerned with payment and settlement systems for banks and securities transactions used by nations and private groups around the world. The volume of cross-border financial transactions had grown tremendously during the 1980s. The risks involved in these transactions included foreign currency risk, credit risk, solvency risk, systemic risk, settlement risk, operational risk, as well as political risk. Payment and settlement systems were needed to increase the inefficiency of these transactions and to reduce the risk exposure to international financial institutions.

The BIS and the G10 central banks created the Committee on Payment and Settlement Systems to analyze this issue and to formulate standards and new systems designed to alleviate the riskiness of international financial transactions, to increase the efficiency of international financial institutions and markets, and to provide national financial supervisory authorities with modern tools to control this growing area.

EVALUATION OF THE BIS 1970–2000

The work of the three permanent BIS committees performed extremely well during this 30 year period. The two Basle Concordats have identified whose nation's banking authority is responsibile for foreign banking failures. The Basle Capital Accord has established a risk-based format for determination of the minimum capital deemed adequate for large international banks and this Accord is now being amended to take into consideration more modern risk measurement models and to delegate some of the supervisory authority to the banks themselves.

Financial risk and the use of derivatives has gained the attention of the BIS and its committees and task forces have formulated new ways of looking at these financial innovations as well as financially engineered products such as securitization of assets and exotic derivatives. Cross-border financial transactions need more efficient payment and settlement systems designed to reduce several of the financial risks which face international financial institutions. The Committee on Payment and Settlement Systems has analyzed this problem in-depth and produced rich reports of what presently is being utilized. The so-called Red Book is a massive compilation of the systems in use in just the G10 countries.

In addition to the work of the three permanent G10/BIS committees, the BIS has rendered a massive amount of research and data gathering over the past several years. The Centre for Monetary and Economic Research has performed much of this research for the BIS. The major documents produced by the Centre are the BIS Annual Report and its Quarterly Reports. The Annual Report, now found in its entirety on the Internet at the BIS web site, is a highly anticipated document with analyses of global foreign exchange markets, international bond market activity, major events which have occurred in the international monetary and financial system, and BIS activities during the preceding year.

During the 1990s, the BIS became quite active in research and analysis of two major problems: derivatives transactions and the Y2K issue. Its research function has developed a periodical report entitled *Central Bank Survey of Foreign Exchange and Derivatives Market Activity*. The growth in volume in the derivatives markets, especially the over-the-counter market in options and swaps, has required more analysis and data gathering of transactions in this area, especially for national banking supervisory authorities. To further this need, the BIS furnishes data on international banking and securities markets for central banks.

The Y2K problem spawned a massive amount of studies by international financial institutions, central banks, and private organizations. Although the problem did not escalate into a massive global financial collapse, it is probable that the massive study of the issue and the massive response to it by upgrading of computer systems worldwide alleviated the problem. The BIS played a role in this effort by initiating its study in 1997 with the publication of *The Year 2000, A Challenge for Financial Insitutions and Bank Supervisors* by the Basle Committee. A BIS task force was established and other reports were produced.

The BIS formed two other groups within its system which have become useful efforts in increasing the stability of the international financial system. These are the Financial Stability Institute and the Financial Stability Forum. The former, for example, established a bank supervisors training program for national banking authorities. The latter's objective is to strengthen international cooperation and coordination in financial market supervision.

These efforts and others have made the BIS one of the more successful international financial institutions. The organization has increased the coordination between not only the G10 central banks but others around the world including those in emerging market and transition economies. It has expanded its operations through its three permanent committees and other groups to cover most areas of international bank supervision. The efforts of these sub-units have not been totally successful in eliminating risk and management problems in international banks but the stability of the international monetary and financial system has increased in recent decades. Much of the improvements in the international banking community can be traced to the work of the BIS.

THE SORDID PAST

Much can and will be said about the successful work of the BIS. Some areas of the international financial system still need more attention. These areas will be discussed in the following section. In spite of the successful work of the BIS during the past three decades, its operations during the six-year period during World War II placed a cloud over its legacy. As discussed in Chapter 12, several investigations, newly declassified documents, and even admissions by BIS officials have pointed to the fact that BIS and other Swiss banks executed transactions in gold and foreign exchange with the Nazi German government during the entire World War II period.

Many neutral countries carried on commercial transactions with the Nazis during World War II. Some of these same countries also dealt with the Allies even though this also meant that these neutrals were doing business with wartime belligerents. Switzerland was one of those countries. The BIS was located in Switzerland. The BIS Board of Directors had members who were either Nazis or Nazi sympathizers.

The extent to which gold transactions by the Nazis with the BIS and the Swiss banks has not been determined precisely. Data released by the BIS states that the institution sold at least 5,480 kilograms of gold to the German Reichsbank and purchased at least 9,142 kilograms from the Reichsbank, all during the war. At that time, the President of the BIS was Thomas McKittrick, a U.S. citizen and alleged Nazi sympathizer, and Emil Puhl, a Nazi, was a member of the BIS Board.

Did the BIS officials know that a large share of this Nazi gold had been stolen from Holocaust victims of the German government? At the time, they said they were unaware that the gold was tainted. In fact, Puhl had told McKittrick and Swiss bank officials that the gold was pre-1939 gold and had not been looted. The BIS and Swiss officials believed Puhl, or they used this guarantee as a rationale for their actions. The Nazi gold had usually been remelted and stamped with pre-1939 stamps and given new certificates of authenticity. Thus, looted gold was mixed with legal gold in a way that fooled most banking officials. Or the means to launder looted gold was made easier by the acquiescence of central banking officials.

After the war, several investigations of the Nazi looted gold matter were carried out and documents became declassified. At the end of the war, the Allies estimated that the Germans sold US$300 million in gold to the Swiss banks and laundered US$140 million through these banks to pay for goods from Portugal and Spain. In 1946, a Tripartite Commission study led to a Washington Accord whereby the BIS transferred US$39 million identified as looted gold to the Commission as restitution. In 1962, a Swiss Federal Council Disclosure Decree asked Swiss banks to identify funds which were owned by victims of the Nazis. Only 26 of 500 banks responded and only US$7 million in lost victims' deposits were found. A Washington Conference on Holocaust-Era Assets was held in 1996–1997 and found that the Swiss did not return all the money it held for the Jewish victims of the Holocaust. Another US$37 million in dormant accounts was found. Shortly afterwards, an Independent Commission in Switzerland estimated that US$444 million in gold had been transferred through Switzerland. Finally, the 1998 Bergier Commission determined that US$316 million of this was looted gold.

It remains to historians researching documents to be declassified in the future to determine the real extent to which the BIS and Swiss banks laundered stolen assets for the Nazis. The current findings have revealed that a large amount of looted foreign currency and gold was transferred through Switzerland. But World War II was a complex international conflict. American companies collaborated with the German government in the production of war materiel in their German subsidiaries. The Portuguese furnished bases for Allied planes. Sweden, Spain, and Turkey, all neutral countries, furnished important war materiel to the Germans.

The rationale given for these actions was as varied as the nations that collaborated with the Nazis. Some of the European countries, including Switzerland, were afraid of Nazi occupation, as had happened in Poland and Czechoslovakia. The historical Swiss neutrality and the Alps could not have kept the Germans from overrunning the country. So they carried out the financial transactions which the Germans needed to prosecute the war. No doubt the BIS officials rationalized that the by-laws of the agency gave it the right to deal with any governments no matter which side they were on. And the Nazis were not eager to occupy Switzerland when they could use Swiss banking institutions to launder their gold and foreign exchange needed to prosecute their military machine.

The important international goal is to determine the truth of what happened during the war and to insure that such will not happen again. Adequate compensation should be made to the victims, if that is ever possible. And the BIS needs to continue the work it has done for the past 30 years in making the international monetary and financial system more stable and efficient.

A BIS AGENDA FOR THE FUTURE

The international financial institutions have developed a number of international codes and standards designed to advance a set of good practices in areas such as policy transparency, data dissemination, and financial regulation and supervision. The objective of these international codes and standards is the maintenance of a stable international financial system so that national economies can operate efficiently with relatively low risk. The BIS is among these multilateral financial institutions which have formulated these codes and standards through its committees and other groups.

The three permanent BIS/G10 committees and the other Basle groups, including the International Association of Insurance Supervisors and the International Organisation of Securities Commissions, have produced a vast amount of rules, standards, and proposals designed to bring more stability to international banking and to reduce the riskiness of global financial markets.

What should the BIS future agenda contain? Four areas seem to need more work. These are: (1) the due diligence in banks problem, especially with regard to illegal money laundering; (2) better supervision and control over the relationship between hedge funds and reinsurers; (3) better supervision of offshore captive insurers; and (4) more transparency in financial and banking transactions. These issues will be discussed in this section.

Illegal Money Laundering

The practice of money laundering began at least 3,000 years ago when Chinese merchants hid their wealth because they feared that rulers would take profits and assets they had made from commercial trade. The practice has not always been a criminal activity. In modern times, illegal money can be moved in many different ways and cross-border financial transactions by electronic means makes transfers of illegal funds difficult for bank supervisory authorities to track.

A number of international efforts to track illegal money flows are in their infancy. The Financial Action Task Force on Money Laundering (FATF) is a 31-member intergovernmental organization established by the Organisation for Economic Cooperation and Development (OECD) and its objectives include gathering data on illegal money laundering. The FATF estimated the volume of illegal money laundered in 1996 ranged from US$590 billion to US$1.5 trillion. This is about 2 to 5 percent of total world output.[1]

All laundered money, legal or not, must pass through the financial system including financial institutions and markets. Most of this is probably moved through the banking system. It is very difficult for banks to separate the good money from the bad. Thus, banks must establish control systems which include know-your-customer rules. It is insufficient to know only the names and addresses of customers. Their background and activities must be known by banking officials. In the European Union, so-called suspicion-based reporting has been instituted and this practice has been adopted recently but reluctantly by the United States.

The BCCI debacle, discussed in Chapter 4, was an excellent case study for banking supervisory authorities in discovering how lax some major bank regulatory agencies were in the acquisition of ownership interests in foreign banks by BCCI officials. When these supervisory agencies finally became aware of the problem, they acted quickly to close the BCCI banks and bring the BCCI officials to justice. The Foreign Bank Supervisory Enhancement Act of 1991 was passed by the U.S. Congress to make it more difficult for criminal banks to gain access into the mainstream banking system. However, this did not stop illegal money laundering.

Money launderers, especially those who are criminals, move their funds between different banks and financial institutions, and invest them in tangible assets of honest businesses. They use different currencies to change the size and shape of the holdings. With the aid of computers and wireless electronic transfer equipment, they are able to move large amounts of money anywhere in the world in a matter of seconds.

The BIS is in a key position to give the leadership necessary to stem the flow of illegal money laundering. A successful effort will necessitate international coordination of financial institutions and financial supervisory authorities. Otherwise national regulatory agencies operating from nation to nation, some of them exercising lax controls over financial services systems, will be unable to stem the flows of these funds. The perpetrators have become much more sophisticated than many of the supervisory authorities.

The Basle Committee has made a start toward alleviating this problem. As discussed in Chapter 4, it has recently published a consultative paper on customer due diligence for banks. Hearings will be held during 2001 on this issue. The best work toward a global standard on illegal money laundering has been initiated by the FATF. Its efforts have culminated in "Forty Recommendations" which have furnished the foundation for counter-laundering legislation in its 31 member states. The FATF has also promoted the estabishment of a Caribbean FATF and an Asia/Pacific Group on Money Laundering.[2]

One of the cultural problems found in many countries, especially those that are developing or transition economies, is the dislike of financial transparency. Most of these nations are controlled by wealthy citizens who are among the elite in their societies. These people are not interested in the degree of financial disclosure found in the western world, particularly the United States. One of the more successful organizations established to promote financial transparency is Transparency Inc., a German organization which compiles indexes on global corruption by country as well as rankings of countries by the extent to which bribery is practiced. Its rankings, utilized by multinational corporations, government officials, and academicians, are found at its Internet web site, www.transparency.de.

The problem of money laundering is at the stage where a host of national and international institutions are beginning to discuss new international rules to reduce the problem. Governmental, intergovernmental, multilateral, and supranational organizations have become involved and these include in addition to the BIS and its Basle Committee, the OECD, G7, G8, G20, the European Union, some United Nations agencies, the World Bank, the IMF, and the Financial Stability Forum. The work of these organizations, if coordinated, should produce anti-laundering rules which, if enforced, can eliminate the practice. The BIS can play a large role in coordinating the efforts of these agencies.

The Hedge Fund/Reinsurance Problem

Another area in which the BIS should take a leadership position is the role in which reinsurance firms play in hedge fund operations. The tax implications of hedge funds using reinsurance firms in their funds for tax advantages points to the need for more government regulation of this activity.

Actually the tax avoidance method works this way: wealthy individuals invest in private placement offerings of offshore reinsurance companies. These companies, many headquartered in Bermuda, buy insurance policies written by name-brand insurers in the life, health, and property/casualty area and the reinsurers collect and invest the premiums. The reinsurer may then make a private placement issue of stock which is bought by wealthy individuals who gain a tax advantage from the income received from the reinsurer's investments. The reinsurer may then invest its stock issue returns in a hedge fund.

A U.S. taxpayer is liable for annual taxes on realized profits, usually at a high ordinary income rate, if he/she invests directly in the hedge fund. But the reinsurer that invests in the hedge fund pays no taxes on the trading profits until it sells the fund shares and then the reinsurer is taxed at a lower capital gains tax. The tax savings are passed on to the individual investor.

The problem for supervisors of this activity is that insurers are exempt from registering as investment companies under U.S. securities laws even though the activity described above is investment business. These reinsurers do not have to make annual distribution of profits as mutual funds do and they are not taxed by the Internal Revenue Service as investment vehicles. Although in the United States, Congress passed the Passive Foreign Investment Companies Act in 1986 mandating that offshore companies be treated for U.S.

taxpayer purposes just like domestic investment funds, since their principal business activity is insurance, they do not have to pay taxes in the manner of an investment company. In short, the activity herein described is a method for wealthy investors to reduce their tax burden as a result of a tax loophole.[3]

Since these insurance companies are mixing insurance business with investment business, they need more supervision, especially on the insurance side of the business. The major conclusion reached in Chapter 10 was that the insurance business is inadequately supervised in almost every country. The BIS has worked closely in recent years with the International Association of Insurance Supervisors (IAIS) to formulate standards and rules for better international supervision of insurance companies. This is one area in which the IAIS can strengthen regulation and supervision of one area of insurance activity.

The other side of the coin in this activity is the hedge fund itself. As discussed in Chapter 4, the case of the Long-Term Capital Management Company (LTCM) in the 1990s brought the international financial system to the brink of collapse in many areas from the systemic risk generated by the failure of LTCM. U.S. banking authorities came to the rescue of LTCM with funds that saved it from taking several banks and investment companies into bankruptcy.

As mentioned above, hedge funds work with reinsurers to reduce tax liabilities for their wealthy clients.[4] The process is as follows: U.S. hedge fund managers and investors form a tax-advantaged reinsurance company offshore in, for example, Bermuda, which has no corporate income tax. The Bermuda-based reinsurer writes insurance policies or reinsures other insurers' policies and sends investment assets to the hedge fund to invest. Investors return to the United States with shares of the reinsurer and pay no taxes until the company goes public. At that time, investors sell their shares in the reinsurer company and are taxed at a lower capital gains rate.

Aside from the tax loophole problem, the real issue in these cases is the added underwriting risk incurred in the process. Several groups have attempted to form Bermuda-based firms that are hedge funds acting as reinsurance companies. These firms have insufficient insurance expertise on the liability or underwriting side of the balance sheet. Much of this activity has stemmed from financial engineering and deal making of the 1990s. The reinsurance business is a wholesale business and requires a small staff. The traditional reinsurance industry is dominated by very large companies. Four of these firms account for one-third of the reinsurance business volume.[5]

When the LTCM failure occurred, many reinsurance companies had trouble selling their stock if they placed a large amount of their assets in a hedge fund. Again, without the bailout of LTCM by national bank regulatory authorities, many banks and reinsurers might have collapsed as well. Much of the regulation of these companies since the LTCM debacle has been generated from within the firms in the form of stronger control systems established by the firm or by insurance trade association activity. This is an activity in which the BIS, with IAIS, can generate standards and rules with the cooperation of national bank supervisory authorities and, in the case of reinsurer/hedge fund operations, national tax authorities.

Insolvency is a significant risk in hedge fund activities. The insurance industry, particularly in the reinsurance part of the business, is fraught with the issue of asymmetric information when the consumer is considered. The Basle Committee could extend its efforts with regard to capital adequacy to the insurance industry using the IAIS as a conduit. In other words, the Basle Capital Accord rules should be extended to the insurance industry and particularly to the reinsurance/hedge fund operations.

Other Insurance Regulatory Issues

The WTO and Its Influence. As mentioned in Chapter 10, the World Trade Organisation (WTO) has promulgated an agreement in world trade among the WTO members which includes services, among them the insurance industry. A global capital market is being created, especially in the services sector. The large U.S. insurers want to enter European markets with their insurance products but the European Union has its own set of rules. In fact, European insurers have actually acquired many large U.S. insurers in recent years.

Many countries have state-sponsored insurance companies. For example, in China, the People's Insurance Company is the major state-owned insurer. However, China is slowly opening its doors to foreign insurers as it becomes a member of the WTO. The regulatory differences in these regional environments need to be harmonized to maintain stability and efficiency in the global insurance industry.

Captive Offshore Insurers. A number of insurers have established offices outside their countries of origin and are classified as captive insurers. This issue was discussed in Chapter 10. These captive insurers operate in tax haven countries and can offer lower insurance costs, access to reinsurance, and tax advantages. Captive insurers can offer many advantages but the fact that they operate in countries with little or no supervisory authority over financial service firms leaves them prone to operations which may not be appropriate or even legal. This is an area in which the BIS in conjunction with the IAIS can formulate codes and standards which will result in better supervised captive offshore insurers' operations.

Transparency in Financial and Banking Transactions

A third agenda item for the future of the BIS is the reduction in the asymmetric information problem by the encouragement of more transparency in financial and banking transactions. The practice of financial disclosure is almost forbidden in many countries because the practice of secrecy in financial transactions has become a part of the local culture.

Some countries have begun to attack this problem. In the United States, a Financial Disclosure rule has been implemented in 2000. This rule attacks the source of much corporate financial information in that it prohibits companies, through Securities and Exchange Commission enforcement, from giving out financial information in a piecemeal fashion to financial analysts. The rule essentially prohibits anyone from gaining an advantage from advance publication of financial information which is relevant to a company, particularly information which might affect the company's stock price. But this rule has been put into effect in a country that already practices a great deal of financial disclosure. In many other countries, financial disclosure is a dirty term.

An increase in transparency of company operations would result in more fairness for consumers and investors, particularly in the insurance business. It would level the playing field in the financial analysis of equities on the securities markets. It could reduce corruption and criminal activities in global commercial and financial activities. It, thus, could reduce political risk for foreign investors.

The WTO was mentioned in the last section in its standard setting for financial services. The WTO itself will need to become more transparent in its operations in the future. As this organization's operations become more transparent, its constituent banks, insurers, and other financial services firms will also need to become more transparent.

One solution recently proposed to deal with the supervisory problems of transparency and bank regulation is the formulation of international banking standards (IBS).[6] These are voluntary rules which may cover a variety of problems and include: (1) more transparency by excessive government involvement/ownership in banking systems; (2) better public disclosure of banks' financial conditions; (3) upgrading banks' internal controls; and (4) subjecting national bank supervisory systems to international surveillance.

This is an area in which the BIS can demonstrate leadership. The Basle Committee could promulgate rules for financial disclosure much like the American rules. The BIS could work with the IAIS and IOSCO to bring more transparency to insurance and securities market operations on a global basis. And the BIS could cooperate with the German organization, Transparency Inc., to utilize the country rankings of global corruption and its bribery index to identify the countries which are the worst offenders.

The BIS is already working with the IMF, OECD, and the World Bank to develop guidelines to consolidate financial statements and to achieve more cross-country harmonization in accounting and auditing standards, as well as information disclosure. These groups have also identified and closed gaps in regulatory arbitrage whereby weaker regulations on some type of institutions are taken advantage of in order to reduce capital requirements without a similar reduction in risk.

CONCLUSIONS

The BIS is the oldest operating international financial institution still in existence. It has concentrated its activities on, first, the G10 central banks and, second, on other central banks around the world. In short, its financial activities have been concentrated on acting as a bank for central banks in terms of gold and foreign exchange operations and asset/liability management tools needed by central banks.

Its permanent committees and other groups have concentrated on the formulation and implementation of rules designed to increase the stability of the international monetary and financial system and to reduce its inherent risks. The organization has been sufficiently successful although it has gained many critics. Its work with the IMF, World Bank, and regional central banks to alleviate the economic and currency crises that have occurred in regions such as Asia, Latin America, and Russia has not had the totally successful results that some would have desired.

Criticism

Most of the blame for any failures in solving regional economic crises probably lies with the IMF. But since the BIS is involved and is instrumental in the coordination of the efforts of several multilateral financial institutions and central banks, it has deserved its share of the blame. Some of the strongest criticisms aimed at the BIS and other institutions involved in these bailouts have made the connection of Wall Street creditors with monetary policy formulated and implemented by these multilateral cooperative efforts. This was true of the Brazilian economic problems of the 1990s and their implications for the rest of Latin America.[7]

Other criticisms aimed specifically at the BIS have been concerned with the secrecy of the organization. The discretion practiced by the BIS when it deals with other central banks was discussed in Chapter 8. The BIS must practice confidentiality when facilitating transactions with other central banks. Some of the financial operations in foreign exchange and gold transacted by the BIS can have severe consequences on international financial markets if their impact is known in advance. However, some students of international financial markets have labeled the BIS as an international organization so obscure and secretive that its control lies with the heads of more than 30 central banks who are able to shift billions of dollars and alter the course of economies at the stroke of a pen.[8]

The Praise

On the other hand, some analysts have praised the BIS for its ability to predict regional and national economic downturns. Its ability to forecast these downturns happened before the Mexican peso and Asian currency crises of the 1990s. Some financial markets which experienced "irrational exuberance" during those crises did not heed the BIS. But, according to *Handelsblatt*, the leading German economic daily, the BIS has had a record of being very accurate in its economic forecasts.[9]

The work of the BIS in coordinating global efforts to reduce the effects of any Y2K computer problems should also be praised. Although no serious events occurred to create instability in the international financial system, the planning by the BIS for any likelihood and its coordination of central banking and multilateral agency officials in the analysis of potential breakdowns in the system contributed to a successful campaign with the Y2K issue.

The Future

A successful future for the BIS lies in its ability to cope with innovations in the international financial system. The four issues discussed earlier, illegal money laundering within the international financial system, the hedge fund/reinsurance firm connection, the use of captive offshore insurance firms, and the absence of financial transparency in company and banking operations, are 21st-century issues and are candidates for BIS consideration. The agency can promote new rules for financial supervisory authorities to reduce the adverse effects from these activities. Its relationship to the Basle Committee and to the IAIS will be especially helpful in producing solutions to these problems.

Finally, this "obscure and secretive" international organization has quietly carried out its major objectives. It has expanded from a regionally-oriented agency to a financial institution with global outreach. Its work in the past three decades may never offset the cloudy past of six years of "facilitation" of the Nazi war machine during World War II. But what other institution now operating can work with central banks, bank supervisory authorities, organizations such as the OECD, IAIS, IOSCO, IMF, and World Bank to improve the efficiency and stability of the international monetary and financial system and to reduce the risks of cross-border financial transactions? The Bank for International Settlements, perhaps misnamed, is the only such institution which is prepared for international finance in the 21st century.

NOTES

1. Nigel Morris-Cotterill, "Money Laundering," *Foreign Policy*, May/June 2001, p. 16.

2. Ibid., p. 20.

3. Hal Lux, "The Great Hedge Fund Reinsurance Tax Game," *Institutional Investor*, Vol. 35 (April 2001), pp. 52–53.

4. Ibid., pp. 54–55.

5. Ibid., pp. 55, 57.

6. See Morris Goldstein and Dennis Weatherstone, *The Case for an International Banking Standard* (Washington, DC: Institute for International Economics, 1997).

7. Michel Chossudovsky, "Brazil's IMF Sponsored Economic Disaster," *Heise Online*, December 2, 1999, p. 9.

8. "Questions Concerning the Protocols," *Winds: The Protocols of the Learned Elders of Zion*, April 25, 2001, pp. 24–25, and found on the Internet at http://the winds.arcsnet.net.

9. "Editorial," *Australian Alert Service*, June 8, 2000, p. 1, and found on the Internet at http://www.nex.net.au/.

Balance Sheet: Bank for International Settlements

(Year ended 31 March 1996–2000) (in millions of gold francs: 1 gold franc = US$1)

	1996	1997	1998	1999	2000
Gold					
Held in bars	4,364.2	3,547.3	3,037.1	2,801.5	2,265.4
Time deposits	637.3	956.7	1,122.4	1,077.2	1,240.4
	5,001.5	4,504.0	4,159.5	3,878.7	3,505.8
Cash on hand and on sight account with banks	9.8	384.4	7.8	8.3	11.4
Treasury bills	4,105.7	2,813.4	1,863.9	7,314.0	7,853.9
Time deposits and advances in currencies	37,328.1	42,355.1	34,862.2	32,423.0	41,853.9
Securities purchased under resale agreements	1,652.2	884.2	2,781.0	276.0	1,268.1
Government and other securities at term	10,488.1	15,651.1	18,517.1	22,167.9	20,139.9

Land, buildings and equipment	—	—	—	124.7	120.7
Miscellaneous assets	32.8	200.8	258.7	44.5	82.0
Total assets	58,618.2	66,793.0	62,450.2	66,237.1	74,835.7
Paid-up capital	295.7	323.2	323.2	323.2	330.7
Reserves					
Legal reserves	30.1	32.3	32.3	32.3	33.0
General reserves	803.3	974.9	1,016.3	1,156.4	1,259.1
Special dividend reserves	56.5	59.5	62.5	65.5	68.5
Free reserves	893.6	995.1	1,157.4	1,351.4	1,550.9
	1,783.5	2,061.8	2,268.5	2,605.6	2,911.5
Valuation difference account	373.5	351.1	247.2	265.4	192.0
Deposits					
Gold	4,245.0	3,836.4	3,473.7	3,192.6	2,820.2
Currencies	49,649.2	57,585.6	54,023.6	57,705.8	65,903.7
	53,894.2	61,422.0	57,497.3	60,898.4	68.723.9
Securities sold under repurchase agreements	376.6	674.8	30.7	121.5	103.0
Staff pension scheme	283.1	252.6	257.0	—	—
Miscellaneous liabilities	1,558.3	1,658.7	1,773.7	1,965.6	2,519.9
Dividend	53.3	48.8	52.6	57.4	54.7
Total liabilities	**58,618.2**	**66,793.0**	**62,450.2**	**66,237.1**	**74,835.7**

Source: Bank for International Settlements, 70th Annual Report (Basle, Switzerland, Bank for International Settlements, 2000).

Profit and Loss Account: Bank for International Settlements

(Year ended 31 March 1996–2000) (in millions of gold francs: 1 gold franc = US$1)

	1996	1997	1998	1999	2000
Net interest and other operating income	254.3	263.8	314.9	370.4	376.6
Less costs of administration					
Board of Directors	1.5	1.3	1.3	1.3	1.2
Management and staff	46.6	42.9	39.4	40.9	40.6
Office and other expenses	18.3	16.3	15.0	18.6	19.4
Costs of administration before depreciation	66.4	60.5	55.7	60.8	61.2
Depreciation	—	—	—	6.0	7.6
	66.4	60.5	55.7	66.8	68.8
Net operating surplus	187.9	203.3	259.2	303.6	307.8
Less amounts transferred to					
Provision for exceptional costs of administration	3.5	3.0	—	—	—

Provision for modernization of premises and renewal of equipment	3.1	6.0	—	—	—
	6.6	9.0	—	—	—
Net profit for the year	181.3	194.3	259.2	303.6	307.8
Dividend	53.3	48.8	52.6	57.4	54.7
	128.0	145.5	206.6	246.2	253.1
Transfer to general reserve fund	38.4	41.0	41.3	49.2	50.6
Transfer to special dividend reserve fund	3.0	3.0	3.0	3.0	3.0
Total	**86.6**	**101.5**	**162.3**	**194.0**	**199.5**
Transfer to free reserve fund	86.6	101.5	162.3	194.0	199.5

Source: Bank for International Settlements, *70th Annual Report* (Basle, Switzerland: Bank for International Settlements, 2000).

Selected Bibliography

Abken, Peter A. "Over-the-Counter Financial Derivatives: Risky Business?" Federal Reserve Bank of Atlanta *Economic Review*. Vol. 79, March/April 1994, pp. 1–21.

Allen, Linda. *Capital Markets and Institutions: A Global View*. New York: John Wiley & Sons, 1997.

August, Ray. *International Business Law: Text, Cases, and Readings*. Englewood Cliffs, NJ: Prentice-Hall, 1993.

Baker, James C. *International Business Expansion into Less-Developed Countries: The International Finance Corporation and Its Operations*. Binghamton, NY: Haworth Press Inc., 1993.

———. *International Finance: Management, Markets, and Institutions*. Upper Saddle River, NJ: Prentice-Hall, 1998.

Ball, Donald A., and Wendell H. McCulloch, Jr. *International Business: The Challenge of Global Competition*. Chicago, IL: Irwin, 1996.

Bank for International Settlements. *62nd Annual Report*. Basle, Switzerland: Bank for International Settlements, 15th June 1992.

———. *63rd Annual Report*. Basle, Switzerland, Bank for International Settlements, 14th June 1993.

———. *64th Annual Report*. Basle, Switzerland: Bank for International Settlements, 13th June 1994.

———. *66th Annual Report*. Basle, Switzerland: Bank for International Settlements, 10th June 1996.

———. *70th Annual Report*. Basle, Switzerland: Bank for International Settlements, 2001, found on the Internet at http://www.bis.org.

————. *Central Bank Payment and Settlement Services with Respect to Cross-Border and Multi-Currency Transactions.* Basle, Switzerland: Committee on Payment and Settlement Systems, 1993.

————. *Delivery versus Payment in Securities Settlement Systems.* Basle, Switzerland: Committee on Payment and Settlement Systems, 1992.

————. *Introductory Note on the Bank for International Settlements 1930–1945.* Basle, Switzerland: Bank for International Settlements, May 12, 1997.

————. "Note on Gold Operations Involving the Bank for International Settlements and the German Reichsbank, 1st September 1939–8th May 1945." Basle, Switzerland: Bank for International Settlements, May 12, 1997.

————. *Payment Systems in the Group of Ten Countries.* Basle, Switzerland: Committee on Payment and Settlement Systems, December 1993.

————. *Report of the Committee on Interbank Netting Schemes of the Central Banks of the Group of Ten Countries.* Basle, Switzerland: Committee on Interbank Netting Schemes, November 1990.

————. *Report on Netting Schemes.* Basle, Switzerland: Group of Experts on Payment Systems, February 1989.

Basel Committee on Banking Supervision. *Overview of The New Basel Capital Accord.* Basle, Switzerland: Bank for International Settlements, January 2001.

"Basle Brush," *The Economist.* May 1, 1999, p. 69.

"Basle Sets Off the Fireworks," *The Banker.* Vol. 143, June 1993, pp. 6–9.

Bennett, Rosemary. "Creative Solutions for Interest-rate Uncertainty," *Euromoney.* August 1993, pp. 50–52.

Berton, Lee. "Understanding the Complex World of Derivatives," *The Wall Street Journal.* June 14, 1994, p. C1.

"BIS Annual Report Highlights Organization's Recent Activities," *IMF Survey.* Vol. 24, July 17, 1995, pp. 226–227.

"BIS Quarterly Review: Signs of Global Economic Slowdown Cast Shadow Over International Markets," *IMF Survey.* Vol. 30, March 19, 2001, pp. 95–96.

Blanden, Michael. "Basle Faulty," *The Banker.* Vol. 149, July 1999, p. 25.

Blustein, Paul. "Ambrosiano's Fallout on International Banking," *The Wall Street Journal,* September 1, 1982, p. 12.

Board of Governors. *Symposium Proceedings: International Symposium on Banking and Payment Services.* Washington, DC: Board of Governors of the Federal Reserve System, December 1994.

Borio, C.E.V., and P. Van den Bergh. *The Nature and Management of Payment System Risks: An International Perspective.* Basle, Switzerland: Bank for International Settlements, February 1993.

Bower, Tom. *Nazi Gold: The Full Story of the Fifty-Year Swiss-Nazi Conspiracy to Steal Billions from Europe's Jews and Holocaust Survivors.* New York: Harper Collins, 1997.

Brady, Simon. "How Central Banks Play the Markets," *Euromoney.* September 1992, pp. 49–57.

———. "The Ref Gets Rough," *Euromoney.* April 1992, pp. 25–30.

———. "Structured Finance," *Euromoney.* August 1992, pp. 31–39.

Casserly, Dominic, and Greg Wilson. "Managing Derivatives-Related Regulatory Risk," *Bank Management.* Vol. 70, July/August 1994, pp. 27–32.

Chesnoff, Richard Z. "Banks Profited from Nazi Gold," *U.S. New & World Report.* May 19, 1997, p. 43.

"The Complacent Derivatives Industry," *Euromoney.* August 1993, p. 5.

Cowell, Alan. "Global Bank Says It Held Gold Looted by the Nazis," *New York Times.* May 13, 1997, p. A8.

"Derivatives Bother Basle," *The Banker.* Vol. 144, July 1994, pp. 28–29.

Dwyer, Paula, William Glasgall, Dean Foust, and Greg Burns. "The Lesson from Barings' Straits," *Business Week.* March 13, 1995, pp. 30–32.

Euroclear. *Cross-Border Clearance, Settlement, and Custody: Beyond the G30 Recommendations.* Brussels, Belgium: Morgan Guaranty Trust Co., June 1993.

Federal Reserve Bank of New York. *Annual Report 1999.* New York: Federal Reserve Bank of New York, 1999.

Ferris, Paul. *The Money Men of Europe.* New York: Macmillan, 1968.

Fraser, K. Michael. "What It Takes to Excel In Exotics," *Global Finance.* Vol. 7, March 1993, pp. 44–49.

Goldstein, Morris, and Philip Turner. "Banking Crises in Emerging Economies: Origins and Policy Options," *BIS Economic Papers, No. 46.* October 1996, pp. 1–67.

Goldstein, Morris, and Dennis Weatherstone. *The Case for an International Banking Standard.* Washington, DC: Institute for International Economics, 1997.

Grant, Charles. "Can the Cooke Committee Stand the Heat?" *Euromoney.* October 1982, pp. 39–45.

Gurwin, Larry. "Death of a Banker," *Institutional Investor.* Vol. 16, October 1982, pp. 258–275.

Henry, Marilyn. *Switzerland, Swiss Banks, and the Second World War: The Story Behind the Story.* Somerset, NJ: Transaction Publishers, 1999.

Hirsh, Michael. "Nazi Gold: The Untold Story," *Newsweek.* November 4, 1996, pp. 47–48.

Howell, Kristin K. "The Evolution and Goals of Leading to Developing Countries by the Bank for International Settlements," *Journal of Economic Studies.* Vol. 22, 1995, pp. 69–80.

Independent Commission of Experts Switzerland–Second World War. "Gold Transactions in the Second World War: Statistical Review with Commentary," *Conference on Nazi Gold*. London, England, December 2–4, 1997, pp. 1–23.

International Association of Insurance Supervisors. *Principles on the Supervision of Insurance Activities on the Internet*. Cape Town, South Africa: IAIS Working Group on Electronic Commerce/Internet, October 10, 2000.

Kapstein, Ethan B. *Supervising International Banks: Origins and Implications of the Basle Accord*. Princeton, NJ: Princeton University, December 1991.

Levi, Maurice D. *International Finance: The Markets and Financial Management of Multinational Business*. New York: McGraw-Hill, 1996.

Levich, Richard M. *International Financial Markets: Prices and Policies*. Burr Ridge, IL: Irwin McGraw-Hill, 1998.

Lux, Hal. "The Great Hedge Fund Reinsurance Tax Game," *Institutional Investor*. Vol. 35, April 2001, pp. 52–58.

Machlis, Avi, and Norma Cohen. "Italian Insurer Opens Archives of Nazi Victims," *Financial Times* (London). July 8, 1997, p. 3.

"Major Central Banks Expect an Upturn In 2nd Half of 2001," *The Wall Street Journal*. February 13, 2001, p. A18.

Marki, Susan Ross. *Derivatives Financial Products*. New York: Harper Business, 1991.

Meister, Edgar. "Supervisory Capital Standards: Modernise or Redesign?" *Economic Policy Review—Federal Reserve Bank of New York*. Vol. 4, October 1998, pp. 101–104.

Melloan, George. "Leeson's Law: Too Much Leverage Can Wreck a Bank," *The Wall Street Journal*. March 6, 1995, p. A15.

"More Meddling," *Euromoney*. February 1992, p. 5.

Morris-Cotterill, Nigel. "Money Laundering," *Foreign Policy*. May/June 2001, pp. 16–22.

Ogden, Joan. "The 'D' Word: A User's Update," *Global Finance*. Vol. 9, June 1995, pp. 60–63.

"Recent Trends in Foreign Exchange, Derivatives Markets Detailed in New Study," *IMF Survey*. Vol. 28, May 24, 1999, p. 176.

"Revised Basle Concordat on Bank Oversight Clarifies the Division of Supervisory Roles," *IMF Survey*. Vol. 12, July 11, 1983, pp. 201–204.

Rickman, Gregg J. *Swiss Banks and Jewish Souls*. New Brunswick, NJ: Transaction Publishers, 1999.

Sancton, Thomas. "A Painful History," *Time*. February 24, 1997, pp. 40–41, 44.

Saunders, Anthony. *Financial Institutions Management: A Modern Perspective*. Burr Ridge, IL: Irwin McGraw-Hill, 2000.

Saunders, Anthony, and Marcia Millon Cornett. *Financial Markets and Institutions: A Modern Perspective*. New York: McGraw-Hill, 2001.

Sayer, Ian. *Nazi Gold: The Story of the World's Greatest Robbery—and its Aftermath*. London, England: Panther, 1984.

Schloss, Henry H. *The Bank for International Settlements*. New York: New York University, 1970.

Seeger, Charles M. "How to Prevent Future Nick Leesons," *The Wall Street Journal*. August 8, 1995, p. A13.

Siegman, Charles J. "The Bank for International Settlements and the Federal Reserve," *Federal Reserve Bulletin*. Vol. 80, October 1994, pp. 900–906.

Skipper, Harold D., Jr. *International Risk and Insurance: An Environmental-Managerial Approach*. Burr Ridge, IL: Irwin McGraw-Hill, 1998.

Smets, Frank. *Measuring Monetary Policy Shocks in France, Germany, and Italy*. Basle, Switzerland: Bank for International Settlements, 1997.

Smith, Arthur Lee. *Hitler's Gold: the Story of the Nazi War Loot*. New York: Berg, 1989.

Smith, Roy C. *The Global Bankers*. New York: E.P. Dutton, 1989.

———. *Global Banking*. New York: Oxford Press, 1997.

Stehm, Jeff. "Analyzing Alternative Intraday Credit Poicies in Real-Time Gross Settlement Systems," *Journal of Money, Credit, and Banking*. Vol. 30, 1998, pp. 832–848.

Strange, Susan. *Mad Money: When Markets Outgrow Governments*. Ann Arbor, MI: University of Michigan Press, 1998.

van der Vossen, Jan. "Basel Committee Presents Proposals for New Capital Adequacy Standards for Banks," *IMF Survey*. Vol. 30, February 5, 2001, pp. 37–40.

———. "The New Basel Capital Proposal for Banks," *Finance & Development*. Vol. 38, March 2001, pp. ii–iii.

Vicker, Ray. *Those Swiss Money Men*. New York: Charles Scribner's Sons, 1973.

Vincent, Isabel. *Hitler's Silent Partners: Swiss Banks, Nazi Gold, and the Pursuit of Justice*. New York: William Morrow and Co., 1997.

Walker, Marcus. "Nothing to Fear but Fear Itself," *Euromoney*. September 1999, pp. 34–38.

Westlake, Melvyn. "Into Basle's Inner Sanctum," *The Banker*. Vol. 144, March 1994, pp. 14–19.

Ziegler, Jean. *The Swiss, the Gold, and the Dead*. New York: Harcourt Brace, 1998.

WEB SITES USED

http://www.bis.org/ (June 2000, pp. 1–7).

http://www.bis.org/about/profforum.htm (April 25, 2001, pp. 1–3).

http://www.bis.org/cbanks1.htm (March 6, 2001, pp. 1–3).

http://www.bis.org/fsi/index.htm (March 21, 2001, p. 1).

http://www.bis.org/press/p010108.htm (March 19, 2001, pp. 1–4).

http://www.bis.org/press/p010116.htm (March 19, 2001, pp. 1–5).

http://www.bis.org/publ/cpss42.htm (January 2001, pp. 1–2).

http://europa.eu.int/ (April 25, 2001, pp. 1–2).

http://www.federalreserve.gov/boarddocs/speeches/1999/19991001.htm
     (October 1, 1999, pp. 1–6).

http://www.iaisweb.org/1/pas.html (April 16, 2001, pp. 1–2).

http://www.lib.uchicago.edu/ (March 21, 2001, pp. 1–9).

http://www.monde-diplomatique.fr/ (November 1998, pp. 1–6).

http://www.state.gov/www/policy_re . . . 1998/980602_eizenstat_
     nazigld.html (April 9, 2001, pp. 1–16).

http://www.transparency.de.

Index

About the Author

JAMES C. BAKER is Professor of Finance and International Business at Kent State University. A fellow of the Association for Global Business, Baker has published widely on a variety of topics in international finance and business, and his articles appear frequently in such publications as the *Journal of World Trade*, *International Journal of Finance*, and *Journal of International Arbitration*. Among his more recent books is one published in 1999 by Quorum, *Foreign Direct Investment in Less Developed Countries: The Role of ICSID and MIGA*.